THE
WIVES

THE
WIVES

—

A Memoir

SIMONE GORRINDO

SCOUT PRESS

New York   London   Toronto   Sydney   New Delhi

Scout Press
An Imprint of Simon & Schuster, LLC
1230 Avenue of the Americas
New York, NY 10020

Simon & Schuster: Celebrating 100 Years of Publishing in 2024

Interior design by Hope Herr-Cardillo

Manufactured in the United States of America

ISBN 978-1-9821-7849-9

For the wives,
who know this story as well as I do

AUTHOR'S NOTE

In writing this book, memory was only one of many guides. I consulted books, news articles and reports, as well as emails, letters, journal entries, and social media feeds. I also spoke extensively with several of the people who appear in its pages.

Out of respect for its ethos of privacy and quiet professionalism, I refrain from naming the unit I write about and refer to it, only, as the Unit. For similar reasons, most names and some individuals' identifying features have been changed. Occasionally, I omitted people or events, but only when doing so did not affect the narrative's accuracy.

PART I

I'd rather live in his world than live without him in mine.

—"Midnight Train to Georgia"

CHAPTER 1

A RAPIDLY DEPLOYABLE COMBAT UNIT

November 2012, Columbus, Georgia

In the photo Andrew had texted, the little brick house looked out of another time. *Just call me June Cleaver*, I'd captioned the shot when I'd sent it to my oldest friend, Reina. In person, though, the 1940s home looked more like it had been forgotten entirely, the front lawn patchy, no shrubs or flowers bordering the foundation, not even a small porch to sit on. I hadn't realized that I'd hoped for these things, but I'd lost an apartment next to a reliable subway line in the only city I had ever loved. A porch swing would have softened the blow.

"Maybe we should have gone with base housing?" I asked Andrew, who was standing next to me on our new driveway in the dusk. I didn't have a driver's license, had never had a need for one in New York City, so he'd driven all one thousand miles here. Over the course of two days, we'd had six hours of sleep and lukewarm showers at a Motel 6 in southern Virginia, but he looked untouched by exhaustion, his dark hair combed perfectly into place.

"Trust me, at my rank, it would've been worse," he said, rolling up the back door of our U-Haul. "Plus, this place is $700 a month. We get to pocket a little bit of that BAH." He looked at me with a mischievous grin, the evening light catching the flecks of gold in his green eyes, and I felt a surge of excitement. We were going to live in a *house*. We had never lived in a house before.

The Army issued you a "basic allowance for housing" to cover rent and utilities, calculating the amount allotted by looking at the cost of living in your area, your rank, and whether you had any dependents. Ours was $1,100 a month. After utilities, we probably wouldn't be pocketing much. Still, I could not get over this number. $700. That had been my rent for a basement bedroom in Brooklyn when I was twenty-one. My view had been a brick wall.

"I wish we could leave this stuff out here for the night, but I don't think it's a great idea," Andrew said, looking around. Getting off the freeway, the roads we'd driven had been lined with used car lots and fast-food restaurants. Then, when we got close to our street, a neighborhood park had appeared like an oasis, shaded by tall oaks, maples, and southern pines. The old homes bordering it were in good shape, even stately, but they had become smaller and more run-down as we'd driven up the hill toward ours. We were just two houses in from an intersection, after which the neighborhood dissolved into a wasteland of empty lots and old warehouses. Among them was a small clapboard church with an old marquee in front, one of its letters gone—SIN ERS ARE WELCOME.

"Oh, look," I said to Andrew, pointing. "They knew the New York heretics were coming."

He laughed as he picked up a box. I grabbed it from him and turned away from the truck.

There was a woman standing at the end of our driveway.

She looked about my age, late twenties, thin and freckled, her face red as though she'd been out all day in the wind. She wasn't wearing a speck of makeup. Her long chestnut hair looked dry at the ends, like it needed a cut.

"Let me get that!" she said, rushing toward me and grabbing the box from my arms. "I'm Rachel, it's so nice to meet you, can we help you unpack?" The words trailed after her, rushed and breathy, as she walked up to our front door and placed the box on the stoop. It was like she had been waiting for us.

"Maybe we should let them get settled in, babe," said a guy standing at the curb. Rachel was so excessively friendly, so overwhelmingly *there*, I hadn't even registered him until now.

I looked over at Andrew. A smile was spreading across his face.

This had to be Boyd.

Or Daniel, as Rachel introduced him now, rejoining him at the end of the driveway, her hand curled around his forearm in a way that was both tender and possessive. Wisps of blond hair peeked out from under his Mets cap.

"Dan," he gently corrected, and shook my hand. There was something old-fashioned about Dan or Daniel or Boyd, with his ruddy complexion and white sneakers and big, toothy smile. Andrew had met him at Fort Benning, the Army base ten miles from our new house, at a selection process for an elite, rapidly deployable combat unit that was part of the Army's Special Operations. After they'd made it in, both of them had gotten stationed here, and when Dan found the nearly identical brick house across the street from ours, he told Andrew about our place. The landlord, a plumber named Frank, had bought both for cheap during the height of the Recession. Theirs was nicer, I noted with some jealousy. It had a covered porch, some well-kept bushes, a feeling of having been recently loved.

That was where June Cleaver actually lived.

"Well, if you need anything, anything at all, we're right here,"

Rachel said, pointing at their house as Dan practically dragged her off our driveway. Even their walkway was lined with petunias. I had never before wanted petunias, but suddenly I was painfully envious of Rachel and her tidy flowers.

"Apparently, the last tenants trashed the place, but it's been renovated, sort of," Andrew said as he fished the keys out of his pocket, unlocking the front door as we reached the stoop. He turned on the overhead light, illuminating a small, box-shaped living room with shiny wooden floors. The smell of fresh lacquer hung in the air.

"There's even a mudroom," Andrew said, opening a windowed door just off the living room. I peeked in. On one of the walls were appliance hookups. "We'll need to get a washer and dryer," he said, pointing.

"We won't have to go to the laundromat," I countered before walking back through the living room to the dining area and turning on the light, bringing to life a chandelier that hung from the ceiling. It was plastic, but it shimmered beautifully. At the back of the house I found three bedrooms. *1,300 square feet*. Just being inside it made me feel like someone had opened a window in my mind and let in the breeze.

Once we'd brought in every last item from the truck, Andrew and I lay down on the living room floor. My body ached. The last week had been a conveyor belt of boxes to pack and goodbyes to say and a thousand loose ends to tie up at my office in the Flatiron District, where I'd worked as an editor for the digital division of a publishing company. By the time we'd finished loading the U-Haul, we'd probably walked a half-marathon up and down the four floors of our Harlem building.

Reina had helped us move out of our one-bedroom. I'd known her since I was twelve. She was like my sister. I didn't know when I'd see her again, when I'd even next be in New York. Would I ever get another chance at an editing job like the one I'd just given up? It seemed unlikely. I'd only had it for a year and a half, still couldn't believe I'd even landed it.

And now, here I was, twenty-eight years old, an *Army wife*.

Andrew found my hand and fingered my wedding ring, a tiny diamond that had belonged to his grandmother. We had married nine days before he left for almost eleven months of training. During his ten weeks of boot camp, he'd been allowed just three five-minute phone calls, so I had survived on his letters. In them, he had sounded happy, like something that had been jostling around inside him his entire life had clicked into place. It was strange, the way time had both expanded and compressed while Andrew was gone. I had been living with this ring on my finger for close to a year now, but my husband was still getting to know my hand with it on. My *husband*. The word, as comforting as a hearth, sent a warmth through my body every time I said it.

A knock came at the door. Andrew and I looked at each other.

"That's odd," I said, and got up.

It was Rachel. She had pulled her hair back into a bun. There was blush on her cheeks and color on her lips. She was holding a plate full of chocolate chip cookies covered in Saran wrap. "I just thought you guys might like some cookies. I baked a bunch earlier. I like to bake—a little too much." She laughed nervously.

I didn't know if she was doing this because we were new neighbors or the only people she'd met in the Unit, but no one had ever, in all the apartments I'd lived in during my decade in New York, brought over cookies when I'd moved in.

I took the plate from her. Even through the Saran wrap, I could smell the warm butter and chocolate. "Wow, thank you," I said, smiling stiffly, standing there for a moment before remembering that I should invite her in. I inched back from the door and opened it farther so she could enter, realizing, as I did this, that there was nowhere for her to sit.

But she was already backing away, looking toward her house, as though she could hear her husband from across the street: *Leave them be, babe.*

"I'll let you guys unpack!" she said. "But please, please let me know if I can help."

"Of course," I said. "Thank you so much." I smiled again, relieved that the expression felt more natural this time, and closed the door. When I turned around, Andrew was standing behind me.

"She seems really nice," he said. "You should be friends."

"I've never been friends with someone just because they're nice," I said.

"Maybe you have some things in common," he said. "I mean, other than your husbands."

Our husbands were exactly why I doubted we'd have much in common. Because I had nothing in common with the Army. Even the language of this world—*rapidly deployable combat unit*—was so foreign to my ear, we might as well have just unloaded a spaceship on the moon. The South, too, was new territory for me. Before today, Virginia was the farthest I'd gone beneath the Mason-Dixon line. *Columbus, Ohio?* New York friends had asked when I'd told them where I was moving. No, not that Columbus. The one in Georgia. The one no one had heard of. It was a city of nearly 200,000 people, but when I'd called the *New York Times*' customer service to transfer my subscription, the woman on the line had told me they didn't offer delivery here. There just wasn't the demand.

"Give her a chance," Andrew said. His voice sounded hopeful, but his eyes were pleading. He was leaving for Afghanistan in two weeks.

I had a high tolerance for loneliness. Andrew and I had just spent almost a year apart. But I'd had a life in New York—a career, friends, more than a decade of history.

I looked across the street. Through the Boyds' window, I could see

Rachel gliding across her kitchen. She looked so at home in the space already. There had been an urgency in her voice, though, when she'd dropped off the cookies, like she needed something she didn't know how to ask for.

—

"Sometimes I think about joining the military."

That was what Andrew said to me one evening in the winter of 2007, when he was twenty-four and I was twenty-three. We'd just moved in together and were out walking in Annapolis, the colonial Maryland capital where Andrew was studying the classics at a small liberal arts college.

"I would leave you," I said, without thinking. The air was cold enough that I could see my breath.

Andrew's face went still.

"Join the Army? You would never want to do that," I continued uneasily. The Global War on Terror had been going on for six years already. We were in the midst of the Iraq surge, the deadliest year for US forces since 2004. I had moved to New York for college just two weeks before the Twin Towers fell. By the time I graduated four years later, it was hard to imagine not being at war. But it wasn't *my* war. Everyone I knew was against the invasion of Iraq, which seemed, in every sense, like a costly conflict with no clear rationale, and I had marched with friends in protest of it. Afterward, we'd gotten drinks at an East Village bar. That had been the extent of my involvement. It wasn't like my generation was being drafted. US soldiers fighting this, I thought, must either be true believers, from military families, or out of options. Andrew was none of those things.

He always had an answer or an argument. This time, though, he'd said nothing.

Two years passed. Andrew finished his degree, working as a bartender while I waitressed at an Irish pub and freelanced for the local weekly paper. He dropped the Army idea, or so I thought. As he finished up school at age twenty-six, he considered his options. He was fascinated by geopolitics. Maybe the State Department could be a fit? Then he discovered how much paper-pushing the job entailed. The Peace Corps was an exciting post-college idea, but he needed a decent income to repay his mountain of student loans. He also felt like he didn't have time to dally.

When most of his peers had gone off to college, Andrew had chosen to dedicate himself to Wushu, a modern martial art China was bringing to the 2008 Olympics. He'd started practicing traditional Chinese martial arts when he was four, becoming so invested in it that, by the time he was a teenager, he was waking at 6 a.m. to instruct classes alongside his teacher. In late high school, he began working with a coach who trained members of the US team for Wushu. He didn't love it the way he'd loved Shao-Lin, a practice based in Buddhist philosophy that had been much more than a sport to him—it had been his purpose, his cosmology, his spiritual center. But the Olympics was an athletic goal he couldn't pass up. He trained seriously for three years in the Bay Area before leaving, at age twenty, to spend six months practicing Wushu full time in Beijing. When he returned to California, he was so burned out on the sport that he quit martial arts entirely and became a bartender, renting a studio above a taqueria on Market Street in downtown San Francisco, where he spent his mornings diving into books by Western philosophers and twentieth-century American novelists and questioning the limits of the narrow world he'd grown up in. By the time he entered college at twenty-two, he had already worked hard for and given up on a lifelong dream.

The spring Andrew graduated, I noticed an Army recruitment pamphlet on our nightstand. I intended to ask him about it but forgot in the tumult of moving. We were heading to do forestry work in the Ontario outback for a summer, where we would live without electricity or running water, a last adventure before we moved back to New York so that I could attend Columbia's graduate school for journalism. Life was so busy, and the Army seemed such a far-fetched idea to me, it was easy not to think about it. Maybe because I didn't want to.

Then, sometime in the fall of 2011, when I was knee-deep in school, I found an extremely detailed workout regimen scrawled on a pad of paper on our coffee table. Andrew was so devoted to the gym that he often went at 3 a.m. after work, but there was something about the specificity of the goals, and the goals themselves—X number of push-ups, two-mile-run in X time—that made me pause.

"Are you planning on running away and joining the Army?" I asked that night. It was Wednesday, the only weekday evening he had off. We were at our neighborhood park. It was June and steamy out. Shirtless men were grunting and sweating, doing pull-ups on rusty equipment. Bill Withers wafted from someone's giant boom box.

"Not running away," he said, smirking. "But yes."

"You haven't stopped thinking about this," I said.

"I haven't," he said. "It's what I want to do."

And suddenly, I understood what I hadn't wanted to understand two years prior: This was real, whatever this was. A desire—a calling, even? For the next month, I came at him with the same question over and over: *Why?* I asked, riding back with him to our apartment on the subway at night, drinking whiskey at a neighborhood bar, sipping coffee out of paper cups on our stoop. Why did *he* have to get his hands dirty with these wars?

Andrew's grandfather had fought in World War II, like mine. Otherwise, his background was about as far afield as you could get from the military. He had been raised in California by children of the '60s. His mother was a modern-dancer-turned-marriage-and-family-therapist. His father, who died when Andrew was eighteen, had been a charismatic ecumenical spiritualist. He had run a commune where Andrew spent the first six years of his childhood. But Andrew had also grown up on a steady diet of *Rambo* and *Predator* and *Saving Private Ryan*, and felt drawn, as a kid, to the Vietnam vets who came through his life, like his father's friend, a helicopter gunner who loved to show Andrew his war wound, the gunshot to his stomach; and a boyfriend of his mother's, a limo driver who lived with a bullet lodged next to his spine that had traveled there after he'd been shot during a firefight. In Annapolis, he lived on the same block as the Naval Academy, bartended with Iraq vets, and watched college friends commission as officers in the Marines. His vision broadened, and he became increasingly curious about the war, inhaling books like Robert Kaplan's *Imperial Grunts*, about American Special Forces soldiers, and *Where Men Win Glory*, John Krakauer's biography of Pat Tillman, the football player who left his sports career after 9/11 to become an Army Ranger.

All of these influences stirred in him a possibility that had maybe always been there. Still, he struggled with the ethics of this impulse. He'd been raised to do harm only as a means of self-defense. If he didn't have to hurt or kill people, he reasoned, then wasn't remaining a civilian the moral choice? He knew there were no clear-cut answers, but he mulled this conundrum for years as though it were a hard but not-impossible-to-solve math equation. Eventually, he came to this: Soldiers were as necessary to a society as shelter was to an individual. If he had both the aptitude and proclivity to be one, then maybe enlisting *was* the moral choice. And a soldier, he decided, was no more responsible for a country's war than a tax-paying civilian. He also felt it was his duty as a citizen to vote and be informed, but it wasn't a soldier's job to weigh in on political decisions. Once he'd clarified this thinking, he spent months looking at photos of seriously wounded vets, soldiers who'd lost both their legs or all of their limbs, fates that scared him more than the prospect of death. He thought that in doing this, he might burn out his desire. But it remained. He was willing, he decided, to take the risk.

There was the matter of the particular conflict, though. Like me, he had been against the war in Iraq. But after thinking and reading about our involvement in Afghanistan, he came to feel that responding to 9/11 in the way we had was important, even imperative. And he understood our need for a presence in a country that shared borders with strategic competitors like Iran and China.

"Countries are in a constant power play with one another," he told me when I asked what he meant by "strategic competitors." I was romantic and naïve. Countries, to me, were beautiful patches on a quilt, mountains to ride trains through and beaches to sleep on, not chess pieces vying for dominance on the board of geopolitics. "Countries need armies, and armies need soldiers," he explained, though he admitted it wasn't quite *that* simple. But he believed in owing your country rather than it owing you. He believed it was meaningful to be a soldier. He wanted to be part of history, to be, as he told me once when he was feeling lofty, "at the beating heart of the world." He longed to be of service, to get high on purpose. And, despite his unerring decency, he wasn't soft. He had an edge, a restlessness, an outsized energy that filled any room.

"Andrew? The Army?" people would say when they discovered that he was enlisting. Usually, they'd pause, then nod to themselves. "He's intense," they'd admit. "It does make a weird kind of sense." His mother was the most worried but least shocked of any of us. Once, when he was in the first grade, she found a piece of paper on which he'd scrawled the words *I love WWII.*

When it came down to it, for Andrew, the Army was like anything else we can't talk people out of: He wanted it.

And I wanted him.

We fought hard about his desire to join, winding up in a therapist's office together in downtown Manhattan, not far from where the World Trade Center had once stood. He had proposed just weeks before. In therapy, I found out that in his past two years of silence, he had been fighting with himself. He worried that maybe he wouldn't make it out whole and alive, but mostly, he worried that I would leave him, just as I'd threatened.

"If I have to choose between you and the Army, it's the Army," he said during one of our sessions. The words hit me with the force of a physical blow. We had been together for four years by then. He had wanted to marry me from our very first date.

"I'd give up my writing for you," I said without thinking. What had I even meant by that? I didn't have to sign away my civil rights to be a writer. I didn't even have to take a shower. But I meant it, at least in the way that people mean things when they feel desperate and terrified. *Don't leave. I'll do anything.*

"Well, you shouldn't," Andrew said, frustration contorting his face.

"What if we just don't get married at all?" I asked after the session as we walked back to the subway, pushing against the autumn wind. I had never been sure about marriage anyway, had been a skeptic of the entire enterprise since watching my parents tear theirs apart. Even the most ordinary marriage seemed designed to fail, and this would be no ordinary marriage.

"What do I do with all my stuff? Just stick it in storage?" he asked.

"No, leave it! We'll still be together," I said.

Andrew stopped suddenly, just a block from the subway entrance. Leaves skittered across the sidewalk. "We need to get married, Simone. Girlfriends don't count for shit in the Army. If something happens to me, no one's gonna be calling you, no one's gonna take care of you. And we've been together four years. It's time to shit or get off the pot."

I looked at him. His face was calm, no longer twisted with emotion, and I felt every impulse I'd ever felt toward him. I wanted to slap his cold, rough cheek and touch it, softly, just to warm him.

"How romantic," I said, looking down at the feet rushing past us.

"You could stay here, keep your job," he said.

"So, what? We break up?"

"No, I could just do one contract, then get out."

One contract? That was more than three years. "A long-distance marriage?"

"People do it," Andrew said.

"People are idiots," I said. "It would crumble. We would crumble. Can you imagine? With how much you'll be deployed and training? It would be like saying goodbye for the next three years. And then what?"

"We're strong," he said.

Were we? I had always thought we were. I knew, somehow, from the beginning, that our relationship wouldn't be one to just run its course. This fact had intimidated me at first, but once I'd summoned the courage to commit, being with Andrew had been like building a home from cedar and cement. Time wouldn't tear it down. You'd need heavy equipment, a fire fed with kerosene. You'd need violence. That's how I'd felt about our relationship. And then Andrew's single-minded ambition about the Army came blowing into our house, threatening to knock it down. It was a force of nature I hadn't foreseen, a decision he was making that required me to make my own tough decisions: Could I marry a soldier? Could I support him in a war with a purpose that seemed more gray than black and white? Could I reconcile that man with the man I loved? And was it worth it to leave behind a life I'd made for the life he'd chosen, simply because I loved him?

—

CHAPTER 2

QUIET PROFESSIONALS

December 2012, two weeks later

ndrew stood over the moat of gear surrounding our Christmas tree, ticking off items from a packing list—a sub-zero winter jacket, wool glove liners, things he was required to pack but unlikely to actually need for winter in Afghanistan. It was early December, and this was our version of Christmas morning. In eight hours, Andrew was leaving. So was Dan, though he would be heading to a different forward operating base. Rachel and I were not allowed to know where in the country they were going. She would be giving us a ride for the drop-off.

"Can I help you?" I asked Andrew from our love seat, though I wasn't sure how I could.

He glanced at the stack of papers sitting on his dad's old trunk: the living will, the power of attorney, and the pink book, which was still blank, asking for information I didn't have to give, like an emergency contact or the name of my local doctor.

"Why don't you fill out the pink book?" he suggested.

Every time I'd try to sit down with the booklet, I'd found something more pressing to do, like clipping my toenails. If anything happened to Andrew and I was too out of my mind with grief to deal with life's mundane details, someone could go to it to fill in the gaps. But who?

"Why pink?" I'd asked Andrew when he'd brought it home from work.

"Because you're women?"

"Shut up."

"I'm serious. Our book of regulations is blue. Not because we're boys or anything. The Continental Army's first training manual was blue."

"So, we're pink, like babies in a nursery? What happens if women are eventually allowed into the Unit?"

"I guess they'll have to change the colors."

"Yeah, I'm sure that's all that will need changing," I'd said.

Andrew handed me the pink book and I opened it, flipping through the pages until I reached the item that had stumped me most of all. *Emergency contact, if I am notified that my husband has been injured or killed.* This would be the person notification officers would call to come to my side after they knocked at my door. My stomach was suddenly uneasy. All morning had been like this: I'd feel fine, and then, reality would hit with a blunt force that made me sick. I closed the book.

"Do you think they'll let you go on missions, since you're new?" I asked. I was hopeful that maybe they'd keep the dumb private back at the forward operating base, but he nodded.

"I think so. I need the experience," he said.

I had only a vague idea of what happened on these missions. I had asked about them only once, the morning after Andrew enlisted. We'd been eating greasy take-out plates of eggs and bacon from the short-order diner beneath our apartment in Harlem. It was July, and President Obama's surge in Afghanistan was just coming to an end. There was such a backlog of enlistees that Andrew would have to wait until the end of January to leave for boot camp.

"So, you were able to get a Special Operations contract?" I asked.

"I was," he said. The contract ensured that he would have a chance at the Unit, though it was no guarantee. He had to pass a rigorous selection process. It was not necessarily his first choice, but it felt to him like the best choice. He'd originally thought of joining Special Forces, also known as the Green Berets, but he was already twenty-seven. The pipeline felt too long. A friend he'd gone to college with had joined the Green Berets two years prior, and he was still in preliminary training. What if the war was over by the time Andrew made it onto a team? The unit Andrew chose required a shorter selection process than Special Forces. It was also one of the most extensively used combat units in the military. And he wanted, more than anything else, to be in the fight.

"What do these missions entail, exactly?" I'd asked, trying to keep my tone light. For months, I had avoided this question, but now that the deed was done, I found that I had to know. I was trying to frame it as just one more logistical query. *When do you think you'll leave for boot camp? What day should we schedule our courthouse wedding? Will you be killing anyone this time next year?*

"Well, I don't actually know. But, I watched this documentary about special operations leading manhunt missions. Kill or capture. That kind of thing, I guess," he'd said, trying to sound casual too, as he averted his eyes to 116th Street outside our windows. The word *kill* curdled my stomach instantly. It was state-sanctioned killing, but that didn't make it any more palatable to me. I didn't like *manhunt*, either. It made me think of that disturbing Hemingway quote: "There is no hunting like the hunting of man, and those who have hunted armed men long enough and liked it, never care for anything else thereafter." Why did he want to put himself in a position where he might have to kill another person? Did he *want* to kill another person?

"*Why* would you want to do that?" I asked. He'd enlisted; I had stayed. I was trying to stop interrogating him about his motivations. But this had been my main question all along, one I was brave enough to ask only after there was no way out.

Andrew slowly put down his toast, considered my face for a moment. "You look ashamed," he said sadly.

I'd thought then that he was right. But sitting here, watching him move swiftly around our half-empty living room in Georgia, I understood what I'd felt was fear. I was an adventurer, but Andrew was a seeker, the type of person who opened doors not just to peek behind them, like I did, but to step all the way through. His enlistment was a door I never would have considered opening, not even for just a glimpse of what lay waiting on the other side.

Now, we were both about to find out.

I looked past the Christmas tree and through the living room at the Boyds' house. Since that first evening when Rachel had brought us cookies, I'd only seen her in passing outside, each of us waving awkwardly to the other across the street. I wondered if their place was as comically disappointing as ours. Over the course of the last two weeks, it had become abundantly clear that whoever had renovated it had left in the middle of the job and never returned. When I went to pull up the blinds to let the sun in, they fell clean off the window, clattering to the floor. The first time I plugged in my hair dryer, the outlet shocked me. At every threshold, tacks poked up from beneath the carpet, and a persistent leak dripped beneath the kitchen sink. But it was ours. Or at least, it already felt like ours in a way no apartment ever had.

Andrew turned away from the mess of gear on the living room floor. "I need a break," he said. "And I have something for you." He took my hand and guided me down the hallway.

"I see where this is going," I said, but he bypassed our bedroom and opened the door to the spare room next to it.

"Merry Christmas," he said as my eyes fell on a lean black desk beneath the window. It was simple, with just a single drawer in the center. I walked over and ran my hand across its surface.

"I put it together this morning," Andrew said. "It isn't much. It's from Walmart. But you'll need a place to write while I'm gone. I was thinking this could be your office."

For as long as I could remember, I had loved to write—stories in elementary school, poetry in high school, short fiction in college. In Annapolis, looking for a viable way to turn my passion into a profession, I started writing for the weekly paper. I loved interviewing sources and hunting down stories and thought maybe I could be a tough-as-nails reporter. In journalism school, though, I discovered I was too enthralled with the slow burn of creative work, too obsessed with language, more interested in the guy who owned the bodega that was robbed than the news of the robbery itself.

With my graduate degree, I found work as an editor and decided I would carve out time to write on the side. That was when I discovered essays. Writing them gave me a profound sensation most people seemed to take for granted but I'd never quite understood: that of being at home. I stole moments to write before sunrise, or late on Saturday nights at a cramped table in McNally Jackson's café, drinking coffee as people streamed by outside. But the responsibilities at my editing job, where I worked hand-in-hand with the editor to publish three 5,000-to-30,000-word pieces each week, were all-consuming. I was doing everything from sifting through slush to soliciting work from big-name authors to developing pieces with newer writers. I loved this work, could not believe I was even getting paid to do it, but it left almost no room for my own essays, so I decided that writing would likely always be a side note to my life, a kind of mischief I committed when no one was looking. I'd never truly believed I could be a *real* writer, anyway. Being a writer was something for other people. Luckier people. People who believed in themselves blindly. That wasn't me.

Andrew believed in me, though. He always had. He thought I shouldn't rush to find a traditional job in Columbus, at least for now. Instead, I could build my own freelance editing business and write— still on the side, but there would be no more answering to a boss at any hour or staying up until 2 a.m. responding to emails, no more relegating writing to the farthest edges of my life. Andrew made less in the Army than he had as a bartender, but our expenses here were easily half what they'd been in New York. Still, he was a low-ranking enlisted man. Money would be tight. He couldn't support us both entirely. But he insisted that I didn't need to make a full salary, at least not yet.

"Here's your chance at a writer's life," Andrew had said to me. I had been suspicious of his glass-half-full argument, but now, looking at this little desk, I thought that maybe he was right. This wasn't the airy loft I'd imagined when I'd moved to New York. The window across from me looked out at a diseased tree stump and a rusted clothesline. But nothing was ever what you imagined.

I turned to face Andrew in the doorway. He looked so hopeful. The desk was an offering, I understood—both an apology for leaving me in this place and a hope for what my future might hold here. This desk was Andrew's way of saying, *I believe in you.* It demonstrated, too, just how much he wanted—needed—this new life to work for both of us. *I'm leaving you*, it said. *But I'm giving you something else in return: a room of your own. The precious commodities of solitude and time.*

"It's perfect," I said.

In the afternoon, we sat on the floor in front of the Christmas tree and opened our stockings. The tree was plain, decorated in uniform bulbs we'd picked up at Walmart. The one exception was an ornament Andrew's mother had sent, a stained-glass yellow ribbon. I hadn't known what it stood for when I first opened the package, but over the last two weeks, I'd seen that yellow ribbon plastered on bumpers around Columbus, hanging from front doors, peeking out from the windows of small businesses. It signaled that someone the ribbon-hanger loved was deployed overseas. The gift felt like a symbol of Andrew's mother's effort to know his new world, which was as foreign to her as it was to me. She had even signed up to be in a support group for local parents. "None of their kids are deploying, though," she'd said to me over the phone, and her voice had cracked.

Andrew talked about the war as two wars. He had joined the second, which was, in a sense, Obama's war. Under Obama, the war's primary combat strategy changed from daytime foot patrols to night raids. For the previous few years, we'd been slowly handing over control of territory we'd seized from the Taliban to the Afghan National Army. We continued to support and train them, but had shifted the focus of combat operations to killing or capturing leaders of terrorist units that the Taliban had given safe harbor to, like Al-Qaeda and the Haqqani Network. This kind of work was the purview of Special Operations. They owned the war now, which meant Special Ops families were feeling the burden of continual combat deployments in a way that the families of conventional soldiers no longer were.

Andrew found the silver St. Michael's medal I'd put in his stocking, and I kneeled behind him to fasten it around his neck. He'd worn a St. Christopher's medal when we'd first started dating. Times had changed. He needed a saint with a sword and shield, not just a walking stick. Neither of us was religious, but I was superstitious, and I had decided that the patron saint of soldiers would keep him safe. I would keep him safe.

"This is harder than I thought it was going to be," he said.

Andrew lived in the present, facing down obstacles only as they approached. And now that this one was finally arriving, I could hear in his voice that he was fully realizing, maybe for the first time, where he was going, and that I wouldn't be there.

"This is exactly as hard as I'd imagined," I said, forcing a laugh.

Andrew looked at his watch. "Shit, we have forty-five minutes before we've got to be at the Boyds."

The sex was rushed and sweet, lips brushing against collarbones, hands grasping at each other's necks. We kept avoiding each other's eyes, like we were afraid of getting too close. After, when we were lying side by side, I was surprised to reach down and feel a wetness on my chest. Somehow, I knew it was Andrew's tears, not sweat, though I had only seen him cry on a few occasions.

"We still need to talk," he said.

I'd known this conversation was coming. He'd filled out the paperwork, answered questions like, *What music do you want played at your funeral procession?* (The opening aria of the Goldberg Variations, the frequent soundtrack to his paper-writing in college.) But there were things he hadn't written down.

"This is just another thing to check off the list," he said.

And so, minutes before leaving, he began to tell me the things he wanted, if anything were to happen to him: his best friend to officiate at the funeral, a burial, no talk of God or the military.

"It is important to me that you and my mom receive a flag, though," he said.

My chest tightened. I had seen those flags in videos and photographs, folded meticulously, placed carefully in the hands of spouses.

"And I want you to live a full life, get married again, all of that." He said this slowly and deliberately, as though he wanted me to remember it.

He turned to me and put a hand to my cheek, and, even though our bodies had just been pressed against each other, his touch was almost unbearable. I rolled away from him, wrapping myself into the fetal position and closing my eyes. If I could disappear, maybe this entire moment could disappear too. There would be no goodbye, no deployment, no returning to an empty house and plugging in the Christmas tree lights to ward off the darkness.

"Simone." Andrew's voice was soft. I opened my eyes. My nightstand was just inches from my face.

"Simone." His voice was more insistent, but nowhere near forceful enough to drive out the sick feeling in my stomach. Maybe this was just how life would feel now.

"It's time," he said.

—

On the way to headquarters, Dan fiddled anxiously with the radio until Rachel asked him to please turn it off. Then, there was silence, Andrew and I holding hands across the backseat as we each looked out our respective windows at Victory Drive, the state road that led to base. It was worn out and colorless, bordered by bail bondsmen, tattoo parlors, and motels. Eventually, we turned onto a wooded road, and the seediness fell away as we drove toward the gate.

Before we'd arrived in Georgia, I'd expected the base to feel like part of the greater city that surrounded it, a neighborhood among neighborhoods. But when we'd come to get my ID, I'd been struck by how stark the transition from city to base had felt. Fort Benning was an orderly 182,000 acres, with a brick post office and hospital and four elementary schools, even its own zip code. It was the home of the infantry, which meant it was a base dominated by men. Women were stationed here, but they weren't allowed in combat arms or Special

Operations, so it was men I'd seen marching down the side of the road, their M4s clutched to their chests; men with high and tights standing at attention in parade fields; men buying tins of Copenhagen at the gas station where I'd stopped for a soda water.

When it was first established, Fort Benning's primary purpose was to provide basic training for soldiers in World War I. By World War II, Benning had become the primary infantry and airborne training center for the Army. All of those details had led me to believe that the base would have a real center-of-the-universe vibe, but, at least as it stood today, it felt so utilitarian, with its enormous motor pools of strikers and Humvees and beige buildings lining the roads, that driving through it had the mind-numbing quality of traversing an endless cross-country route. The jump towers at Airborne School reminded me of oil towers, and the massive complex of barracks looked, from the road, like the world's most nondescript outlet mall. Even the commissary, the base's grocery store, had the feeling of a brutalist 1970s DMV.

We went through the gate, driving for a few minutes down a two-lane road before reaching the "white elephants," the most elegant and oldest neighborhood on base. These white stucco homes with Spanish tile roofs were the one aspect of Fort Benning that matched the cinema of my imagination. Porch lights glowed in every entryway and weeping willows shaded yards that looked so soft I wanted to lie down on them. The homes were, reportedly, prone to mold and badly in need of repair, but I had fallen in love with them immediately.

"Why don't we to move to one of these houses?" I'd said to Andrew that afternoon we'd come for my ID. He had driven, then, a mile or so farther on to an enclave of apartments. Their exterior paint was peeling, and through one unit's open door, I could see that the places were small and dark, the floors throughout a yellowish linoleum. Outside, a few residents sat on their stoops smoking. Others were getting in and out of cars parked in assigned spaces. Every single one of them looked depressed as hell about the life choices and circumstances that had landed them there.

"This is where we would live," he'd said. "At least until I move up in rank."

We'd reached the parking lot behind Andrew's and Dan's companies. Since most of the guys had already been overseas for six weeks, there were just a few other couples saying goodbye to each other. I'd expected deployment farewells to happen at airfields, with crowds of well-dressed women holding the tiny hands of their children. But we weren't allowed anywhere near the airfield, and the women I saw dropping off their husbands now were a mess—red noses, smudged eyeliner, sweatpants, and unwashed hair. They didn't look brave or scared. They looked like they'd been through this too many times, their expressions tired and resigned as they gave their husbands a hug and a kiss goodbye before retreating to the safety of their cars.

Other than Rachel, the only spouse I'd had any contact with so far was Andrew's company commander's wife, Charlotte Adams, the leader of A-company's Family Readiness Group, a collection of volunteer spouses that existed entirely to support the families of soldiers in Andrew's unit. I'd received a few cheery mass emails from her. *Leave no trace behind!* Charlotte reminded us at the end of each one. Of what? Were we collectively committing a crime of some kind? Cleaning up after ourselves at a campsite?

"She means on social media," Andrew had told me. "When we're leaving, coming home, that kind of thing. It's a big problem."

"So, you're telling me I should take down that photo I posted on Facebook of the flight schedule?" I'd joked. Of course I had no flight schedule. There was very little I could put on Facebook if I wanted to.

This was all I knew: Both Andrew and Dan would be joining their companies somewhere in Afghanistan. Andrew would be gone for roughly two and a half months. The guys in Andrew's unit called themselves "quiet professionals," and they expected the families they left behind to be equally discreet. The Unit told us just enough, but nothing more, leaving us almost as clueless about the war as the rest of the American public, but with a whole lot more at stake.

When we were about fifty yards from Andrew's company, his name hit the air with a smack. I looked around. There was a moment of silence, and then, there it was again, louder and more urgent. I felt Andrew stiffen against me like a dog responding to a whistle.

"Where is that coming from?" I asked.

"One of the Rear D sergeants is calling me from inside."

I looked toward the open door and saw only darkness. "How can you tell?"

"Oh, I can tell," he said, and then he turned to me in a swift motion and brought me to his chest. He smelled elemental, like sweat and dirt and the fresh air breathed in after a long run.

"I love you," he said, pulling away just as someone shouted his name again. He hitched up his pack and ran toward the open door. And then, he was gone from sight, and I found that I couldn't move. Maybe I could just wait out the next couple of months right here in this parking lot. I had gotten quite good at waiting this past year.

"I hope you have patience, because you'll need it where he's going," Andrew's drill sergeant had said to me at boot camp graduation. In his letters, Andrew had spent whole passages talking about Drill Sergeant Brown, who was always chewing tobacco and clicking his black military knife open and closed, saying things like "you look like hammered dog shit" and "sense is common, but common sense ain't." In one letter, Andrew wrote about the "twenty-one comrades" Brown had lost on his three deployments to Iraq. Thousands of soldiers had been killed in these wars. But twenty-one. That number seemed fathomless.

A breeze moved through the air, and I felt myself go tense as a skinny arm laced itself through mine.

"Let's get in the car."

It was Rachel. Her face was streaked with mascara, and she wasn't even trying to wipe it away.

"I'm not sure I can move my legs," I said. She smelled sweet, like sugar and butter.

Rachel laughed. "I know just what you mean."

When we got to her Corolla, she stopped with me at the passenger side. "You know, when Dan asked if we could give you a ride, I thought it might be weird," she said. "I told him I wanted to cry alone, damn it." She was still crying, I saw, as she unlocked the doors. She was also laughing. "But crying together is better, isn't it?" She handed me a crumpled Kleenex. I touched my cheek and realized that I was crying, too.

Was it better? I rarely cried, and almost never in front of anyone other than Andrew. And yet, oddly, I wasn't mortified.

"But fuck, I definitely will need to cry alone when I get home," she said.

CHAPTER 3

MORALE, WELFARE, AND RECREATION

After just one day by myself in our new house, my body began to ache from the quiet. I missed people—longed, even, for the crush of my old subway commute, the edge of someone's newspaper grazing my arm, the sharp-smelling breath of a hungover man wedged against me. Andrew had told me it would likely be a few days before I heard from him, but I kept my phone with me every moment, the ringer on high, in my pocket or my purse or clutched in my hand. When I caught Rachel looking out through her living room window, I remembered the warmth of the cookies under the Saran wrap, the brush of her fingertip as she'd handed me a tissue, and understood that it was my move.

But how should I make it? And did I even want to? In the two weeks Andrew and I had been in Georgia together, I had just once woken early enough to say goodbye to Andrew at 5:30 a.m. when he left for Fort Benning, and I had seen Rachel in her kitchen window, washing dishes. According to Andrew, she made Dan breakfast every morning. Andrew did not expect or even hope that I'd wake to make him breakfast, because he couldn't stomach food or conversation before the sun rose. But I still wondered if Rachel was made for this life in a way that I wasn't. She was a devout Christian, according to Andrew. What would I have to say to her? Since I'd arrived in Georgia, and especially since Andrew had left, I'd had the sensation that all the mirrors I'd once checked myself in were gone. What were the rules of propriety? How did I greet another person? How should I arrange the features of my face? Suddenly, I had no idea how to be a person in the world.

Around lunchtime on the second day, I dropped off our rent check, riding my bike the quarter mile to our landlord's office, an aluminum-sided shed on a depressing block of what looked like mostly vacant warehouses. Inside, I found our landlord, Frank, standing among walls covered in *Sports Illustrated* swimsuit calendars and tear-outs of women with *Baywatch*-era bikinis. He was the size of a refrigerator. His short-sleeved button-down exposed a chest full of gray hair. When I put out my hand to shake his, he didn't take it, just left it hanging there in the air.

"How's the house workin' out for yah?" he asked. His accent was thick.

"It's great," I said. "Though there are a couple of things that still need doing."

"Oh yeah?" He was looking at my chest, I was pretty sure.

"Just a leak under the sink. The blinds need to be installed properly. A few other things."

"What's that, suga'?"

I winced a little at that, but kept on going.

"The sink has a leak. And the blinds don't work very well."

He took his glasses off and looked at me like I was an amusing little puzzle. He didn't want to admit it, not again, but I could tell he couldn't understand me. Did I have an accent? I thought I had the very absence of one. Maybe he thought the same of his own speech.

"I'll call you," I said finally, and handed him the check.

"Thanks, suga'," he said, looking—I was sure this time—squarely at my chest.

I rode the two miles to downtown and walked Columbus's main drag. It was lined with trees and nineteenth-century brick buildings and quaint shop fronts, and full of wrought-iron benches where strollers could stop and sit. Except no one was in them. And half of the shops were shuttered. Downtown had long ago been Columbus' commercial center, but, like many American cities, it had grown outward as it expanded, with residents abandoning its historic center and leaving it prone to crime. Much of the middle class now concentrated itself in the northern end of the city, where suburban subdivisions and outdoor malls filled with Starbucks and Panera Breads had taken over the once rural landscape.

The city was working to revitalize downtown, Andrew said, and I saw some signs of this: a brewery, a dress boutique with exposed brick walls, a wine and beer shop where a handkerchiefed pit bull lay in a heap at the open door. But there was a strangeness in the air, a sensation that everyone was hiding from a looming storm except for me. When I got home in the early evening, I was so lonely I rifled through the hamper to find Andrew's T-shirt at the bottom. I inhaled deeply and cried, briefly, before throwing it back in.

That night, I held the phone into the late hours, preparing witticisms I knew Andrew would laugh at, imagining the sensation of his eager voice in my ear. While I waited, I scrolled through Honor Them, a Facebook feed that provided nightly updates on American casualties overseas, even though I knew the information was stale and useless. If he died, I'd find out about it well before any social media feed. Still, it was a comfort to see the words *No New Casualties*. It was December 2012, the end of the second surge, and US troop numbers in Afghanistan had dropped to fewer than seventy thousand. We were past the height of the war, or at least that's what news outlets seemed to think, but there had been nearly three hundred US deaths in Afghanistan this year. That was a drop from 2011's count, but it was still one of the highest since the war's start.

By the time I fell asleep on the couch at midnight, the phone had never rung.

The next day, I decided to brave the bus ride to the big-box stores in north Columbus. A man in a lifted pickup truck stopped me as I ran to catch it. "Are you okay, miss?" he asked, as if I were running from, not to, something.

"I'm just late to catch the bus," I told him, and he looked confused. He was white. Nearly every single person on the bus aside from me was Black. The ride, which would take fifteen minutes by car, lasted an hour and twenty minutes. Going back and forth took up most of the day. By the time I got home, it was evening and I was exhausted. I curled up on the love seat that had filled our apartment living room but felt, in our new house, like a raft in the middle of the sea, and picked up a Stephen King novel I was trying to make my way through. Since Andrew had left, my mind had been as anxious and noncommittal as a butterfly, landing on a thought or a TV show or a page in a book for only a moment before flying on to something else.

I was wondering what I'd just read, or pretended to read, over the last twenty minutes, when my phone rang on the end table next to me. It was a number I didn't recognize. My heart jumped. *Andrew.*

"I'm finally settled in." His voice was clear and resonant, almost painfully loud in the silence of the house, but he sounded formal and detached, like he was talking to a customer service representative.

"How are you?" I asked.

"Doing fine," he said. "How are you?"

"Pretty good," I said. Yesterday, I had cried into his dirty T-shirt like he was dead, but you were supposed to put on a brave face for your soldier. I scanned my mind for a question to ask as though I were navigating explosives. *What did you do today?* was no longer a safe question. *What do you have going on tomorrow?* had become off-limits.

"Are other people nearby?" I asked. For Andrew, a conversation without privacy was no conversation at all. I tried to picture his surroundings. He'd told me he'd be calling from the forward operating base's MWR, a kind of bare-bones internet and phone café. MWR stood for Morale, Welfare, and Recreation, the name of the program in the Army that ran the movie theater, bowling alley, gym, and summer camps on base. Its slogan: *We are the Army's Home.* I imagined Andrew sitting in a metal folding chair, soldiers walking past him, fluorescent lights buzzing above. I wondered what the phone looked like. It had been so long since I'd even held a receiver.

"A couple," he said. Maybe it wouldn't even matter if he were alone. The calls were monitored. Andrew was terrified of slipping up and saying something he wasn't supposed to say. He was twenty-nine years old, an adult who'd been on his own for years, but, in the Army, he was just another nervous private.

"What'd you have for dinner?" I asked. Food was safe. No explosives there.

"Breakfast," he said. Andrew's missions happened at night. He woke to darkness and meat loaf and went to bed after orange juice and scrambled eggs.

"What kind of breakfast?"

"You know I can't talk about my day."

"Andrew, it's *breakfast*," I said, laughing.

He exhaled loudly. "I try to make it feel like dinner," he said. "I take these eggs, they're premade, they come in a little sack, and put them in a tortilla and roll it into a burrito." He stopped then. I thought he'd go on, but he didn't. This was all I was going to get, and the paltriness of it, of both the meal and of his offering to me, made my chest ache.

"I went downtown," I said, trying to move the conversation forward. "I saw this monument on one of the side streets. It was huge, as tall as the houses. I don't remember exactly what it said, but it was for the Confederate soldiers. Something about '. . . and the cause tho' lost, is still just.'"

"There are a lot of Confederate monuments in Columbus," Andrew said. I felt my phone buzz and resisted the urge to look at the screen. I wanted to talk to Andrew, but I could feel that so much of him was elsewhere, and so I could feel myself beginning to wander too.

"'But the cause tho' lost, is still just'? Isn't that spooky?"

"It's . . . history," Andrew said. I could tell he was getting uncomfortable. He didn't want to talk about the Civil War on a monitored call from a windowless room in Afghanistan. "It's kinda like that in the South. At least the parts I've been in."

"Like they still wish the Civil War had gone another way?" I asked.

"I don't know if I'd say that," Andrew said. "You talk to Rachel yet?"

"No," I said.

"You should," he said.

"I will."

"I've gotta go, but I'll call again soon," Andrew said, and then he was gone, the silence of our house even louder than it had been before. For a moment, I felt like I might cry—where was his hamper when I needed it?—but then I remembered the buzzing of my phone.

It was a text from Rachel. *Want to come over for TV and wine?*

—

I was ten years old when I met Andrew. He was eleven. I had seen him on the school playground before then, showing off the moonwalk to a circle of spectators, but he didn't know I existed until we were assigned seats next to each other in fifth grade. That first day, when he threw a pencil at my shoulder to get my attention, I stayed focused on the book beneath my desk. But then he whispered a joke in my ear, and I couldn't help myself. I looked up and laughed. Andrew was a spring-coil of energy, with a big, goofy smile and wild eyes, the dominant color in the beige-walled classroom. He was impossible to ignore.

We lived a couple miles away from each other in Marin County, an affluent, progressive enclave north of the Golden Gate, where the seasons were temperate, the light had the quality of golden hour, and residents gave "Peace a Chance" on their bumper stickers. In my own household, war was a dirty word, and my father, a gifted storyteller, loved to regale us with tales of the adventures he went on when his bad feet saved him from the Vietnam draft—hitchhiking across the west to see Creedence Clearwater and The Doors; trying every drug under the sun; cheating death when he fell from a cliff in Switzerland on his nineteenth birthday. He had a temper that got him into trouble at the private schools where he taught, but his core philosophy was pacifistic, and I'd inherited it, whole cloth, straight from the protest song that shouted out from our record player:

War. What is it good for? Absolutely nothing.

My parents were born into the golden age of California when rent was low and college was affordable. They spent their twenties dropping in and out of different UCs along the coast, living on restaurant jobs and jasmine-scented ocean air, breaking up and getting back together until wandering, eventually, into marriage and children. By the time they arrived in Marin in the late '80s with my six-year-old brother and three-year-old me in the back of their old Honda, they were in their mid-thirties and broke, and hoping, without really trying, to repair an already fragile marriage.

California, at this point, was no longer affordable. My father had a master's in music composition, and my mother had a BA in dance, which qualified them, mostly, for coffeehouse and construction work positions. Rent in Marin was steep, but my mother managed to find a two-bedroom house right around the corner from the local high school. At $900 a month, it was a stretch for my parents, more expensive than the home Andrew and I were renting in Georgia two decades later. But it was a steal for a rental in a county the *New York Times* later called the "most beautiful, bucolic, privileged, liberal, hippie-dippie place on earth."

After five years, my father got a job teaching seventh-grade math at a private school, where no credential was required. His teaching brought a bit more stability to our lives, but the salary was too low to support a family in Marin. Often, we were late on rent. My dad taught music lessons in the evenings and my mother worked a carousel of jobs. I loved visiting her at the San Anselmo Coffee Roastery, where she flitted behind the counter, laughing with customers, her blond hair catching the light. When she worked the Macy's makeup counter during the holidays, she came home quiet, her face drawn as she took off her heels. Her favorite job was the flower shop. The customers could be uppity and exhausting, but she filled our house with lilacs and hydrangeas at the end of each day.

My parents didn't have the means, support, or foresight to build a life in the way I saw families doing around us. Mostly, they survived. My father, who had grown up in Lake Tahoe, was practiced at this. He'd spent a lot of time in the wilderness, and he prepared for daily life the same way he might prepare for a backpacking trip or a natural disaster. Every time we broke down on the freeway in one of our used cars, his trunk was ready with flashlights and water and Mexican blankets. I knew that these breakdowns, among many other small but consistent crises in our lives, were a sign of our family's precariousness, the kind of thing I never discussed with friends. But, in secret, I loved those afternoons on the shoulder of the freeway, my hair whipping around my face as the cars flew past. Much of the time, my father's presence felt more like an absence, but on the freeway, he was right there, tall and defiant and broad, lit up by struggle. *There he is,* I'd think. And here *it* is—that *zing,* that feeling I was always trying and failing to catch and pin down, the bone-rattling sensation I couldn't get, even, from books. *This* was being alive.

While my father prepared, my mother hoped, and she tended to hang that hope on impossible people and places and things—my moody father, an expensive county, and the sense that everything would work out, despite all evidence to the contrary. She was deeply, almost inappropriately compassionate. When she heard a baby cry a few aisles down in a grocery store, her eyes filled involuntarily with tears. She was also beautiful, her step as buoyant as her optimism, and she possessed a gift for flirtation that was utterly guileless. Men fell in love with her at every one of her jobs, and women fell in love with her too. But I loved her the most. At night, I'd hold her hostage in my twin bed, reading to her until she fell asleep. In the morning, I sat on the toilet seat, watching her apply makeup, drinking her in, inhaling the powdery scent of her perfume, relishing even the way her hairspray stung my eyes. *I love you, sweet pea,* she'd say every morning when she hugged me, and her voice sounded like song.

By the time I was eight, my parents could rarely stay in the same room for long without starting a fight. My mother turned to drinking, and my father became increasingly withdrawn. While I lost myself in books, my brother escaped into a large network of friends who were always shooing me away. We spent less and less time together as a family, but sometimes, on hot summer weekends when our bedsheets stuck to our backs with sweat, we'd pack into the car and drive out to the beach. My brother and I would beg to go to Stinson, the fun beach with ice cream cones and kids splashing on boogie boards and the kind of beer-swilling mediocrity my father loathed. My father insisted on taking us, instead, to Limantour, a cold beach on West Marin's wild peninsula, where the riptide was fierce and the wind howled. There, he would disappear on a long walk while my mother stewed on a blanket, my brother complained to go home, and I traced words into the wet shore with my toe. Slowly, without any of us really noticing, this had become the layout of my family: separate not just from the world around us, but from each other, four lonely individuals trying to figure out how to make being alive a little bit more tolerable.

One night at home, in the springtime of my eighth year, my mother told me she was going for a walk. She'd just had a brief but tense argument with my dad. It was twilight, a mild evening that didn't require the thick winter coat she'd thrown on before letting the screen door slam behind her. *Where was she walking to? How far would she go?* I stood for what felt like hours at the front windows, asking myself these questions and getting no answer, willing her to arrive as the sky grew dark outside.

"We should look for her," I finally told my father.

I caught sight of her feet first, peeking out from beneath the peony bush in our front yard. Then, the fifth of gin lying next to her arm. I hadn't seen her return to the yard. Had she been there all along, just out of my vision from where I'd been standing at the window?

My dad rushed to her and picked her up the way a groom would his bride. "Oh, Lynn," he said. It was a different voice than the one that had been yelling earlier. It was a different man, one who could remember loving this woman, who maybe still loved her. *Oh, Lynn.*

I followed him to their bedroom, where he turned on the bright overhead light, gently lay her down and took off her panty hose, briskly, as though he hoped it would rouse her. Her face went red, and her eyes flew open. She began to thrash, snarling, and looked at me in the doorway. Or through me. It was like she couldn't see me at all. She wasn't my mother. But she was, at least, alive.

After that, I took on the role of family watchman, always listening for the slur in my mother's voice, the rise in my father's temper, the stillness of the house the morning after a fight. I worried about everyone in my family, but especially, I worried about my mother, who seemed, suddenly, impossibly delicate, like a passing breeze might knock her off her tiny feet. Every night, I waited for her at the living room window, longing for her headlights to fill the drive. Sometimes, she'd come through the door and the house would hum with warmth and completion. But, more and more, she walked in tipsy and ready for a fight. When my father ultimately retreated to the backyard shed, she would crumple onto the floor in tears, and I'd hold her and wait for her pain to ebb, which was so big and boundaryless it became my pain, too. I loved my parents. I felt for them with an intensity that consumed me, and I wanted to believe that I could save them from the sorrow that hunted them as ferociously as the creditors my father told me to hang up on.

When I was thirteen, they finally split up. They fought so bitterly and constantly that it was, by then, a relief. My mother moved out, crashing with different friends until she eventually got a one-bedroom apartment of her own. I stayed there every other week. There were times of relative calm in that place, when my mother didn't have a boyfriend coming by. The two of us would talk and laugh, interrupting each other like old friends with too much to say. When the triangle-shaped living room filled with light, it felt like we were inside a glowing prism. In the summertime, the big window and front door were always open, letting in the scent of orange trees.

But my mother was unpredictable, and I watched her the way one might watch the clouds for a storm coming in. One night, when I was fifteen, she drank too much and sobbed inconsolably, throwing herself against the wall in frustration. I realized, for the first time, I had the option to leave. I *needed* to leave. I had chemistry homework. I had to read *The Crucible*. I had an after-school job at the local library. I didn't have time to fix an unfixable situation anymore. I called my dad. Twenty minutes later, my mother ran after me as I got into the passenger seat of his Geo, tripping and falling to her knees in the gravel driveway. *Please*, she said. Her face was so full of pain, I couldn't even take it in. I could only see her knees digging into the gravel. *That must hurt so bad, Mom,* I thought. And then I slammed the door.

As my father drove, I let the silence of the car fill me so completely that it crowded out the well of feeling I'd always had for my mother. It was a relief, and with that relief, came a new clarity: As soon as I could, I was getting out of the most beautiful place on earth, taking myself as far away as I could go.

CHAPTER 4

—

DEPENDENT

With painstaking care, Rachel removed two wineglasses from a set of six stored in its original packaging.

"It was a wedding gift," she said, sheepish, as she gave us each a generous pour. A drop spilled on the kitchen counter, the red stark against the beige laminate. She wiped it up quickly with a sponge and handed me a glass. "You want to see the house?"

Their renovations had actually been finished, it looked like, and they had a gas fireplace in the living room. Even their blinds were sturdier than ours. "I'm sorry, it's such a mess when Daniel isn't here to keep it tidy for," Rachel said as she took me down the hallway, the low murmurs of the cop show on in the living room following us. Mess? The place was so clean, fresh vacuum marks stood out on the cream-colored carpet. I didn't even own a vacuum yet. The kitchen smelled like Lemon Pine-Sol. Rachel was clearly a real domesticated adult in ways I was not. New York could grow you up quick while also keeping you young and stupid, with its absurd conveniences of twenty-four-hour bodegas and 11 p.m. dinners and laundromats that would wash, dry, and fold your clothes for you.

"Wow," I said when we got to the en suite bathroom at the back of the house.

"I know, a double tub," she said.

"No, it's just that you have a second bathroom," I said, feeling that faint ripple of jealousy I had when I'd seen her petunias.

Peppered throughout, on walls and end tables, were photos of Rachel and Dan on their wedding day. Andrew had told me they'd met in a Florida bar six weeks before he'd gone off to Basic and married a few months later at one of his training bases, in Lawton, Oklahoma. It was a story of speed and convenience and hormones and, yes, love that was exceedingly common in the Army. Enlisted soldiers were forced to live in the barracks until they were either married or became staff sergeants. "That really speeds up the whole marriage thing," Andrew said.

A few months before she met Dan, Rachel had quit her stressful post-college job doing in-home investigations for Child Welfare Services in San Diego and moved to Florida, where her father had retired and was on dialysis for kidney failure. It was an opportunity to pay down some credit card debt and to spend some one-on-one time with her father, who had always connected more easily with Rachel's sister. A month after she arrived, he had a heart attack. During the day, she managed a Clinique counter at Macy's, and in the evenings, she cooked him chicken breast and steamed broccoli, hunting through the trash for the greasy Wendy's bags he tried to hide from her.

"Your wedding dress is lovely," I said, sitting down on the couch as Rachel disappeared into the kitchen to grab the bottle of wine. Across the living room, Dan's German pointer snored softly from a dog bed.

Like us, like so many military couples, Rachel and Dan had married in a courthouse. At my own ceremony, I had worn a silver cocktail dress, Andrew a tweed sport coat and olive-colored slacks. Reina was our witness. She brought me a bouquet of white peonies and Andrew a white rose for his lapel and took candids of us while we waited awkwardly in line with other couples, a succession of Barry White and Marvin Gaye songs playing in the lobby, all of us clutching numbered tickets like deli patrons. Rachel's photos were clearly professional, staged on benches and in front of fountains, with Dan in a tux and Rachel in a strapless white wedding dress, the kind I'd seen a thousand times before. She really looked fantastic in it, though.

"I wanted a real wedding," Rachel said when she got back, taking a seat next to me as she muted the TV. "I had this vision of getting married under the banyan trees in Selby Gardens in Sarasota. I'd been dreaming of the day for what felt like my whole life, you know?"

I had never once dreamed of my wedding day. But I nodded because I recognized the disappointment in her voice, so fresh I could feel it in the air between us. I had imagined marriage would look different than this too.

"He proposed the day he graduated from Basic," she said. "It wasn't a proposal, actually. We were sitting in his car, and I thought he was breaking up with me because he kept going on about how it just wouldn't work for me to move wherever he did. And then finally, he asked. Or really, told me. He said: 'We have to get married.'" She laughed, remembering.

My chest warmed as the merlot traveled through me. I wasn't sure what I'd have to say to Rachel, but it felt so good to be this close to another human, I wasn't particularly worried about it.

"Are you going to the spouse retreat?" Rachel asked.

I looked at her questioningly. "Spouse retreat?"

"Didn't you get an email? The retreat in Birmingham."

Right. Charlotte, the FRG leader, had sent a mass email about a weekend retreat. On each day there would be a talk of some kind. The only that had been named was the optional one: "God's Ultimate Design."

"Aren't those run by the chaplain?" I asked. *The God thing in the military is huge*, Andrew had written in one of his boot camp letters. *Every Sunday we have four hours for religious services. There's every kind you can imagine on base: Protestant, Catholic, LDS, Jewish, Muslim, etc. My first Sunday, I was one of only four out of the twenty-six in my barracks who didn't go to services.* At the start of boot camp, an Army chaplain offered recruits pocket Bibles and religious pendants to add to their dog tags, if they wanted them. Army chaplains were, in theory, nondenominational, and the services on post were diverse, but the overwhelming religious flavor of the Army was Christian. Andrew had read one of the Bibles lying around cover to cover, because he wasn't allowed any other reading materials. One of his bunkmates, he'd told me in a letter, had even gotten baptized at one of the base churches.

Andrew considered himself an atheist. I wasn't ready to commit to that label, but the existence of a God did seem doubtful. Life was too random, too cruel, too absurd and unfair. I had always worried, though, that faith might be life's one true rudder, and without it, I would be lost. This scared me when I was young, and I'd gone to the nature I was spoiled with for comfort—Mount Tamalpais's wooded trails, silent groves of redwoods, the cold, fierce riptide of Limantour that, eventually, I grew to love. On rare hot days, my father would walk into the icy surf with me on his shoulders. From there, I could see all the way out to the boats at the edge of the ocean. In those moments, I felt like I understood what the religious felt. In those moments, I felt like the luckiest kid in Marin.

"Oh, there will be some guest speakers, but no one's going to preach to you," Rachel said, refilling my glass. We were moving through this wine fast. *A church-every-Sunday-and-Bible-study-every-Wednesday kind of Christian.* That was how Andrew had described Rachel. I had never before known such a Christian. Was I allowed to swear around her? She had said *fuck*, hadn't she, at the deployment drop-off? It wasn't that Rachel seemed innocent. There was too much knowing in that disappointment I'd heard in her voice a moment earlier. She was earnest, though, in a way that I was unaccustomed to, so clearly *trying*—in those vacuum marks, the carefully stored wineglasses, the wedding photos so thoughtfully placed, her brave late-evening text to me.

"I'm not too worried about that," I said, though, of course, that was exactly what I was worried about.

"Dan told me you guys don't go to church," she said. Her tone was gentle but not casual. She was clearing the air. "He doesn't either. Or he didn't. But he goes for me."

"You've found a church here already?" I asked. The question felt strange coming out of my mouth, like it belonged to someone else.

She nodded, her eyes on the quiet television. "I like it. Except for one thing."

"One thing?"

She looked at me, hesitating. "So, technically, gay people are welcomed to the congregation."

"Technically?" I raised my eyebrows.

"But the church sees them as sinners who need to be reformed, forgiven, whatever," she finished, her tone almost apologetic.

"So, you don't agree with the church?" I asked nervously.

"Absolutely not," she said. There was an edge in her voice, and I understood that I'd just come close to crossing a line. "I'm not *that* kind of Christian. I'm a Democrat. I believe love is love. I'm pro-choice. I just. I need a church. This is the most liberal one I've found here, you know?"

I didn't know, but I recognized the urgency in her voice, the same urgency that had been there when she'd dropped off the cookies that first evening. A need. A loneliness. A wanting. I felt it too. Since Andrew had deployed, I'd started praying at night when I was trying to fall asleep. I hadn't done that since I was a kid waiting for my mom to come home late from work.

Please, keep him safe. Bring him home to me.

"Have you talked to Dan yet?" I asked.

"Oh, every day," she said, brightening visibly.

"Every day?" Andrew and I had never been the kind of couple who constantly texted and checked in with each other, but suddenly, I felt like we should be. Before he had left, he'd written down his social security number. "Since I'm your sponsor, you can't even make a doctor's appointment without it," he said. I didn't want to be a *dependent*, my presence in this world *sponsored*. But dependent I was. Already, my days revolved around waiting for him to call.

"Oh, well, they're short a lot of the time," Rachel said, draining the last of the wine in her glass. "But I'm so relieved every time he calls."

"So you worry?" My voice came out quieter than I had meant it to. I knew I'd worry, of course. But, when I'd decided to marry Andrew, I'd had no idea that I was inviting such a primal, constant fear into my life. I wanted to know if she felt it too, and if it had changed her already, if she had developed the same new dark compartment in her heart that I had, and, if she did, how well hers managed to contain her worry. I could dwell in that compartment or ignore it, but it was always there, and I had a sense that whether or not Andrew was deployed, a new permanent detail in my architecture was taking hold.

"Every single day," she said definitively. "But it's hard to imagine it happening to him." I'd seen that line more than once from military widows in news articles. *I never thought it could happen to us.* I had hoped I'd feel the same, that sending my new husband off to war would either make me noble and brave or just plain blind with rose-colored denial. But that would have required a seismic shift in my foundation. I was always bracing for catastrophe.

"I told Andrew I'd leave him if he joined the Army," I said.

Rachel laughed dryly. "I guess that didn't happen."

"No, it didn't," I said. "But we spent months in couples therapy going back and forth about it. He told me if it was me or the Army, it was the Army." I couldn't believe I was telling her this. The words were just releasing themselves the way a body releases heat. I'd had two glasses of the wine now, and felt flush with it, but alcohol never loosened my tongue to this extent.

Rachel said nothing, but I could feel her looking at me. On the television, a cop was cuffing a man, facedown, on his weedy front lawn.

"The thing is, Andrew is the most loyal person I know. Until he said that, I took for granted that he would just . . ." I paused, remembering the way all the air had gone out of my chest when he'd said those words.

"Be the ground beneath your feet?" Rachel asked.

I looked over at her and nodded.

People disappointed you. They fucked up and failed you, even when they loved you. My parents loved me, but they were often bad at it. Most people were. But Andrew wasn't. Andrew had follow-through. Grit. Andrew's love was as consistently true as the light of the sun, so reliable and strong that I'd let him touch my long-guarded soft spots, eventually allowing him to protect them for me. It had been such a relief to hand over the job to someone else. But then he'd gone and enlisted, abandoning the post. And suddenly, I was the one standing guard for him. It seemed so obvious now that this switch would be inevitable, and yet, I felt utterly sideswiped.

"Thanks for opening up to me," Rachel said, smiling. She had a cute, child-like smile that made her face scrunch up so that her freckles gathered around her nose. I couldn't remember anyone ever thanking me for being vulnerable.

"Thanks for being so easy to open up to," I said. "I am not usually this forthcoming." I wondered if Rachel was always this generous-spirited. It was impossible to imagine her any other way, but she needed me as much as I needed her, and needing and being needed, I was finding, made people do surprising things.

"So, will you come?" Rachel asked, her voice hopeful. "To the spouse retreat?"

I paused, thinking. It wasn't like I had much going on. Who was I to turn down a free trip, especially when the alternative was sitting alone in a half-empty house?

"Yes," I said. "But can you do something for me?"

She looked at me questioningly.

"Would it be okay if I made you my emergency contact?"

She furrowed her brow.

"In the pink book, I mean."

She burst into laughter, loud and raucous, like a punch-drunk kid up past her bedtime.

"Fuck, are you kidding me? Of course. You're already mine."

—

The summer I turned seventeen, I made good on my promise to myself to leave home, and I went big: On the final day of my junior year, I dropped out. Two months later, I moved to New York with no distinct plan for how I'd support myself in a city that was entirely a fantasy to me. I'd never been east of Nevada.

The previous summer, the doors of my life had blown open at a government-funded summer school for the arts, where young actors, painters, animators, and writers spent four weeks working on their craft at CalArts. I had been writing poetry since middle school, but I did not consider myself to have a craft. I did not consider myself a writer at all.

I was a fifteen-year-old hiding away bad poetry in her math folder. And summer camps, even local offerings at the YMCA, had always been out of my family's reach. But after I saw a flyer for the program at the library where I worked, I landed a scholarship. There, I heard myself read lines of my own poetry aloud for the first time. I met my first love. And I made a hilarious, intimidatingly whip-smart friend who told me, point blank, that writing was worth planning my life around. Before meeting her, I had never considered writing as a viable career, had never even thought about any kind of life plan. I only knew I wanted out, wanted more. Months later, when she applied to the New School, a university that offered admission to a small pool of applicants without high school diplomas, she told me I was applying too.

In New York, I made and lost friends, dated the wrong men, drank too much, worked too much, and moved constantly, living in eight different apartments over the span of four and a half years. I was never once late on rent, but my bank account always hovered just above zero. Every day felt a little bit like walking that shoulder of the freeway, only without my father there to act as a guardrail. He had taught me well, though: Life was just a series of breakdowns, and I only needed to be ready for them with enough money to get by and an endless store of resilience.

I didn't understand, though, that resilience is just like money. Eventually, you run out.

My freshman year of college, I contracted a spate of urinary tract infections. Though the acute infections disappeared, the pain and urgency stuck around. Doctors mostly shrugged at these symptoms, or prescribed antibiotics that solved nothing. Sex left me bruised and burning, and there was something about my pain, springing up seemingly out of nowhere, that overwhelmed men and made them feel hoodwinked. Some got angry and frustrated with me, sulking afterward as though I'd done something to wound them. One left me curled up on my futon because he figured I "wanted to be alone" with my pain. I had learned in childhood to survive an untenable reality by escaping through a soothing daydream, but it was during my early years of adulthood that I discovered how to split myself in two, jumping between partners, ignoring the pain that simmered beneath my days, and drinking to numb it when I couldn't shut it out. Slowly, the pain increased, month by month, year by year, until, by the time I graduated, it had become fiery and throbbing, radiating out from my pelvis to my lower back and thighs.

"Come home," my mom said one night, six months after I'd finished college. It was winter, and I was sitting on the cold sidewalk outside of work, my flip phone pressed to my ear. Finally, I'd gotten a diagnosis: a severe case of interstitial cystitis, a bladder condition that had begun with an infection that had burrowed its way into my nerves. I was sick, broke, working three different jobs yet barely staying afloat, sitting on a pile of student loans, and addicted to a guy who exclusively showed up at my door at 2 a.m.

It was suddenly clear that I could not keep living like this.

There was no childhood home to return to, though. The year before, my father had put his stuff in storage and left to travel around Indonesia, chasing a long-held dream none of us fully understood. My brother had recently graduated with a degree in economics and was living in an old Victorian in Oakland with five of his friends, loading rich people's junk into trucks for $12 an hour. And my mother was renting a bedroom from a longtime family friend, working as a middle school aide to a blind girl. "Coming home" meant sharing a bedroom with my mother in a town I'd told myself I'd never go back to. Still, I was hopeful. My mother wasn't drinking. She'd filed for bankruptcy, so was no longer treading the waters of debt. Over the phone, she'd been talking me through the ups and downs—mostly downs—of the 2 a.m. boyfriend. After a string of bad relationships herself, she was, for once, single. I felt closer to her than I had in years. I also didn't have another option.

When I'd left for New York, I'd written in Andrew's yearbook: *Of everyone here, I wanted to know you better.* Throughout middle school, Andrew and I had moved in the same group of friends, but it broke apart at the start of high school, everyone falling into their separate tracks. Andrew emerged as startlingly good-looking, landing a straight-A, well-off ballet dancer girlfriend who provided him entry into what I thought of as the PTA-curated crowd, the kids who had family dinners, piano lessons, and French tutors. These students' mothers ran the elementary school, middle school, and high school PTAs, and their children ran the schools too. I was a straight-A student. I probably could have found my way into that crowd. But just sitting next to them in pre-calc made me feel like a hungry kid pressing her face up against the window of a lavish bakery. Often, I spent lunch hour alone, sitting on a cement ledge with a book. At some point each week, Andrew would appear, still wild and beautiful, smiling goofily, and sit down next to me, trying, as he had in the fifth grade, to yank me out of my head.

"You weren't a loner exactly," Andrew told me later. "You were friendly with everyone. But you were always alone. That's how I remember you."

In the years I'd been in New York, we'd seen each other just once, when I was back for Christmas. I'd run into him at a café where he was working. His back was to me when I reached the counter, and when he'd turned to face me, my jaw had actually dropped a little. And I thought, for a moment, that his did too. But he was so out-of-my-league handsome it didn't cross my mind that he could be interested in me. I wasn't a monster or anything. My eyes were a warm brown, my almond-colored hair had a natural wave. People complimented my smile that curled up and in, like a cupid's bow. But I was missable, in part because I had made an art of hiding in plain sight.

"You're very pretty up close," one guy I dated said. "But I'd never notice you across the street." Andrew was across-the-street handsome.

He was the only person I called when I got to California. I wasn't sure why, but I dialed his number without even thinking twice, inviting him to the condo where I was staying with my mother. We sat on the cement patio out back, drinking tea, and he made intense, almost unbroken eye contact, like he was trying to hold me still with his gaze. I found it a little unnerving. He had a girlfriend. Was he into me? I wasn't sure until he asked if I would read a poem of mine. I laughed before I realized he was serious. I would have kissed him, would have slept with him, even, were he not dating someone else at the time. But read him a poem? He insisted. So, in a shaky voice, under my family friend's patio light, I did.

Much later, Andrew told me he'd been willing me to reappear ever since that chance run-in at the café. He had even written me a letter from Beijing that had never arrived at my Brooklyn apartment. He didn't really believe in fate, but he felt like my sudden reappearance was something akin to it. Throughout the winter, I took the bus from Marin to San Francisco. We sat on Fisherman's Wharf drinking coffee and smoking cigarettes, watching the ferry unload and reload as the seagulls swooped into the bay. Between their calls was a kind of silence I'd never experienced. It wasn't heavy or awkward or laden with meaning. It wasn't drafty and cold like the silence that had pervaded my childhood home on mornings after nights of screaming. It was as expansive as the bay before us.

"These birds sound like home to me," Andrew said.

I didn't know where my home was. I was beginning to wonder if I'd ever find it. But sharing that bench with Andrew, our thighs barely touching, for the first time in my life I didn't feel the need to search for one.

In February, after Andrew ended things with his girlfriend, we wound up in his loft bed. I was, by this point, practiced at performing intimacy. But for the first time, I found I couldn't fake my way through. The sex lasted maybe ten minutes. There was a lot of "oh no, ow, stop, sorry." He didn't come.

"I'm sorry," I said, rolling into the fetal position so I didn't have to look him in the eye.

"There's no need to apologize, Simone," he said, and, for a moment, just hearing him say my name drove out my shame as though it were an evil spirit.

After that, I stayed on my side of the bay. I was well enough to return to work, and had started doing early morning shifts serving breakfast at an Italian restaurant in Sausalito. Setting up bistro tables outside as the sky lightened around me, I'd look out at the water and remember that morning in Andrew's loft bed, recalling his kindness, the gentleness of his touch, the way he'd said my name, like the word itself was something rare and precious, his gaze a statement of intent: *I'm looking at you because you're worth looking at.* Revisiting that morning felt like pressing on a bruise. I liked being looked at, but only if I was standing in the very best light. He had seen the roiling part of me that I tried to keep hidden—the pain, but also the shame.

I stopped returning Andrew's calls. Briefly, I dated an Italian vegan. Along the front of his torso were four of his seven chakras tattooed in little spirals, like tiny tumbleweeds. He spoke limited English. In the afternoons, I smoked high-grade medical marijuana and listened to a lot of Nick Drake on my father's old record player. I tried a slew of medications for interstitial cystitis until finally, I found one that actually helped. I did yoga and boiled ayurvedic herbs. Slowly, the pain that had taken up residence in my body began to recede.

At the end of August, ten months after I'd arrived in California, Andrew moved to Maryland for college. We'd seen each other only a handful of times since that night in his loft bed, but his sudden absence made the Bay Area feel strangely empty. My father married a woman he met in Indonesia and became a permanent resident there, and my mother landed a rent-controlled studio of her own. Everyone, it seemed, was restarting their lives, forcing me into a position to do the same. I decided to return to New York, where I had a community of friends to call upon. And, though I couldn't quite admit it to myself, I wanted to stay close to Andrew.

An old coworker got me hired as a receptionist at an Upper East Side salon, where I stayed for two months until Reina helped me land my first "real job" at Bloomberg. The work, technical writing, bored me to tears, but for the first time in my adult life I had private health insurance and could call in sick. I felt like I'd won the lottery. At night, I mostly stayed in and read and began, at twenty-two, to ask myself what I actually wanted. My old friends were still drinking in bars until 4 a.m. and snorting coke in grungy bathroom stalls. I couldn't go back to that life, and I didn't want to. I was ready for something new.

One fall evening after work, I sat on the stoop of a Brooklyn brownstone and called Andrew. It had been over two months since I'd seen him, but the call was as automatic as the one I'd made to him when I'd gotten to California.

"Maybe I could come visit?" I asked, and that Friday, I was on an Amtrak to Annapolis. It was different this time. *I* was different. I was willing to be seen and held, but even more, I could see him—he was so immediate, so right there when he spoke to me, nowhere else, and that made the trees and sunlight and bedsheets around him feel more immediate too. Since I was a kid, I'd felt shut out by the world in some fundamental way, and here was Andrew, inviting me in.

We wrote each other letters, handwritten and snail-mailed. And when I came up for air from work, I'd shoot straight to him on gorgeous fall weekends. Warm in his bed, I was safe from both the outside world and the interior one in which I had struggled to stay afloat my entire life. He came to the city, too, holding my hand on the ice-skating rink at Central Park as I fumbled to mirror his graceful steps. Late one snowy night, I called him and asked him to come. He did, no questions asked, boarding a 1 a.m. train in the dead of winter because I needed him.

When summer arrived, he came to New York, subletting a friend's apartment in Morningside Heights and bartending at a busy SoHo restaurant filled with beautiful people. It was a good way to save up money, he said. It was also an excuse to be close to me. We spent evenings lying on the cool wooden floors of his sublet just talking, forgetting ourselves to the point that we'd neglect to turn on the light until well after the sun had fallen. We drove up to Bear Mountain, sharing Häagen-Dazs and reading books to each other on the lake. I talked politics with him more than I ever had with a guy. He was closer to the center than I was, and sometimes we argued fiercely, raising our voices in Polish cafés in Greenpoint. We walked miles through Brooklyn on "Expedition Sundays," discovering new corners of the borough. One afternoon I went to a concert with Reina and returned to find my books, which had been sitting in stacks for months, lined up neatly on bookshelves. Andrew had gone on a secret mission to find an eight-foot-tall bookcase for me at a neighborhood furniture store, carrying it up the avenue in the brutal summer heat.

At the end of August, he offered to stay in the city, transfer colleges.

"Or you could come back to Maryland with me," he said, when I was silent. We were lying on the bed in his airy sublet, looking up at the ceiling together. I had seen the summer's end as an expiration date, a built-in ending that had allowed me to relax into being with him.

"Separation is always painful," he said. "But this just doesn't feel right."

It didn't feel right. But I had always been better at doing what felt a little bit wrong. Because this kind of right required courage, faith, a leap into the unknown I wasn't sure how to make. The thing was, I could see no natural ending with Andrew. If we really did this, went all in, and we did break up down the line, it would be brutally, unnaturally painful, like moving through life afterward without some fundamental part of myself. I wasn't sure I could survive such a loss.

"I miss him," I told Reina a month after he left the city. His birthday was coming up. Reina and I were smoking outside the high-rise where we worked, standing in a huddle under the awning to protect ourselves from the wind. Lexington Avenue was clogged with cabs, people hustling themselves across the intersections to get to work. Wind carried trash down the sidewalk. I had always loved the way I could hide inside the chaos of the city. But I missed locking eyes with Andrew in the morning. I missed feeling found.

"I was wondering when it was going to hit," she said.

Later that night, I drank most of a bottle of wine and called Andrew. "Can I visit to wish you a happy birthday this weekend?" I asked, sitting on the edge of my bed, looking at myself in the full-length mirror. My lips were stained purplish red.

There was silence on the end of the line. After what felt like an unendurable lapse of time, he broke it.

"I love you, Simone. I probably always will. But you can't come in and out of my life like this anymore." He sounded tired, like something in him had been pushed to its limit. And I had been the one to bring it there.

I willed myself to say the words that were stuck in my throat.

"I'm in," I said, my voice small.

"What did you just say?"

"I'm in," I said again, and this time, the words were clear and strong.

CHAPTER 5

—

SPOUSE RETREAT

Rachel and I stood by the entrance of the Hilton conference room, taking in the perfumed sea of dangling earrings and blown-out hair. At least fifty women had come to Birmingham, and all of them, hugging and laughing and finding their seats, looked like they knew this world and their place in it.

"I feel like I'm crashing someone's high school reunion," I said, inching closer to Rachel. When I'd left New York, I'd had my editing job for only a year and a half, and there were days I worried someone was going to escort me out of my office and tell me a terrible mistake had been made. But I'd relied on the Senior Editor title as a crutch. It was shorthand that communicated my place in the world. Here, I was just a private's wife. I didn't know much about the Army, but I knew it didn't get any lower than that.

"It looks like you two still need name tags," said a pregnant woman, smiling at us with a mayoral distance. I guessed she was around thirty. She had a long Mona Lisa nose and was so tall I wondered if she could dunk a basketball. A delicate strand of pearls hung around her neck, accentuating the broadness of her shoulders. "Is this your first retreat?" she asked.

What had given us away? Certainly not our age. Rachel was twenty-seven and I was twenty-eight. By the standards of the Unit, we were old. It was probably the way we were practically clinging to each other, quietly refusing to budge from the doorway.

"It is." Rachel nodded eagerly. "We're neighbors, our husbands just joined the Unit, and I dragged her here, convinced her to share a hotel room with me." I couldn't believe how much information she was giving this woman. Behind us, a long line of spouses was beginning to form.

"Go ahead and get your name tags," the woman said briskly, trying to move us along. "I'm Charlotte, by the way," she said. "Charlotte Adams." Adams. That was Andrew's company commander's wife. The leader of the FRG who'd been sending all those emails.

"You have been assigned key callers, right?" she asked, as though she'd just thought of it.

I nodded. "I got a text from someone, Katie?"

"Yes, Katie is one of our key callers. She's great; she's been doing it for a few years now."

"Doing what exactly?" Rachel asked.

"Oh, the key callers are spouses who volunteer to be your main point of contact during the deployment. Mostly, they call if something happens overseas that doesn't involve your husband." She smiled stiffly, as if to say the discussion was closed, because any more questions would lead to more explicit language, like *injured* or *killed*. She paused a moment, then, appraising us. "Do you want to join my group?" She turned and pointed toward a table at the front. It was right across from the speaker's podium.

"We'd love that," Rachel said, her grip so tight on my arm it was beginning to hurt. We would? *Shit.* I didn't want to sit next to the commander's wife. Wasn't that like sitting next to the teacher? You had to behave.

Charlotte smiled, with more warmth this time. "I remember my first Army wife friend. You'll be friends forever." And then she was on to the next wives shuffling in behind us, and Rachel and I were moving toward the table of name tags, pushed forward by the current.

Friends forever? Rachel and me? We were both from California, both married to guys in the Unit. We lived on the same street in more or less identical houses. Maybe friendship, now, functioned like arranged marriage: Rachel was clearly my best available match.

"She was nice," Rachel said as she leaned over to write her name on a tag. I found a Sharpie and did the same.

"She's the company commander's wife," I said, like this meant something to me. "Andrew's company, I mean." We stood up together, facing the crowd as we stuck our names to our chests.

"Oh, wow," Rachel said, like that also meant something to her. And it did mean something, but neither of us was exactly sure what.

Today's speaker was a "retired pastor's wife," according to the pamphlet I found on our table. Not a pastor, or retired pastor, or, even, I was pretty sure, a retired wife, which seemed the most enticing option. But the wife of a retired pastor. This was a role that landed you speaking gigs? Holding the leaflet, I looked over at Rachel in the seat next to me, but she assiduously avoided my gaze, focusing instead on the Unit chaplain at the front of the room, who was introducing the speaker, a short middle-aged woman setting up a projector behind him. She wore her pale blond hair in a razor-sharp bob.

"Get ready for some good practical advice on navigating marriage," the chaplain said before giving her the stage. I wondered if our husbands were receiving a similar talk on marriage-strengthening in Afghanistan. It seemed unlikely.

The speaker put on the glasses hanging from her neck and looked out at us. "Y'all are *gorgeous*!" she said in a deep Alabama accent.

"Well, have you seen our husbands?" one of the wives yelled from a table in the back. Snickers went through the crowd. A few women hooted in agreement. Across from me, Charlotte smiled tightly. "Oh, good lord," said a freckled woman next to her under her breath.

"My husband, a retired pastor, will be talking later today," the speaker started. "But first, I wanted to talk to you all, woman-to-woman, about self-care. Though now I'm not so sure y'all need this talk, good gracious." The crowd laughed. "Still, I know how much your husbands are gone, and I know y'all must be *tired*." Women were nodding their heads, Rachel included.

"Once upon a time, when my children were small, I certainly needed this talk. I forgot myself; I let myself go. And I let my marriage go too."

Let myself go?

"My husband would get home from work and I would have dinner on the table, but you know what I hadn't done?"

The room sat quiet and expectant. I could hear faint laughter from the restaurant on the other side of the hotel.

"I hadn't taken care of myself," she said. Her voice had softened, just slightly, and I could feel myself soften too as she said, "I'm gonna talk to y'all today about taking care of yourselves."

I had always marveled at Andrew's ability to know exactly what he needed and then give it to himself, without hang-ups or cloying terms like "me-day." I rarely knew what it was I wanted or needed, and even when I did know, I often wouldn't give it to myself. Maybe I could actually learn something from this woman.

"Because I'd greet my husband at the door, excited to see him, and he'd take one look at me and his face would fall a little, like he was disappointed, you know?" She paused for effect. Or maybe she was waiting for a reply.

"I mean, I hadn't looked at myself in the mirror once. I probably hadn't even brushed my hair. Y'all know what I'm talking about."

"Mm-hmm," someone said from the back of the room.

"I needed that mirror. I needed to put on some heels, some lipstick. I needed to take care of my marriage," she said, her tone shifting again, this time to triumphant.

I looked to Rachel. I wanted to nudge her, ask, "Did you hear that?" But her gaze was fastened to the speaker. The woman's words were like a skip on a record player. I wanted to put the needle back where the song started and listen the whole way through, because I had missed the crucial moment when we'd all walked through a portal and found ourselves in the pages of an article from the December 1958 issue of *Good Housekeeping*. When I couldn't catch Rachel's eye, I surveyed the other women at my table. Every face was impassive, except for one—it was the woman who'd said "good lord" under her breath. We locked eyes and she rolled hers, hard. I smiled despite myself, and she grinned back, revealing an endearing gap between her two front teeth.

A little disappointed? Not once had I ever felt disappointment coming from Andrew when he looked at me. Frustration or confusion, maybe. But never disappointment. I didn't need to hide who I was from Andrew. I hoped I never would.

—

"That was crazy, right?" I asked my eye-rolling compatriot in a near-whisper. The talk had finished and we were in line for the catered buffet.

"Completely nuts," she said. "They're not all like that, I promise.

This is my husband's eleventh deployment, and trust me, I do not put on heels or lipstick for his return. He's lucky if I pick him up at all."

"Eleventh?" I said, incredulous. All numbers, it seemed, were suddenly unbelievable in their size.

"Maggie's husband is the first sergeant," said Charlotte, who was just ahead of us.

Maggie shrugged. "He runs the company and still can't manage to pick up his wet towel from the floor." She pointed at Charlotte. "Now this lady, she could run a company. She was a military intelligence officer. Played basketball at West Point."

I looked over at Charlotte. "Wow," I said. So I was right about the dunking.

"I was only in for five years after college," she said. "Once we started trying for kids and John kept moving up in his career, I left." This seemed like a stark trade-off to me, but her voice was matter-of-fact.

As we made our way down the line, Maggie and I chatted. She was *witty*, describing the laissez-faire midwife who hadn't wanted to treat her high blood pressure during pregnancy as "Kevorkian." Talking to her, I felt excitement blooming in me.

"Are you a writer?" I asked hopefully, as she plopped a heap of mashed potatoes onto her plate.

She put back the serving spoon, then looked at me like I'd just said something both fascinating and surprising. Her eyes were a shade somewhere between green and brown, but richer than hazel. "I used to be a journalist," she said. "Why do you ask?"

"Just the way you talk," I said.

"Well, I'm keeping that compliment in my back pocket for a while," she said. "These days the only thing anyone ever calls me is 'Mom.' Which, trust me, is all I ever wanted. But . . ." She trailed off then. We had reached the end of the line. She locked eyes with me a last time and an emotion flashed across her face. Longing? It was hard to say. A group of women enveloped her and she gave me a little nod as she disappeared. My plate was warm and heavy in my hand.

"It's nice you have a little friend," I heard a voice say, and I turned to see Charlotte towering over me. I followed her gaze to our table. Rachel was waving to me with such eagerness she looked like a marooned sailor putting out a Mayday signal.

A little friend?

A petite woman in heeled boots walked past us. Her long silver earrings glinted in the fluorescent light.

"Hi, Charlotte," she said, flashing us a smile. Her dark chin-length hair was so shiny it looked as though it were coated with lacquer. She was the most beautiful woman in a room full of beautiful women.

"You should be friends with Mira," said Charlotte, nodding in her direction. "She's great."

I looked up at Charlotte's strand of pearls. Why was she trying to orchestrate my life like this? Was she taking me under her wing? But there was that distance. We weren't ever going to go for drinks or dinner. It just felt obvious, somehow, that this was not an option. Was she seeking me out as a consolation, then, a way of saying that in another world, if she weren't a commander's wife, we'd become friends? If she couldn't be my friend, at least she could clarify this world for me.

"I like Maggie," I confessed. "But I'm not sure a private's wife is supposed to hang out with a first sergeant's wife."

Charlotte laughed good-naturedly. "Oh, Maggie is wonderful, don't worry about that." I smiled stiffly, relieved but also newly confused. Maggie's husband was high on the food chain, high enough that she and Charlotte were clearly peers. They could be friends—they *were* friends, it looked like. My husband was low on the food chain, so Charlotte, who was married to an officer, could only be my guide. But, since Andrew and Maggie's husband were both enlisted, even though they were leagues apart in their responsibility and ranking, we could be friends. None of this made any sense.

I'd heard that the Army had, in many ways, shed its outdated caste system. But I was sensing that in the Unit, at least, the old system was very much alive, though its rules, like all social rules, were mostly unspoken, at least among the wives. Charlotte walked away to talk to a group of women, and, as I headed back to Rachel, I caught sight of Maggie, who was sitting at a different table now, laughing with friends. *Eleven deployments.* Charlotte had given Maggie a reverent nod when she'd said this, as though Maggie had done the deployments herself.

And she had. This is what I was starting to understand. For years, she'd walked the tightrope of monitored phone calls, corralled her worry, carried one-sided conversations. It had only been two weeks since Andrew left and he'd told me what he wanted for his funeral if something happened to him overseas. Looking back now, it felt almost unreal, like a still frame from a film. We had been actors, feeling through the scene, trying to make the lines that had been given to us our own. *I want you to have a flag. I want you to remarry.* It struck me that both of us had just barely understood what those words meant. We had miles to travel to reach where Maggie and her husband stood.

I didn't want to be where Maggie was. And yet, I watched her from across the room, now, the way I'd watched crushes as a teenager—like she was not just a person but a whole world, one I wanted to understand and maybe even be a part of.

—

A few days after we got back from the retreat, Rachel came over in the morning with to-go coffees when I was still in my pajamas. She walked past the pile of shoes by the door, glanced at my sad little love seat, and said, "We need to get you more furniture. And some art for the walls." She pointed to the blank space above the shoes. "And maybe a mirror, right there, by the door? You know, somewhere to check yourself on the way out?"

"Check myself?" I asked dubiously.

"You know, make it a home," Rachel said. She was makeup-less and her hair was pulled up into a messy bun, but she looked well-rested and ready to take on the day in a way that I was not.

Making a home appeared to come so naturally to Rachel, maybe because she had lived in the same one for most of her childhood. Her family went to church every Sunday, and her boisterous mother cooked big Italian meals, all of them laughing and talking over each other at the table. Both of her parents sang beautifully, and on road trips, the family would harmonize with each other on easy songs like "99 bottles of beer on the wall." Still, it wasn't as if Rachel's early years had been particularly stable. At times, her mother had been physically and emotionally abusive, and after her parents split up the summer before she started college, Rachel left to live in her next-door neighbor's house, gathering her most crucial belongings in her old Radio Flyer and walking out the door.

"We don't have a lot of money right now," I confessed, nervously thumbing at the plastic lid of my coffee as I watched her dart around the house, a vision of some kind playing out in her head. Before Andrew had left, we'd bought a used Hyundai hatchback, and had very little left in our account to spare.

"That's why God created thrift stores," she said.

When I was growing up, most of our furniture had been ancient, but my mother splurged, occasionally, in an effort to make our place presentable. Once, she put a new oak dining table on a credit card, and when it arrived at our house wrapped in plastic, it had felt like Christmas. It wasn't fancy, but the pristineness of its blond finish made it special, and it elevated the entire house, which was always in disrepair, with scuffed wooden floors and a leaky bathroom faucet and brown shingles falling from the siding. The chain-link fence was rusted, and oil leaks from our used cars left a permanent ink blot stain in our driveway.

There was beauty in that house, though. Deer in the early morning dew of the backyard. Zinnias my mother and I planted together in the spring. And the lush peony bush that bloomed reliably every May. When I was three and my father was laid off from his adjunct job teaching electronic music at UC San Diego, my mother had driven to Marin to see about starting a life up north closer to her parents, who lived in San Jose. That peony made her fall in love with the house. My mother adored peonies. Most of all, she adored something beautiful to wrap that hope of hers around, like that dining table, like the gentle hills that surrounded Marin County as a buffer from the rest of the world.

After being late on rent too many times, we were evicted from that house when I was twelve. We moved into a larger, more expensive place that my mother was petrified we could not afford, a 1970s Eichler-style home with two bathrooms and an atrium at the entrance. My dad brought me to see it, and the landlady, who had a soft spot for kids, decided to rent it to him without checking his abysmal credit. My mother took on more hours at the deli where she was working, and my father added clients to the after-school tutoring business he'd started to supplement his income. My parents hoped, maybe, that the Eichler would be another new start.

Instead, from almost the moment we arrived, it became clear that our cramped rental had been keeping us together. After less than a year in the new place, my mother left. A few months later, my father moved in a new girlfriend, who had a knack for homemaking. She began to decorate the still-bare walls of the house, framing old black-and-white photos of Basque family ancestors on my father's side. It was a gift to my father. To me, it felt like an invasion.

My dad stayed in the Eichler until a couple of years after I left for college, when he moved to a tiny one-room cottage isolated at the top of a hill in rural West Marin. I visited him there one winter when I was back from New York. His desk had been covered in a mess of papers, and, among them, I'd caught a glimpse of lyrics to a song he'd written: *I could have even tried to love my wife.* There was so much sadness in that cottage, you could feel it like a draft.

I'd recognized that draft because it had followed me too, to every apartment and rented bedroom. All of those places had been way stations. Decorating, questions of paint colors and mirrors by front doors, were afterthoughts, or thoughts I'd never had at all. As I watched Rachel flit around, I decided that this house in Columbus would be different. I had to make it mine, maybe precisely because nothing else here was.

—

Over the next couple of weeks, Rachel dragged me to thrift shops and estate sales and stores selling refurbished furniture, all of which were abundant in Columbus. She had a nose for shopping and relentless energy for negotiating. The woman could *haggle.* I became desperate, sometimes, to find things for cheap. At an estate sale just up the street from us, I found a tan linen couch that looked passable. Rachel walked slowly around it, inspecting the cushions as I talked to the seller.

"I think it's too big for your place," Rachel called to me.

I looked over at her. "You do?" I was getting rid of the tiny love seat Andrew and I had inherited from friends, and there really wasn't much else in my living room other than a chest Andrew had inherited from his father when he died, which we were using as a coffee table. Of course it would fit. I went back to talking to the seller.

"Crap, I totally forgot about an appointment I have," Rachel called out to me as she walked briskly toward the exit.

"That thing stunk of cigarettes," she said when I met her outside. "You don't want it anywhere near your house."

Every day, nearly, we returned with something new: a shoe rack, a bookcase, a chocolate-brown couch and love seat set I purchased from a couple on base. I'd had no idea what pleasure there could be in making a home, watching it take shape. I was giddy, sometimes, looking around at what Rachel and I were creating together.

We drove all over Columbus in her Corolla, along the back roads and interstates, behind oversized pickup trucks blasting country, getting a feel for the lay of the land. It was a majority Black city with a diverse range of income brackets, but a high poverty rate. Not far from downtown were vast sections of public housing, empty lots home to only dumpsters, brick apartment buildings with tarp signs that read: *Move in special: FREE RENT.* The city felt small to me, but it was actually midsized, with higher-than-average crime, a public university, and a 15-mile riverwalk along the Chattahoochee, the river that formed the border between this part of Georgia and Alabama.

Rachel and I never knew when our husbands would call, and we had no way of calling them back. A missed call was a lost call, and so we clung to our phones. It would never have occurred to me to just walk out of Rachel's house when mine rang, but she gave me explicit permission, a strong push toward the door. "Go!" she'd say, waving me away. With most people, I always had the sense that if I left, they wouldn't be there when I returned.

But miraculously, Rachel always was.

One day, Rachel took me out for a driving lesson in her Corolla.

The used car Andrew and I had found was a stick shift, and I had far from mastered it.

"There's good old Frank's," she said as we passed our landlord's plumbing company on the way out of the neighborhood.

"Oh god," I said. "Does he call you suga'?"

"He calls you suga' too?" There was a note of something in her voice. It sounded surprisingly like jealousy.

"Yes, I hate it," I said.

"I think it's kind of sweet," she said.

"Yeah, well, I think it's gross," I said.

She laughed. "You know, Dan said we should be friends, and I told him it's not like that with women, we don't just automatically get along." She paused for a moment. "But he was right about you. I'm so happy you're across the street."

A car cut in front of me and I wasn't sure if it was driving nerves or the effect of what Rachel had just said, but I felt an excited heat spread across my chest. I didn't know what I'd thought about her spending all this time with me—that maybe she was not terribly discerning? That she was lonely as hell, just like me? But I hadn't really understood that she genuinely liked me. Did I like her? Strangely, I hadn't once thought to ask myself that question. I had just known that when I was with Rachel, I felt a restlessness ease that had been with me since Andrew had left.

When we reached a stoplight, I breathed a sigh of relief. "Good," I said. "Because I think you're stuck with me."

CHAPTER 6

—

REAR D

A couple of weeks later, I was sitting in bed with my laptop, reading a Facebook message I'd just received from Maggie, when Andrew called. It was evening, which meant it was morning there, the end of his workday. He was either just back from a mission or had spent the night on base.

The longer he'd been over there, the less he called. Still, I waited hopefully every night to hear from him, and this was the first time in nearly seventy-two hours that my hope had been answered. It was a huge relief to hear his voice, which was easy and soft, almost satiny. I couldn't remember the last time I'd heard him sound like that.

"Guess what? The first sergeant's wife wants to be my friend," I said, still looking at Maggie's message. Charlotte had passed along my interest like a love note.

Andrew's laughter was so close in my ear it almost felt like he was next to me. Almost. "I don't think you can be friends with the first sergeant's wife. I mean, we definitely won't be having her and her husband over for dinner, I can tell you that much."

"Well, good thing I have absolutely zero interest in her husband," I said. "And she makes no mention of him. Listen:

'*I want to personally assure you that I don't prescribe to the caste system that is the old Army. Are you going to the company party this weekend? If so, please, I implore you to seek me out and save me from standing against the wall awkwardly like I'm at a middle school dance.*'

She's funny, really smart. I think you'd like her," I said.

"I bet I would," Andrew said. "But like I said . . ."

"Yeah, yeah, we're not all going to become best friends, I know."

"I gotta go in a couple minutes," he said. There was reluctance in his voice, and I couldn't tell whether he was nervous to disappoint me or hesitant to go.

"Already?" I asked. I'd been clingy like this with other guys before Andrew, but never with him—until that evening in couples therapy when he'd told me he'd choose the Army over me if he had to. That moment had activated a latent fear of abandonment I'd thought maybe Andrew had cured. But it was still there, and I was always accidentally touching it now, shocking myself on it like an electric fence.

"Yeah, I need to get food from the chow hall before it closes," he said.

I tried to imagine the landscape of the half-mile walk from his room to the dining facility. Was there snow on the ground? He had been gone over a month now, and had described only his room to me: plywood walls inside of an industrial tent, a mattress on the floor so old and worn springs poked through, a sleeping bag for a comforter, and, for a sheet, his *woobie*—a standard-issue nylon poncho liner that guys used as a blanket because it was universally beloved for its magical ability to provide warmth and comfort in even the shittiest of conditions.

Missions I tried not to imagine. During my year alone in New York, I had obsessed over the war, poring over books and articles about our involvement in Afghanistan, like Sebastian Junger's *War* and Luke Mogelson's *New York Times Magazine* cover story "A Beast in the Heart of Every Fighting Man." I compulsively checked the news on Afghanistan, tracking the number of soldiers that had been killed in a given month and how many civilians had died in the most recent open-air market bombing. I practically memorized these numbers, asking myself whether Andrew would be the reason someone lost a child or got to live their life, or both.

Since Andrew had left, though, I had mostly put such questions on mute. I couldn't help but think about the missions sometimes, but the details that filled my imagination were the crunch of snow underfoot; the neon green of the landscape seen through night vision goggles; the sun rising in the windows of the helicopter on the way back to base. Less palatable visions made their way in when I was trying to sleep: soldiers kicking in doors, men yelling, civilians huddled in the night, an IED missed by a single step.

"What are you reading right now?" Andrew asked. He asked everyone, always, what they were reading, an icebreaker that he used with both cashier and wife.

"Poetry, actually," I said. "Robert Hass." I turned to poetry when I felt unmoored, and Hass was one of my favorites, a Marin poet who transported me back to Tomales Bay and Heart's Desire Beach. Poetry also didn't require too much of an attention span, and mine was still short and flighty.

"Will you read some to me before I go?" Andrew asked, his voice tired and slack. It was the sound of all his defenses down, and it made the nerve endings on my neck come alive in the way they did when he combed his fingers through my hair. I missed his touch. I missed sex. I wanted, all of a sudden, for him to tear my pajama shirt down the front, simply because he'd asked me to read to him. My shell was that thin. He only had to lightly tap and I would crack open.

I picked up the collection and began to thumb through its pages. "'Meditation at Lagunitas' is maybe my favorite," I said.

"Perfect," he said. I knew that would get him. He'd hiked around Lake Lagunitas a thousand times.

And so I picked up the book from my nightstand and read, pausing for just a moment on my favorite line in the whole collection. I'd read it more times than I could count, knew it in my bones the way I knew the sensation it described. I might not understand what home felt like, but this line of poetry I understood so well, better now than ever, that it might as well be my home.

Longing, we say, because desire is full of endless distances.

Andrew had been so silent on our phone calls that it had felt, sometimes, like I was talking to myself in our empty living room. But his silence felt different now—receptive, welcoming, the way it had been when I'd read to him over the phone in our early days, me curled up in my bed in Brooklyn, him perched against the headboard in his Annapolis dorm room, snow falling outside both our windows, each of us with all the time in the world for the other.

"If it weren't for you," I'd told him one night after reading a passage from *If Beale Street Could Talk*, "I wouldn't believe the kind of love between Tish and Fonny was even possible."

—

A few days later, Maggie picked me up for the company party. Her SUV smelled overwhelmingly of the graham crackers and milk her toddler, Emmie, was dining on in the backseat. She smiled at me around the straw of her sippy cup as I got in.

"I love your shirt," I said to Maggie, nodding to her black-and-white striped blouse. She wore a gold crucifix around her neck.

"I just lost fifty pounds on Weight Watchers, and I'm going a little wild at Target these days," she said, pulling out of the driveway. "It's my alternate universe. My potential perfect self exists within its walls." There was that wit, just as I'd remembered. And a brazen kind of honesty.

"So, Charlotte's email about the company party mentioned beer, but I didn't see anything about wine," I said.

"Beer, sweet tea, and Country's Barbecue, baby. You're in the South now," she said. Maggie had only the slightest southern accent, mixed with something else. "My dad grew up in the Bronx," she told me when I asked. There *was* something of a New Yorker about her, brusque and no-bullshit.

Each company's Family Readiness Group, or FRG, put a few of these parties on every year, Maggie explained. They were tame and kid-friendly—there was usually a bouncy house or a bean bag tournament. This one was in the "activity center" by the Uchee Creek Campground on base. I still couldn't believe Fort Benning was big enough to have a 400-acre park with lodges and hunting and fishing access.

"I typically dread them," Maggie said. "I'm so socially inept."

"Socially inept? You're hilarious."

"Well, that makes one person who thinks so," she said, a smile in her voice.

"Sometimes I skip them. But it's good to show face. I am, after all, the first sergeant's wife," she said in a phony upper-crust accent.

"When I asked Charlotte who my key caller was, she sent me a roster of all the A-co wives. Your name was in bold at the top, right next to hers."

Maggie snorted. "Charlotte's sweet like that. I do almost nothing for the FRG, but she always puts my name on those things. I do have to attend the monthly officer wives' teas, though. They'll notice if I don't show. Now that Mark is first sergeant, they're trying to inculcate me into their world."

"Officer wives' teas?" The enlisted wives didn't have teas, at least not any I'd been invited to so far.

"It's strange, I've been an enlisted wife for more than a decade, but suddenly, now that Mark is the first sergeant, I'm supposed to hang out with the officer wives. No thanks."

College graduates became officers rather than enlisted men, generally, because they made more money, and the job garnered more respect in the white-collar world. But if you wanted to spend most of your career in Andrew's unit, you had to enlist. In the conventional army, enlisting carried certain connotations: young, no college degree, not a lot of options. And some of the guys who came into Andrew's unit fit that description. They'd enlisted just out of high school, mostly, for the steady paycheck and benefits, and decided somewhere along the pipeline of preliminary training to try out for Special Ops. But many had set their sights on the Unit early on in their lives. A few of the guys had left behind careers in finance and sales and even law. Some were racking up experience that would help them get a foot in the door of the FBI or CIA. There were also athletes who had done stints in professional rugby or DIII football or Minor and Major League baseball and gotten restless, hungry for something more. Restlessness might have been the men's main common denominator: a searching, a feeling of too muchness—too much energy, too much need to win.

"It sounds like you'd rather stay out of that whole scene?" I asked.

Maggie nodded. "My name was never at the top of an FRG roster before, and that was how I liked it."

She pointed, then, to a squat building with a satellite dish on its roof. "I did production for the local TV news there when we first moved here," she said as we passed it.

"Really?" I asked. "Why did you leave?"

"Mark got stationed at Fort Lewis for a little while. By the time we returned to Benning, I finally got my Emmie." Her toddler let out a squawk from the backseat as if on cue. The implication was that Emmie had been the end of her career, though Maggie didn't seem upset about this. Her voice, in fact, sounded dreamy.

I stole a quick glance at the crucifix on her chest. It wasn't small. Since she had been a journalist, I'd assumed, without really thinking about it, that her politics were toward the left. But, perusing her Facebook profile, I'd stumbled on a photo she'd taken of demonstrators at a pro-life rally she'd marched in. Maggie was not just pro-life. She was sign-carrying, march-down-the-avenue pro-life. Socializing here seemed to be an exercise in trying to figure people out, to wedge them into what felt like the appropriate box. So far, no one fit anywhere, least of all me.

Just weeks after Andrew and I had moved in together, I'd gotten pregnant. He had offered, immediately, to quit school and move back to California to be near his mother. "Whatever you want," Andrew had told me. I hadn't wanted a baby. I hadn't wanted an abortion either, but it was the decision I made. It broke my heart, and for a brief time, threatened to crush our new relationship. I had never felt shame about it, but, looking at those photos on Maggie's profile, I'd felt something like it, a familiar prickling hotness creeping up my neck.

When we reached the gate to base, I fished my military ID out of my purse and handed it to Maggie. It was federal identification, but, with its grainy black-and-white photo and done-in-the-office lamination, it looked flimsier than the fake ID that had gotten me into New York bars when I was seventeen.

Maggie rolled down her window and handed the IDs to the soldier at the gate.

"Good evening, Mrs. Corbin," he said before returning them to her.

"He liked you, I guess," I said after she rolled up her window.

"He liked my husband's rank," she said. She gave me back my ID, and I looked down at it. Right. It was front and center: *Sponsor's rank: Specialist.*

I had never been through this gate before. It took us onto a rural two-lane road surrounded by tall metal fences. These were protected lands. Andrew had told me that military bases were home to even more threatened and endangered species than national parks were.

"I wish they'd do more parties in town," Maggie said. "Most of us live off-post anyway."

"I do see the appeal of living on post," I said.

"Yeah, I like to fantasize about it sometimes. Can you imagine? Something breaks and they just come. Or so I hear. And you'll see, it's Murphy's Law: The guys leave, something always breaks. And they're always leaving. Even when they're here, they're not really here."

It was completely dark now, and Maggie had turned on her brights, casting a cold light over the road. "What do you mean, 'not really here'?" I asked hesitantly.

"So many trainings, and, even when they're at Benning, they're usually at night, so they come home at 8 a.m. exhausted, if they come home at all. Half the time, Mark sleeps on the floor of his office. Command is always pushing the guys and they are always pushing themselves. God forbid they ever rest."

The Unit had about seven months at home between deployments. Andrew had told me that during that time, he would be gone for training, spending nights on base, and working long daily hours. I was prepared for absences. But Maggie made it sound like the men were ghosts in their own homes.

"At least I've got Lucas," she said. "Mark's friend from the company. He mows my lawn, drops off groceries. A godsend."

"He's on Rear D?" Andrew had told me about Rear Detachment. It consisted of all the guys in the Unit who stayed home, or, in military vernacular, "in the rear," during a deployment. A certain number always had to stay back to run the Unit at home.

"No. He lost his leg stepping on an IED a while back," she said. "Super capable still, but he medically retired. Another friend of Mark's is on Rear D this time, though. He'll check on me every now and then."

"That's lucky for his wife," I said.

"Not for him," she said. "The only guy I've ever seen openly cry in the Unit was someone on Rear D." We were close now. Lights had come into view. Through the barren trees and southern pines, I could just make out the edge of a parking lot and the brown steepled roof of a building.

"We were at a company party a few years ago. The guys had just returned from a rough deployment. This sergeant, he had stayed back, and one time, he had to accompany the chaplain to a wife's door for notification. The woman wasn't home, and so they'd waited in the car until the woman got back. Her hands were full of plastic bags from a grocery run. He counted down as he watched her walk to her door. '*Thirty seconds, twenty-nine seconds, twenty-eight seconds before I change this woman's life forever.*' He was crying by the time he got to that point in the story."

I felt sick. Andrew was scheduled to come home in a little under a month. It didn't matter how hard I concentrated on my desire for him to return safely. Nothing I said or did or imagined was of any consequence.

A man could park across the street from my house, count down from thirty, and blow up my life.

Maggie pulled her keys from the ignition and looked over at me. "You ready for this?"

We had arrived, I realized. The doors to the cabin-style rec center were open in front of us, letting a warm light out into the night. A mother with three children was making her way up the front steps, her blond preschooler charging ahead of the rest of the group. From where we sat in the parking lot, I could see high wooden rafters and long picnic tables inside. I wasn't ready to leave the car for a bright lodge full of people I didn't know. I wasn't ready for any of this.

Emmie was starting to whine in her seat and Maggie was getting out of the car, moving quickly, opening the back door and shushing Emmie as she gathered her in her arms. I got out and we walked up the steps together through the double doors.

"How do you keep doing this?" I asked. The rec center was vast, with twenty-foot knotty-pine ceilings and a huge brick fireplace at the head. Heavy chandeliers made of what looked like fake deer antlers hung over the sixty or so people who filled the place—families eating together, soldiers on Rear D out of uniform drinking beer, kids dashing outside to play in a bouncy house that had been set up on the lawn.

"These parties?" Maggie asked.

"The deployments," I said, following her to a buffet table in the back.

"Oh, that," she said. "It mostly just has to do with not having any choice."

—

A month later, in mid-February, about thirty other wives and I sat in a cold, windowless room inside Andrew's company, waiting for our husbands to land. We'd been here for two hours and it was pushing midnight.

The dozen or so women who'd arrived early had a place at a conference table in the center, but the rest of us were seated like schoolchildren in plastic chairs against the wall and my lower back was starting to hurt. I wasn't sure what this room was designed for, exactly. There was a small bar in the corner with a few beers on tap. The light was fuzzy and dim. A faded *Terminator* movie poster hung across from me. I had never been inside Andrew's company before, and I wanted to explore, but the sergeant on Rear D had met us at a side door, leading us down an empty hall to this room, as if we were secret society recruits and he was the henchman assigned to keep us in the dark.

The guys returned on a series of flights over the span of ten days or so. Rachel's husband, Dan, was in a different company and due home tomorrow, and Maggie's husband wasn't going to be back for another week, so I didn't know any of the wives here. Maggie had been to enough of these drawn-out deployment pickups, anyway. "He'll find a ride home," she'd told me over the phone. When I'd first arrived, I'd briefly made conversation with the pale, freckled woman next to me, who was engaged to a guy in Andrew's unit. They were planning a winter wedding in the north Georgia mountains. The bridesmaids would wear lavender, she'd have a veil, the lodge she'd booked for the ceremony overlooked the Appalachians. She hoped for snow. "A winter wedding," I'd said, and smiled, and she'd rattled on in a strangely unenthused tone about the place settings, the tablecloths, the shop in Atlanta where she'd gotten her dress, until her words became a kind of background noise to the physical experience of waiting, to the sweat gathering at the small of my back and under my bra line.

Time during this deployment had practically frozen once we'd hit February, but it had picked up in the last few days. Now, it was back on pause. In the lead-up to the company's arrival, I'd received a series of phone calls from Rear Detachment: *Your soldier is thirty-six hours out . . . now he's twenty-four . . . now he's twelve.* I'd gotten here right on time. Where were they?

The wives had all put considerable energy into their outfits. So had I. I'd worn makeup and silver hoops and washed my hair. I'd put on an emerald sweater I liked and a new pair of black jeans. The other women, though, chatted about exotic grooming rituals, spray tans and bikini waxes, caramel highlights and red lingerie. There was talk of a sex toy party a few women had attended at one wife's house. "It's like LuLaRoe, except for vibrators," she explained, without even a hint of laughter in her voice. I was probably older than every woman in here, but I felt like the middle-schooler who hadn't gotten the memo that it was time to start shaving my legs.

"Hurry up and wait, huh?" said a gymnast-sized woman at the head of the table. She was chewing gum impatiently, chomping down so hard and fast it looked a little painful. I'd heard Andrew use this phrase. Hurry up and get your ass to headquarters so we can start this training in another five hours. Hurry up and get into your jump gear so you can sit on the tarmac for the afternoon while the plane you were supposed to be jumping out of got repaired for unexpected mechanical issues.

Hurry up and wait to hold your husband.

Somewhere at the table, a phone dinged.

"They've landed," one of the wives said, and everyone stood up in unison, as if on command, the room suddenly buzzing. The door opened to the outside, and a chill swept across my neck as I caught sight of a white bus rumbling toward us in the dark.

"Oh, the things we are gonna do tonight," a woman in front of me said, a predatory edge in her voice. The vanilla scent of her perfume filled my nose.

The first guy off the bus belonged to the gum-chewer. She lunged at him, wrapping her legs around his waist. The other women raised their arms and hollered. My fingers started to tingle, and the beehive of the conference room moved straight into my chest. The men rushed out with their packs on, practically piggybacking one another.

And then, Andrew appeared.

He stepped onto the pavement and into the spotlight of the bright outdoor bulbs, looking around for a moment before his eyes found me in the crowd. He smiled without hesitation, and the bees in my chest calmed. It was not just any smile. It was that goofy and dopey one that he'd taken months to even reveal to me, a smile that said, *It's you, thank god it's you.* It was loose, relaxed joy, emotion that even he, always so in control, had no idea how to withhold. I didn't run or jump, but I moved fast, almost jogging. And then I threw my arms around him, pressing my cheek to his. I could taste the salt of my tears.

"You're home," I said.

"You bet I am," he said. I inhaled deeply, his new scent just as I remembered.

CHAPTER 7

—

CHARGE OF QUARTERS

I loved the feel of the short, sharp hair at the nape of Andrew's neck, the softness of his tan undershirt, the cool metal of his dog tags falling against my chest, the way he felt just slightly different but also the same. And god, that smell. Loamy and alive, like the air after a fresh rain. Andrew had seemed so far away on the phone, but he was here now, in our bedroom, and so was I, both of us so eager it was overwhelming.

"Slow down," I said, as much to myself as to him.

Afterward, I reached for his hand, interlacing my fingers in his.

"It's too hot," he said a minute later, getting up to shower. I didn't know how to read the moment. Our marriage was still so new, and so was this life, the peaks and dips of each so closely bound together, it was impossible to separate the two. He was always overheated after sex, and he was exhausted, his clock utterly confused by both the time change and the fact that he'd been working nights and sleeping days. He needed space to readjust. But all we'd had since we'd gotten married was space. Didn't he want to be close? Hadn't he missed me like

I'd missed him? I listened as the shower turned on and felt even more alone in our bed than I had the night before.

The next morning, I showed him around the house, telling him the story of each item Rachel and I had bought together: the white bookcase from the estate sale down the street; the Tiffany-style lamp from Joey's Thrift Mall; the washer and dryer off Craigslist that a teenage brother and sister in matching overalls drove from forty-five minutes outside the city to our door. I remembered the price of almost all the items, and I tossed them out like I was making a sales pitch: $25, $100, thrown in for free!

"It looks good, doesn't it?" I said once we were sitting down with coffee at the dining table. "Like a real home?"

"It's beautiful," he said, and his words of validation were like oxygen.

At first, he was unusually quiet. By the end of the first cup of coffee, though, he began to talk. Afghanistan had been cold, with average temps at night around 20 degrees. Spring through summer was fighting season in Afghanistan, he said, so the deployment had been relatively uneventful. He had nothing to compare it to, but that's how the guys had described the missions this time around. And Andrew had been overseas for only two and a half months, a little over half of the Unit's routine deployment length. He was also a dumb private who had little idea of what was going on.

"I'm lucky they even let me go on missions," he told me. "I'm sure they were nervous I was gonna fuck something up."

"So you weren't that busy?" I asked. "I had the impression you were."

"Sometimes I was, yeah. But there was downtime."

"Really?" I asked, unable to hide the hurt in my voice. "Then why did your calls thin?"

Andrew looked away from me and out the dining room window at our barren dogwood tree. "My boss, Wes, he told me to call you once every three days. That way, if something bad happened and there was a communication blackout, you wouldn't, you know, freak out," he said, his voice unusually low, as though he believed that if he just said this quietly enough, I might miss it. "That was his logic, anyway. It's kind of most guys' logic. If you don't expect us to call, you don't worry when we don't."

"Are you kidding me?" I said. "That is twisted fucking logic. I am not some liability that needs to be managed." I wanted to break something. I had waited every evening for Andrew to call. He had never played games with me, never fucked with my expectations. It would crush me if he started now.

"It's hard to explain, the way things are over there," he said.

"You call me every chance you get," I said, and he nodded, but it was a slight, noncommittal gesture. He felt torn, I could tell, or maybe worried that no matter what he did, he'd be letting somebody down.

—

The following day, Andrew returned to work. "They think it's important to reacclimate," he told me, which was code for: Too much freedom is a dangerous thing. Command wanted to save these guys, in whom the Unit had invested so much, from doing something stupid enough to get themselves kicked out, like drive drunk, get arrested for public intoxication, or pop hot on a post-leave piss test. The FRG sent us info on this delicate transitional time in a document titled *5-day Recovery Model: Why does he STILL have to go to work after just getting home?!* "It's a way to slowly integrate," the document began, echoing what Andrew had said. What followed was a list:

- *He smells—get him body wash you like*
- *He cusses . . . a lot*
- *Narrow vision—lived with a tunnel vision about priorities*
- *"Soldier mode"—varies based on experience deployed*
- *Single Soldiers mindset—don't worry, it just means he's on own schedule . . . Not something else*
- *Train, plan, execute mission, rest, do it all over again*
- *Uses a hammer to fix EVERYTHING—messy but it works*

His expectations upon coming home:

- *Naked at the door with a plate of food . . . (not so much)*
- *Slide right back into the role of the "Man" (you were doing it all without him)*
- *Nothing has changed at home (even if he knows things have)*
- *Predictable schedule (family schedule is not his to control or predictable)*

This message didn't actually say anything about recovery, or how to accomplish it in just five days, but its point was clear: What made for a good soldier didn't make for a great spouse. The Unit was trying to micromanage this reality, giving the guys time to reenter the domestic domain slowly so that they wouldn't smash into their homes like wrecking balls.

At the end of this week of reacclimation, Andrew was released for leave, sent home with the first sergeant's safety brief, which included helpful counsel like "Don't beat your wife." The FRG email, spare as it was, more or less prepared me for Andrew's newfound qualities and approaches to life: the impressive number of swear words that flew out of his mouth; the military efficiency with which he showered and cooked dinner and did the laundry; the afternoon he unjammed our bathroom door by kicking it open and breaking the doorframe (*messy, but it works!*). Nothing prepared me, though, for what Andrew did after he got home from the safety brief.

"Don't you love how it flutters in the breeze?" he asked after he hung the American flag from our front stoop.

The rippling nylon fabric was sort of pretty. But my antiwar father had not raised me to be a flag-waving kind of girl. I understood flags at police precincts and post offices, but on a home? How about a hanging plant, a pot of marigolds by the door?

"The sight of it makes me uneasy," I said.

Andrew looked at me, puzzled or annoyed or both, but we didn't have time to get into an argument about the flag. We were busy getting ready for Friday evening drinks with Tyler, a sergeant Andrew had met overseas. I was greedy for time with Andrew and did not feel like wasting the first evening of his two-week vacation on some guy I didn't know. But it was an unusual invitation, one he felt he couldn't say no to. Since Andrew had a college degree, he had technically come into the Army as a specialist. But in his unit, until he went to Ranger School, he was considered a private, and a private couldn't decline a sergeant's overture.

Andrew jetted back to the bathroom to comb his hair, and I walked over to the mirror by the front door that Rachel had found for me at an estate sale and checked myself in it, just as she'd suggested. My own hair needed a cut. It always needed a cut. I had tried to do something with it, but I had no idea how to use a curler or a straightener, so I'd pinned it back in a bun. I was wearing a black dress dotted with blue flowers. It had an empire waist and modest neck. I looked like a librarian.

At least the dress was new. When Rachel had seen my closet populated with winter's pilling sweaters, she had taken me straight to Marshall's. "It may be February, but it will be spring in no time," she'd said. She was right. It was already warm enough to leave the house with only a light open sweater. I grabbed a nude shade of lipstick from the makeup bag sitting on the bookcase next to the front door and put it on just as Andrew came up behind me.

"I love the lipstick," he said, resting his hands on my hips.

He was always pleasantly surprised when I did something even just slightly dramatic. And for me, any lipstick was showy. Andrew was the flashy one. He had styled his dark hair in a pompadour and was wearing a black button-down that contrasted with his fair skin.

"This sergeant, Tyler? He's married, right?" I asked Andrew, meeting his eyes in the mirror. My stomach did a little flip. I could feel a newness to his presence, a heat in his fingertips.

He nodded behind me. "I think her name is Mira?"

I spun around to look at him. "Mira?"

"I'm pretty sure," he said hesitantly.

The Mira who'd been the most beautiful woman in a room full of beautiful women, the wife Charlotte had advised me to befriend? How many Miras could be married to guys in A-co? I recalled how confident she had seemed, her head thrown back in laughter, her earrings catching the light, and I decided she prized both looks and personality. I decided I needed to look on and be on for Mira. I needed to make her laugh. I needed, for some reason I didn't entirely understand, to impress her.

"Shit, I need a better shade of lipstick than this," I said.

—

Mira and Tyler lived on the other side of the Chattahoochee in Phenix City, a town that many of the guys in Andrew's unit chose for its bigger lots, lower property tax, and relatively small population. Its main artery was clogged with used car lots but eventually gave way to green acreage and thick vegetation that, in places, grew over everything—trees, abandoned trucks, the sides of trailers. Occasionally, a church or barbecue spot billowing smoke emerged from the landscape, but there wasn't much out here, it looked like.

"It seems isolated," I said as we passed a single-pump gas station with a spray-painted sign in front: *no firewood 2day*.

"I think that's how the guys like it," Andrew said. "The ones who grew up in the country, anyway. Feels like home to them." I wondered how it felt to their wives.

When Andrew first enlisted, I'd assumed that everyone in the Army lived on base. But most families in the Unit bought a house in town with a VA loan. It was the financially smart thing to do, plus, living on base felt, to most of the guys, like living at work. There were so many restrictions: You couldn't keep a gun in your home, the speed limits were strictly enforced, and, in certain neighborhoods, the grass on your front lawn had to be mowed to a certain height. The Army owned a soldier for the length of his contract, decided where he would live, how often he'd be away from family, whether he could travel to certain countries, or talk to press. The guys savored the freedoms they got living off base, driving their trucks too fast and growing out their beards on leave and shooting guns in the backyards of their homes in unincorporated towns.

"So, Tyler's an E-6?" I asked. That was two rungs—big ones—up from Andrew.

"Yeah, staff sergeant," Andrew said. "He grew up in the Big Army." This was how the guys in the Unit referred to the conventional Army. It was at best, neutral, at worst, derisive. I'd only gotten to know Dan, a private just like Andrew, but I'd met a few of the guys in passing, and already it was apparent to me that arrogance was a trademark of the Unit: The guys made fun of anything "super hooah"—high and tight haircuts, drill sergeant cadences, *I served in Iraq* bumper stickers. They "hooahed" all over the place themselves, but only sarcastically. They felt superior to the rest of the Army, in part because they were treated as such: The Unit received far more funding than any in the Big Army. They got nutritionists and physical therapists and trainers, as well as equipment of far better quality than what the conventional units were issued. They were invested in like the career warfighters they were.

"The guys who grew up in the Big Army, they seem less rigid about rank," Andrew said.

"Humbler?" I asked.

"They're not . . ." Andrew smiled vaguely, searching for the right word. ". . . assholes." Tyler had been kind to Andrew on the deployment, big-brotherly, even though they were probably about the same age. He stood out among the guys who came from small towns in the South, or the mountainous West, because he had style, which earned him points in Andrew's book. "He grew up in Phoenix, an actual city, so he doesn't, like, cut his hair in a straight line across his forehead," Andrew said. He'd been on some long Afghanistan deployments in his conventional unit—in some "historic battles, actually," Andrew said. I didn't know what that meant, hadn't realized it was even a designation in this century.

On our right, a billboard appeared out of the foliage. *Homes starting at $150,000*, it read beneath the back-lit image of a two-story house painted cornflower blue. Andrew turned down a hill and suddenly we were in an orderly neighborhood, each house along the street nearly identical to the one on the billboard. The subdivision reminded me of some of the newer residential areas on base: perfectly-edged lawns, clean cars, and an oddly empty feeling, like it was missing something central and life-giving.

"That's one of our guys," Andrew said, pointing to a bumper sticker on the back of a red pickup truck sitting in one of the driveways. The Unit's crest was on it. "Tyler is trying to get me to buy out here. He wants to get a whole platoon to move onto the street, have our own little security team." For people comfortable with danger, they sure worried a lot about safety.

"Don't they get sick of each other?" I asked. Andrew was one of them, of course. I could have said, "you guys." But he wasn't really, not yet.

"It's like no one knows how to function without each other," Andrew said, pulling into a wide driveway. I noted the American flag hanging from the porch, just like ours, only bigger.

We sat for a moment, each of us waiting for the other to get out first. "Is Tyler intimidating?" I asked.

Andrew hesitated. "He's . . . intense. But not intimidating."

"What did you mean by 'historic battles'?" I asked.

"He was deployed to eastern Afghanistan, back in 2008," Andrew said. "A COP got overrun by the Taliban near where he was, and—"

"COP?"

"Combat Outpost. Anyway, he wasn't actually in the battle, but some of the guys in his company were. Guys he knew pretty well, I think. A couple of them were killed, and he was on the QRF."

"QRF?"

"It's kind of a break-in-case-of-emergency group of soldiers on standby. He was part of reinforcements and cleanup."

Andrew was no longer speaking in acronyms, but I still wasn't quite sure what he was getting at.

"Cleanup?"

"I don't know how it all went down, but in a situation like that, when a QRF arrives and the battle is already over, at least some of what they're doing is collecting and packaging remains."

—

Mira answered the door holding a baby monitor, her purple manicured nails curled around the screen like talons.

"Good timing. Baby girl just went down upstairs," she said, and spun around, leading us through the airy living room, her kitten heels clicking on the wooden floors as we passed a plush sectional. When we reached the open-concept kitchen at the back of the first floor, she put her hand on a doorknob and glanced back at us. "Tyler and I are in the garage," she said. I looked at Andrew. *The garage?*

She opened the door and the screamo death metal hit me like a physical force.

Andrew and I paused together at the threshold of the sound-insulated space. A motorcycle leaned against a homemade wooden bar, Tyler standing at it with his back to us, his hair pomaded and combed. He was tall and wide-shouldered, his traps pushing against his short-sleeved button-down like they were trying to get out. He had full tattoo sleeves on both arms. A POW/MIA flag hung on the back wall over a leather couch. It was cold in here, and I wished I'd worn more than this gauzy cardigan after all. The music sounded like a train chugging too hard and fast to stay on its rails.

"Does your husband listen to this crap?" Mira yelled as she walked to a speaker sitting on a shelf above the bar. She picked up the phone attached to it and glanced up at me. I shook my head sheepishly, my whole body calming as silence filled the space. Then came the gentle twang of a country guitar. *Something 'bout a truck in a farmer's field.* I'd heard this one. I had a soft spot for '90s country and what my father called "real country," like John Denver and Willie Nelson. But this manufactured-in-a-studio stuff was new to me. It was everywhere here, streaming from pickup trucks and grocery store speakers. Andrew had started playing it in the car sometimes. I always changed the station. At this moment, though, it sounded like the harps of angels.

Tyler turned to me and Andrew. Even from across the room, I could see that he was as beautiful as Mira, blond and sinewy, with deep-cut dimples and eyes the color of slate. He walked purposefully toward us, his body bursting with otherworldly energy, then enveloped us both in one tight hug. It was such an open, childlike gesture that I laughed. When he stepped back, his face was full of mischief.

"I'm so glad you guys came," he said, before rushing back to the bar and pulling out a stool for me. This was refreshing. Other than Dan, the few guys I'd encountered so far in Andrew's unit had more or less grunted in my direction by way of hello.

"Me too," I said as I sat down across from a bottle of chilled white wine. Mira grabbed two glasses from the end of the bar and took a seat next to me.

"We're doing shots!" Tyler declared, pulling a bottle of whiskey and a few shot glasses off the shelf. Andrew stood next to him looking skittish, like he was one moment away from finding an excuse to run back home.

"Maybe *you* are," Mira said, pouring two glasses. "We've got our wine."

"More for us, then," Tyler said, and poured two generous shots. I glared at Andrew. On the way here, he'd told me he'd have a beer, maybe two. A DUI meant you were out of the Unit, no question, no special circumstances. I only had a learner's permit. And Andrew had given me just two semi-catastrophic lessons on the stick shift that had tested the strength of our young marriage with perhaps greater ferocity than our year apart had. Even if I could manage to get us home, I sincerely doubted someone who'd been pounding shots of whiskey counted as a licensed supervising adult.

Andrew looked at me, then at Tyler, then back at me. There was apology in his eyes. I was new to all this, but I understood: Tyler was a sergeant. Andrew was a private.

Andrew picked up the shot glass and drank.

"How you liking this one-horse town?" Mira asked, giving me the kind of saleslady smile that is designed to convince you of something. It was working. I could swear there was an actual twinkle in her eye. Mira had grown up in Phoenix. She'd moved here—"the middle of nowhere," as she called it—a year before, not long after she and Tyler had married. They'd met in high school and reconnected online while Tyler was deployed.

"He pulled out all the stops with me, flowers and love letters and balloons sent to my office on my birthday," she said. She eyed him across the room. "I didn't want to marry a military guy, but, god, he's sexy."

I followed her gaze. He *was* sexy. It was hard not to look at him.

"I love his tattoos. But, then, sometimes, I look at him, and, it's too much, like, almost *ugly*." She squinted at him across the bar, like she was trying to decide something. "Nah, never mind, it's hot."

I laughed. "He swept you off your feet," I said.

She swatted the air between us playfully. "Girl, Tyler tells me you're from New York. Did you get married in a library? I could see you two getting married in a library." She nodded emphatically at the idea.

I laughed. Good god, she had me pegged.

"I've never been to New York," she said. "I was a real estate agent in Arizona. I bet I could make some money in that city, what do you think?"

"They'd love you there, no question," I said.

Mira missed everything about home—her family, her mom's rice and beans, her coworkers. "I was good at my job," she told me. "But I needed to get licensed here, and then I had Nora. And now I'm just a thirty-year-old mom." She made a face, like she was mildly disgusted with this fact.

"Do their schedules become more regular after leave?" I asked, taking a sip of wine. It had warmed a bit, or maybe I had.

She laughed. "God no. Just go ahead and eat dinner without him. That's the main bit of advice I can give you about this crazy life," she said.

"I do hate not knowing when to get dinner going," I said. The phrase sounded almost as strange to my ear as my question to Rachel about finding a church. Up until now, Andrew had been the cook in our relationship. Even when we'd both worked nights at restaurants in Maryland, he'd made us midnight meals, each of us still in our black pants and white shirts when we sat down at the oak table that we'd carried up the road to our studio after finding it at an antiques shop. The owner had given it to us for cheap because she had a soft spot for young people, she'd said. Since I was home all day now, I was the one cooking the meals that we ate on it, biking down the hill to Piggly Wiggly for groceries, the full bags banging hard against my knees on the ride home.

"Just try not to take on his moods and stress," Mira said. Her words were more deliberate now, her face serious as she picked up the wine bottle and refilled her glass.

"It was different in the Big Army, more relaxed. The guys there, in his old unit, they were like brothers." She looked down the bar at Tyler, with either wistfulness or sorrow, I couldn't tell. He and Andrew were huddled next to each other and Tyler was reaching for the whiskey in front of them.

"It's not like that here?" I asked.

She shrugged. "They're close, I guess. They'd die for each other and all that. But everything is a competition. Everything is a test. Every day, they worry about getting fired. At least that's what Tyler says, when he's willing to talk about it. Sometimes I think that stress is worse than anything they deal with on deployment. We're going to Arizona on leave, and that'll be great, but then we'll be back in the training cycle, and that's what I'm really worried about." She took a long sip of her wine and looked past me. I followed her gaze. She wasn't looking at Tyler anymore, but at something else I couldn't see. I felt my stomach clench.

"You're worried about the training cycle?"

"It's just a lot . . . I don't know. It was different before," she said. "It was beautiful."

I wasn't sure if she was talking about the beginning of their relationship, the love between the men, or just the way everything used to be and no longer was.

—

Tyler was drunk. It had been, at most, an hour and a half since we'd arrived, but he was unsteady on his feet, and he and Mira were at the end of the bar together, veering between hard-edged laughter and full-blown argument, their voices rising in pitch. It was unnerving. Slowly at first, and then, seemingly all at once, Tyler's magnetic energy had turned aggressive, and Mira's effervescent spark had gone blistering hot.

"You're such a drunk!" she yelled at him, laughing unkindly.

"How did this happen so fast?" I whispered to Andrew, who was now sitting next to me at the bar.

"He's probably been drinking all day," Andrew said, as though this were a reasonable assumption. Andrew's speech was not quite slurred but definitely fuzzy. For a moment, he wobbled on the stool as though he might fall off. Fantastic. I was the only sober person in the room.

Tyler grabbed the motorcycle from the side of the bar and mounted it, taking a swig of whiskey from the bottle. "This is my beauty," he said, suddenly cogent sounding. "If Mira ever leaves my ass, at least I've got her." And then he and the motorcycle clattered together onto the cement floor.

"We have guests, you fucking idiot!" Mira kicked the motorcycle. He grunted as he pushed it off himself in one impressively quick motion, and Andrew ran to catch it before it slammed into the bar. Tyler got to his feet, and for a moment, I thought he was going to push Mira, but instead, he pointed his finger and pressed it against her chest. I thought of their sleeping, blissfully ignorant baby. *Please don't wake up.*

"Don't call me a fucking idiot," he slurred, taking her chin in his hand in a way that looked almost tender. I couldn't see her expression, but her body was tense. He looked at me, Mira's chin still in his palm, and I felt a cold shiver move from my chest down my arms. His eyes were unseeing, and their very absence of light and recognition was far more terrifying than an angry gaze. I knew this kind of drunk. This was the kind of drunk who was not in the same reality as everyone else, not even close. This was the kind of drunk that could not be reasoned with, not even the way one might reason with a three-year-old.

"Get him away from her," I whispered to Andrew. "Now."

"Okay," Andrew said, pulling his hands through his hair. He was readying himself, summoning courage, scared as shit to be who he was about to be—a private talking a staff sergeant down from the ledge.

Andrew approached, careful not to touch him. "Hey, man," he said, stopping about two feet away from Tyler—close enough to be friendly, far enough to remain unthreatening.

Tyler looked at him and smiled lazily, his head listing slightly as he put his arm around Andrew. "This guy is a stud," he said. "Or he's gonna be, anyway. I know it." He stumbled, looked over at me. It was as though he'd forgotten Mira was even in the room. She was still at the end of the bar. She had picked up the baby monitor again and was looking at it intently.

"I've gotta take a leak," Tyler said. He stumbled out of the garage and into the house, and I felt myself go slack on the barstool.

Andrew turned to Mira. "Where does he keep his gun?" he asked. She looked up immediately and locked eyes with him. He had posed this question as though he'd been waiting for the moment to ask it. I didn't hear her answer, only saw Andrew fly out the door and down the hall. Carrie Underwood was singing. *Why, why you gotta be so blind? Won't you open up your eyes?*

"I'm so sorry," Mira said to me. Now that Tyler was gone, it was as though all the fire had gone out of her, and she looked tired and resigned, like she could see how the rest of this night was going to play out and she was already done with it. She got up and I followed her into the kitchen, which was shadowy but warm, a disorienting shift from the bright, cold garage. Mira leaned against the kitchen island, her phone against her ear.

"Who are you calling?" I asked, still trying to wrap my mind around the clean sobriety of Andrew's question, and the fact that he knew to ask it. Where had he gone?

"CQ," she said, like she'd done this before. "Elliott is on shift. He'll take care of this." She guided me to the living room and we sat down on the couch. There was barely any light here and I wondered why she didn't turn on a lamp, but I didn't dare ask why, or who Elliott was, or what CQ meant. All I wanted, with every last molecule in my body, was to get out of here, and to get Tyler out of here too.

"He gets like this," she said into the dark. I wasn't sure what she meant. Gets drunk? Violent? Did he hurt her? Did she feel unsafe? These were the questions I was supposed to ask, wasn't I? But I'd just met her, and I was out of my depth. CQ sounded official, like some arm of the Unit that I hoped would ask her those questions. I wondered how long it would take them to get here. I hoped it would be fast. I listened for some sound from the back of the house, the creak of a floorboard, the sound of Andrew's voice, a sign that things were okay. But there was only the soft static coming from the baby monitor in Mira's hand. I looked down at the ghostly black-and-white image on the screen. The baby was facing us, her eyes closed, her mouth a tiny, exquisite rosebud.

"She's beautiful," I said.

"She's perfect," Mira agreed.

—

Andrew and I left the moment Elliott arrived, but immediately, I stalled on the hill that would take us out of Mira and Tyler's neighborhood.

I swatted Andrew's arm, hard. "Wake up!" I yelled.

After a moment, he lifted his head and looked at me with dazed eyes.

"I'm stalled," I said.

"Okay," he said dutifully, and then his chin fell back against his chest.

Fuck. I looked out into the pitch black, trying to remember what Andrew had taught me the last couple of days, reaching for his voice in my head: *It's all about finding the moments of balance. Remove your foot from the brake as you slowly take pressure off the clutch, then gently press the gas as you release the clutch.* I tried this over and over again, slipping backward each time, until, finally, I lurched forward and laughed out loud, giddy with victory and relief. And then I remembered the journey ahead.

"There are no fucking streetlights out here!" I yelled as I turned onto the main road. I switched on my brights and a cold blast of air from

Andrew's direction hit my face. I glanced over as quickly as I could. His head was hanging out the window. What was he doing?

Then I heard it.

"Are you *puking?*" In high school, my boyfriend had thrown up out the window of his friend's mom's van one night, and I still remembered the painstaking and disgusting process of cleaning out the narrow space between the window and the door. Andrew had returned from his first deployment unscathed, but I was absolutely going to murder him tonight.

Andrew lay back against his seat. "I'm sorry," he said weakly. The cold air of the night felt pretty good, actually. I said nothing, just stared straight ahead. I was leaning so far forward the steering wheel was like a shield against my chest.

"Who was that guy Elliott?" I asked after a few minutes, thinking of how tired and put out and dutiful he'd looked in his uniform as he'd gone into the back of the house to find Andrew and Tyler, like he'd done this too many times before. Maybe this was why Tyler, a staff sergeant, had invited a private over. Maybe he'd burned through all of his friends. Mercifully, he had gone compliantly, as though he, too, had seen the night going this way, and Andrew and I had followed, Elliott saying nothing to us at all.

"He's a team leader, on CQ," Andrew said slowly. I could sense that the puking had helped Andrew wake up a little. I was starting to relax, too, now that we were once again safe among the car lots and streetlights. "He took Tyler to sober up in the barracks, in the cool-down room. Better him than the cops."

"What's CQ?"

"It's, you know, someone . . . manning headquarters . . . at night," he said, struggling to string the sentence together. "They clean up messes sometimes." Maybe they could come clean up my car tomorrow, get the corn chips Andrew had eaten out of its upholstery. I looked at the clock on the dashboard. Somehow, it was 2 a.m. It was so much darker here at this hour than it was in New York.

I stopped at a red light and looked over at Andrew. He was asleep, soft and rumpled, like a boy, and he looked a little like he had when he'd gotten off that white bus with that melted-butter smile, like the deployment had softened instead of hardened him. An hour before, his face had looked so tight and focused as he'd leapt through the garage door. Andrew had always been good in a crisis, but I wasn't sure I'd ever seen him turn like that so quickly, as though he were operating entirely on instinct.

But it wasn't just instinct, was it? He'd had a year of training, a deployment where he'd carried his M4 everywhere and kept a pistol on his nightstand. I was seeing who he was becoming in startling, sudden flashes. I wondered when, or if, I'd get a full picture, and what it would look like, how it might change, even, in the next seven months before the next deployment. What had Mira said about the training cycle to come?

"That's what I'm really worried about."

CHAPTER 8

—

MANDATORY FUN

March 2013

I was in the kitchen packing up the pesto pasta I'd eaten for dinner when I heard Andrew come through the door. It was Friday evening, the end of Andrew's first week back at work. Early that morning, before it was light, I had woken to the sound of him vomiting in the bathroom. This had become his ritual over the last few mornings.

It was nerves. I had them too. Throughout the day, I'd picked up my phone uselessly, hoping for a text that would calm the queasiness in my stomach. Personal cell phones weren't allowed in the building for security reasons. Soldiers broke this rule routinely, partly out of necessity, because they needed to call each other from different training locations. But Andrew wasn't important enough for anyone in the Unit to be calling him.

"There's food in here," I called to Andrew from the kitchen.

"Thanks," he called back. "I'm not hungry." I couldn't see his face, but his voice sounded thin, like it required real effort for him to summon speech. I put the pasta in the fridge and walked over to the door where he was standing with a water bottle in one hand and a backpack in the other. He looked utterly defeated.

"What did those assholes do?" I asked.

Technically, the Army didn't allow hazing, or "smoking," as Andrew referred to it. And overall, higher-ups were becoming stricter about enforcing this rule. It was 2013. In the conventional Army, the tempo of deployments had slowed way down, and a "peacetime Army" was always a stricter Army. But oversight hadn't ratcheted up in quite the same way in Special Operations. They were still deploying overseas every year and the team leaders believed that hazing weeded out the guys who did not possess "intestinal fortitude," a phrase that essentially meant the courage and endurance and grit to continue even when it felt impossible.

In the conventional Army, soldiers and officers moved frequently between bases across the country and world. But in the Unit, guys were allowed and even encouraged to remain stationed on one base for a long time, sometimes for the majority of their careers. This made Andrew's unit unusually insular and inbred. Guys went to war with each other again and again, handing down hazing like a family tradition: Team leaders hazed their privates, and those privates eventually became team leaders themselves, primed to haze the next generation. If privates couldn't handle a little physical and mental torture, team leaders reasoned, how were they going to handle repeat combat?

Andrew's team leader was a guy in his early twenties named Jack. Jack had been deployed to a different operating base in Afghanistan than Andrew, so Wes, another team leader in their section, had acted as Andrew's boss overseas. Andrew had liked Wes then. He had been warm and talkative. Then they'd come home.

"Home, I'm figuring out, is where they test our mettle," Andrew had told me earlier in the week.

Andrew walked past me to the fridge, opened a beer, and retreated to the couch, taking a long gulp. His skin looked waxy, the hollows beneath his eyes dark. I recalled him tossing and turning the last few nights and wondered how much he'd actually slept this past week. I sat down next to him.

"Wes is fucking evil," he said.

"That team leader you met overseas?" I asked.

"Yes, that sociopath," he said.

"What is it exactly that they are doing to you?" It was day five of this, and this was the first time I'd asked him this question. There hadn't been the space until now. Because each night Andrew came home with a force field of tension around him, a static energy that I was afraid might shock me if I touched it. He even smelled different, almost acidic. It was the smell of a very tightly coiled rage that was building inside of his exhaustion. Tonight, though, he looked suddenly drained of all that pressure. He was Andrew again. An Andrew who'd been mishandled and knocked around, but still Andrew. I inched closer to him on the couch.

"I'm getting fucking smoked all day." He took one last pull of his beer and placed the empty bottle on the coffee table. And then, without another word, he lay his head on my lap, closed his eyes, and described the last week. Over the course of each day, his team leaders doled out orders to him and the other private, giving them impossible time hacks to complete alternately complex and menial tasks and quizzing them on facts about the biographical details of every KIA in the company since its inception or the exact weight of a certain kind of bomb. When they inevitably failed to accomplish the tasks or know the answer to every question, the team leaders forced them to do air squats for forty-five minutes straight. And when their muscles failed before the time elapsed, the team leaders ordered them to do pull-ups, sprint to the climbing rope and go up, sprint back, and then repeat, literally ad nauseum.

"Where is all this happening?" I asked, trying to imagine this scene.

"The zoo," Andrew said. The zoo, he told me, was a warehouse-like space with cement floors, divided into several designated areas for teams of junior enlisted. Surrounded by a horseshoe of wall-length lockers, the guys lived and breathed each other in their little space, spitting Copenhagen into plastic bottles, bearing the ups and downs of each other's moods, getting in and out of uniform, yelling "women in the back!" to warn anyone who might not have their clothes on whenever a spouse came by to drop off lunch. There was always country music playing at high volume in Andrew's space, death metal in another across the way, and Top 40 stuff twenty feet down, filling the air with chaos. Each team owned their area; if someone from another team entered, you had to fight them. This meant that team leaders loved to order privates to steal something from another team's space. One private, an experienced Muay Thai fighter, had refused to do this. But the team leaders would not take no for an answer, and he wound up breaking a guy's ribs.

"I don't think they're going to fuck with that private again," Andrew said, finally opening his eyes. The gold flecks in them shimmered. Like butterfly wings, I'd thought, when I'd run into him years before at that café. I wouldn't have likened them to something so delicate now. As Andrew continued to relay the strange details of his new world, I understood that this was one of those sudden flashes of light that revealed him to me, and I felt the tension I'd been holding in my shoulders release, just slightly. I hated knowing that he was being tortured, but I hated being shut out even more.

—

It went on like this for weeks, some days better than others. I stayed home, writing, editing essays for a literary magazine that paid a monthly stipend that was just enough to cover our utilities and gas for Andrew's

106 ∞ *THE WIVES*

commute, sending emails to old colleagues to see if anyone needed copyediting or fact-checking help. Money was suddenly tight in a way it hadn't been for us since I'd been in graduate school. Andrew had made twice as much as a New York City bartender, and I had lost a $65,000 yearly income. His pay here would steadily go up, and I was hopeful that I could grow a viable editing business, but this first year would be tough, even with the $700 rent.

I filled the rest of most days with the business of housework and bike rides to Piggly Wiggly, my mind always oriented toward Andrew like a lighthouse, as though the power of my thinking could shape the trajectory of his days. I'd know if I had succeeded or failed the moment he walked in the door at night. On a good day, his step was lighter. A bad day showed itself immediately on his face, in his whole body. Rachel's husband's leadership was far more relaxed than Andrew's. On walks with her and Dan's dog to the park, I'd describe, in excited detail, my preferred fantasy of retribution—bringing homemade brownies to the team leaders, the way some of the wives did, but adding a little cyanide to the batter.

"I'll gladly lend you my cake tin," she said.

Andrew had never needed to be mothered. When I tried to nag or coddle him, he bristled, wolfish in his independence. Now, though, in the evenings, he put his head in my lap and let me run my hands through his hair. It felt good to be needed like this. I had always worried, just a little, that Andrew didn't need me enough.

"It does make you stronger," Andrew said by the end of the month. It was the weekend. We were sitting at our dining table, drinking coffee in the low morning light. Spring came early in the South, and outside, the day was already warming up. I looked at him. His chest, usually so proud, was drawn inward, like he was trying to protect himself.

"Stronger?" I asked, unconvinced.

"Well, tougher. Maybe this is preparing me for Ranger School in a few months. I seriously can't wait. It's going to be a goddamn vacation from my team leaders." Ranger School consisted of three separate phases in three different places, each one of them three weeks long. Before the first phase, which was here in Fort Benning, there was also a preparatory course that soldiers in Andrew's unit had to pass. All in all, the experience lasted a minimum of three months. But for some, it could go on for much longer. Eighty percent of soldiers who graduated Ranger School "recycled" at least one phase, meaning they had to redo it, and only 20 percent, on average, passed in the end. But in Andrew's unit, the only option was to succeed. Everything was riding on it—your job, your membership in the Unit, your pride. If he didn't pass, we'd be packing up and moving elsewhere, and he'd join some other unit, who knew which one. Andrew was nervous, but he was also excited: Ranger School would be his ticket out of Private hell. In the regular Army, when you returned with a Ranger tab, you were a god. In Andrew's unit, you finally belonged.

"Do Wes and Jack smoke everyone like this?" I asked Andrew.

"I think Wes does. Jack, he kind of just plays along. I'm his first private, so this is new territory for him. I bet he was smoked hard, though. That's how it works. Or that's how it's expected to. Hard leadership makes you harder. And my leadership is definitely harder on us than a lot of the other team leaders are on their guys." He paused, cracked a weak smile. "So we'll see what that makes of me."

Andrew's team leaders could smell that he was different, and the Army didn't like different. Over leave, when Andrew and I were walking downtown after dinner out one night, Wes had called him and said, "Meet us at Buckhead Bar and Grill in an hour." He had to go, he told me apologetically. But first he had to run home and change his shirt. He was wearing a loud, blue Hawaiian button-down that he loved.

"You're going to change?" I'd asked.

"It's not worth the shit I'll get," he'd said. The guys liked to call out any difference they saw—and boy, did they see it—with jokes. They scolded Andrew for listening to that "communist radio" NPR in his car, and called him "city slicker" without even a hint of irony. Guys made racist jokes, too. While over forty percent of the Army's active duty members identified themselves with a racial minority group, the Unit was overwhelmingly white. One of the most revered team leaders in Andrew's company was Black. Guys looked up to him for both his athleticism and tactical skill. They also called him Oreo for dressing and talking "white." He laughingly referred to himself this way too on occasion. "Everyone accepts you if you can do your job, but people say stupid, horrible shit to each other all the time," Andrew told me.

Before that night on leave, I had never, not even once, seen Andrew cow to social pressures. Sitting across from him now at the dining table, the morning light revealing every line in his exhausted face, I wondered if these boys might extinguish something vital and precious in Andrew, and if there was a way that I could carry and protect it for him.

"We're going to a barbecue tomorrow," Andrew said suddenly.

"We're what?"

"Mandatory fun," he said, half-smiling.

I looked at him skeptically.

"I just gotta show my face," Andrew said. "Well, and your face."

"Like, we have to go?"

Andrew sighed. "We don't *have* to do anything. But they expect me to go. To spend my free time on the weekends with them. Wes says relationships matter. Hey, maybe you'll like some of the wives."

Now I sighed. "Fine," I said. "But I'm bringing those poison brownies."

Andrew laughed and his whole face lit up. He was still in there.

—

Jack and his wife, Hailey, lived in a new housing division in Phenix City, similar to Mira and Tyler's, where the homes looked like they'd sprung up together overnight. Jack was one rank lower than Tyler, though, and that slight difference in pay grade showed in the neighborhood the same way it would have in the allotted housing on base. The homes here were smaller, one story instead of two, the cars in the driveway looked older, and there wasn't much landscaping to speak of.

A little girl answered their door. She was freckled and skinny like Pippi Longstocking.

"I'm Chloe," she said, standing aside and sweeping her arm across the living room in welcome. This had to be the five-year-old daughter Andrew had told me about on the way over.

"So polite," I said quietly to Andrew as she disappeared into the carpeted hallway. In the living room, the TV was on low. A baby boy, maybe eight months old, was crawling around on the floor. Asher, Andrew had said was his name. On the car ride over, he had given me a quick rundown on Jack and Hailey's history: The two had grown up in neighboring towns in Idaho and had just started dating when Hailey got pregnant at nineteen. It seemed like most stories that began this way did not culminate, six years later, in marriage, homeownership, and two children, but for Jack and Hailey, it had.

The house was dim, lit only by the afternoon light coming through the sliding glass doors that opened to an unfenced yard. There wasn't much out there. Just grass, one large tree, and a huddle of men on the cement patio, drinking and spitting tobacco into red Solo cups. One of them turned his face toward the front door as we walked in, smiling as he caught sight of us. He was wearing a Methodist University ball cap. Andrew had mentioned that Wes played DIII football there for a year before dropping out. He had a broad smile and eyes so startlingly blue I could see them from across the room. I hated him with such intensity the sight of him made my insides turn to cement.

"Come on in," said a woman who was standing at the sink doing dishes, waving us forward with a sudsy hand. This had to be Hailey, Jack's wife. She was long and thin, with angular features, everything about her spare except for her long, dark hair, which fell down her back in loose waves. Across from her, standing at the kitchen bar with their backs to me and Andrew, were two other women. As Andrew and I began to make our way toward them, a guy in cowboy boots and Levi's walked inside through the sliding door. He approached us and slapped Andrew on the back.

"Beers in the cooler," he said, and then headed down the hallway without even a glance in my direction.

"I apologize for my husband. He was raised by wolves," Hailey said. So, that had been Jack. His eyes did remind me of a wolf's, pale blue and cutting. He was lean and good-looking, with freckles and bee-stung lips, and he was clearly young, all tightly wound potential.

Hailey's decorations were sparse, but I could see she had made an effort to make their new home look lived in. There was a smattering of family photos—a framed school picture of her smiling daughter, her two front teeth missing. A few group shots taken out in a field somewhere, Jack smiling grudgingly in them. There was a maternity photo of Hailey in a gauzy white dress, her daughter leaning against her. She was luminous, framed by light, and looked incredibly young, despite the fact that the pregnancy hadn't been all that long ago. Then again, she looked young now. On the living room wall was a wooden hand-painted sign, an unnecessary reminder of what hung over us: *Live every day like he deploys tomorrow.*

Andrew squeezed my hand before heading out back, and I joined the two women at the granite bar. One of them was extremely pregnant, the other petite, with blond highlights that were growing out, high-top Converse, and a pimply chin. A blond baby in a pink headband sat on her hip. They looked much younger than I was, younger than Hailey. The blond woman stuck a chip into a crusty, orange-colored dip sitting on the bar and ate it.

"What is *in* this buffalo dip? I need the recipe," she said to Hailey, still chewing.

"Honestly, it's canned chicken," Hailey said.

The woman made a face.

Hailey laughed. "I know, but it works. And it's *cheap* at the commissary."

"I shouldn't have asked," the blond woman said, hitching the baby up on her hip.

"Just come over anytime you want and I'll make it for you, and then you don't have to even think about the ingredients," she said.

The blond woman sighed. "Fuck. I need to do a big shop this weekend, and payday isn't until Tuesday."

"I know," the pregnant woman said. I could see beads of sweat along her hairline.

"Commissary," Hailey said, her tone authoritative. "It's the cheapest."

"The meat at the commissary is just funky a lot of the time," the blond woman said.

"WinCo on Tuesdays," the pregnant woman said. "They've got chicken, beef, you name it, two for one."

"The trip to the commissary is worth it for everything else, though," said Hailey, almost defensively.

"Worth it how?" I asked, and the other two women looked over at me as though they were registering me for the first time. Their disinterest did not feel rude, exactly. Instead, I had the sensation that the manners I'd leaned on in every other social situation did not quite translate among these women. I wished, more than anything, that I could go to an officer wives' tea instead. They might be full of fake niceties and women subtly one-upping each other, but at least that was a social dynamic I could understand. I had no idea how to read this one, and it made me nervous.

Hailey looked at me like I was slow.

"It's *so* much cheaper," she said. I nodded, tucking the information into the back of my mind. The Piggly Wiggly wasn't as affordable as I would've hoped, and it was limited, the food always on the edge of spoiling. I liked going there, though. It was comfortingly familiar in some ways, full of mothers moseying the aisles in pajama pants, just as the store across from my old Harlem apartment had been. But the occasional man looking through the mashed potato options with a handgun on his hip reminded me that I was not in Kanas anymore.

"You can take the back roads to base, too. It takes a while, but at least you don't have to get on the interstate," Hailey said.

The pregnant woman looked at me. "When Hailey got here, she'd never been on a freeway before."

"That's not true. I'd been on one. Once."

"Is it hot in here?" asked the pregnant woman.

"No, you're just very, very pregnant," Hailey said.

"How far are you?" I asked.

"Thirty-seven weeks," she said. She looked tired and a little annoyed, as though answering me took more effort than it was worth. Or maybe she'd found the question invasive. What on earth *were* the rules? Talking to Maggie, Rachel, and Mira wasn't like this. Sure, Maggie and

Rachel had gone to college. But Mira hadn't. She was thirty, though. Rachel was twenty-seven. Maggie was thirty-two. These women looked fresh out of high school.

"It must be uncomfortable," I said, smiling stiffly. When she didn't say anything in reply, I added, "No kids yet." Volunteering information seemed like the only viable way to move the conversation forward.

The pregnant woman looked at me and frowned. "How old are you?"

"Twenty-eight."

"Oh," she said, clearly taken aback. She looked at me skeptically, like she was trying to work out what exactly I'd been doing for the last decade. "Well, at least you don't *look* that old."

I stared at this woman whose face shone with youth and perspiration. In New York, when I had married at twenty-seven, my colleagues had been surprised. "But you're so young!" they said, their eyebrows raised, as though I were some kind of teenage bride.

I turned away from the conversation toward the backyard. On an end table by the sliding door was a copy of Robert Caro's tome *The Power Broker*. The book had been on our "strongly suggested" reading list the summer before graduate school and no one I knew had even opened it. Who in this house was reading that book? Outside, Andrew was squirreling away some dip in his cheek. This was another post-deployment change, one I hoped wasn't here to stay. Jack stood up and reached for something on the patio table, and I stepped closer to the sliding glass door to see.

A rifle.

Could you shoot a rifle in your backyard out here? He aimed it at the ground and instinctively, I stepped back. Something soft brushed against my ankle. I looked down to see the baby gazing up at me.

He didn't even startle at the blast.

I'd heard gunshots on base, as common as the song of birds. This one, though, ringing out through the quiet of the subdivision, was different. This was a barbecue. This was ten feet away from the baby at my heels.

Jack handed the rifle to Wes, who fired a shot into the stand of pine trees lining Jack's fenceless backyard. Between the narrow trunks, I glimpsed the back of a house.

Hailey looked over at me from the kitchen, the light from the windows illuminating her bare face. "They're just shooting at the ground," she said, reading my concern.

"They were, but . . ." I said. Wes fired another shot into the trees.

Hailey groaned and walked over to me, sliding open the door. "What the *fuck?*" she yelled in a no-bullshit tone. It was beautiful to behold. I could not imagine ever having that kind of authority with these guys.

The men all turned around with the same slightly amused, slightly bewildered expressions on their faces, and then Jack muttered something under his breath before taking the rifle from Wes. I didn't know if Hailey and I were overreacting, but my whole body relaxed when Jack set the rifle aside.

"Is it legal to shoot in your backyard here?" I asked Andrew when we were leaving the subdivision a couple of hours later. From where we were on the road, I couldn't make out the exit, and I had the irrational sense that maybe it had vanished. We had stayed just long enough to eat burgers and pay our social dues, though the guys still harangued Andrew for heading home so early. The backyard had looked like more fun than the kitchen conversation, with music and laughter and animated storytelling, but the space seemed off-limits, somehow, like not just the men, but also the women, would have side-eyed me if I'd gone out there.

"It's technically outside of county lines, so yes," Andrew said.

"And was it safe for Wes to be shooting at those trees?"

"That was stupid," he said.

"But he hit the trees, right? I mean, he's a good shot," I said.

Andrew glanced over at me. "He could easily miss, Simone. You know that, right?"

I'd said "he's a good shot" with such confidence, but, truthfully, I had no idea what I was talking about.

Andrew paused at the stop sign by the exit. "Maybe it's time to go to the range," he said.

He turned out of the neighborhood and I looked through the window at the lush wall of kudzu vines. Andrew had asked me if I wanted to go to the range before, and I'd declined. I wasn't entirely sure why. I had grown up without guns, and my inexperience had something to do with my hesitation. But there was more to it than that.

Shortly before Andrew had deployed, we'd gotten lunch at a hole-in-the-wall barbecue spot right by base where "today's vegetables" included mac and cheese and mashed potatoes. A few minutes into our meal, the news of Sandy Hook came on the TV bolted to the wall and a profound stillness settled over the restaurant. I had felt that stillness twice before—in the living room of my mother's apartment, when our TV had cut to the news of Columbine; and in the crowd I'd come upon on September 11, 2001, standing utterly silent on the corner of Broadway and East 12th Street, gazing at a flaming hole in the sky. It was the stillness of collective horror. Columbine had made me fear guns, but seeing those children's faces on the screen calcified my fear, turning it into something very close to hate—not so much for guns, but for the people who owned them, championed them, fetishized them. People like the guys in Andrew's unit. People, to some extent, like Andrew himself.

Andrew was not a card-carrying NRA member. He believed in gun control. He supported background checks and thought owning a gun should be a tested, licensed activity, like driving a car. He also liked guns. His father, who had grown up walking to his one-room schoolhouse in the foothills of Northern California with a .22 rifle in hand, bought Andrew his first BB gun at age eight, and his first .22 at twelve. On family road trips, Andrew's father took him out to shoot in the Nevada desert. When Andrew had told me those stories in the early years of our relationship, I was surprised. I didn't know anyone in Marin who went shooting on the weekends. Growing up, I'd only laid eyes on a gun once, at a friend's house in high school, when I opened an old chest in his father's study and found it full of handguns. I was so shocked I gasped. But my friend's father was a cop. Andrew's dad had been the leader of a hippie commune. Like Andrew, though, he had been a complicated, uncategorizable man.

Andrew insisted I should know how to responsibly handle a gun and, in theory, I agreed. Guns were everywhere here, on top of refrigerators, in nightstands, sometimes in every room of the house. Our neighbor who always waved hello from his front porch had a picture of a revolver in his window: *Never mind the dog, beware of owner.* Suddenly, though, driving along this country road, I *wanted* to shoot one. Or I wanted, at least, to stop asking stupid questions about them. I still dreaded the idea of shooting a gun. But this desire, if that's what it was, warming me like the sun in my lap, was stronger than that dread. Since we'd gotten here, I'd been on the outside, standing at that sliding glass door. I wanted to open it. I wanted to yell at the guys, pissed off and affectionate, like Hailey. I wanted to be confident that I knew this world well enough to move through it with ease. I wanted in.

PART II

"Not for the weak or the fainthearted."

—From the cover of the Ranger Handbook

CHAPTER 9

THE BENNING PHASE

September 2013, six months later

A cool breeze came through my window as I rolled it down and handed the soldier at the gate my ID.

"Have a good day, ma'am," he said. Usually the men and women assigned to this task were gruff and granite-faced, but I could swear he smiled at me—stiffly, but, still, a smile. Everything was going smoothly. Even the four dozen glazed donuts I'd picked up on the way here were fresh out of the fryer.

Along with the oppressive heat of summer, Andrew's first phase of Ranger School was over. He'd left in August, the same week the Unit had deployed. I'd gotten my driver's license a few days before he left, and today, I would get to pick him up and smuggle him home for eight whole hours. This was my one chance to see Andrew for the entirety of his time in the school. Well, as long as he'd passed this first phase at Camp Darby. Lots of guys didn't. But Andrew had, I was sure of it. He'd been his company's honor graduate at boot camp. He never failed anything.

Hailey had told me that Ranger School was brutal on the wives.

"Worse than a deployment," she'd said at another barbecue she'd had during the summer. I was starting to like Hailey. She was sarcastic and smart. She could be cold, but when she smiled, a door in her swung wide open and welcomed you in. A friend's husband, she'd said, had wound up in Ranger School for eight months. Jack had gone straight through, which had taken him about twelve weeks. But it still sucked, she said.

"I received one letter from Jack the entire time, on a dirty note card," she said. "It was just a list of all the candy bars he wanted me to send him at the end of the second phase."

It couldn't be worse than a deployment, I'd told myself. Back in the '90s, four soldiers had died from hypothermia in the third phase of the school, in Florida's panhandle, after spending too long in 52-degree chest-high coastal swamp water. But that had been a big deal, an exception. Andrew was safer at Camp Darby on Fort Benning than Afghanistan, and that was what mattered.

I had been right and wrong. I was more at ease knowing he wasn't overseas, but I hadn't spoken to him since he'd left, and the radio silence had been unbearable at times, so constant it became a kind of white noise, numbing me to every other available sensation. Now, though, I could feel everything—the vinyl of the steering wheel, the late-September air coming through my open window, the bright sun pricking my eyes as I drove along a two-lane road lined with skinny southern pines. I hoped I was going the right way. It was so hard to tell in this rural part of base. It was all blue sky and trees and dry, brown grass. The Maps app on my iPhone didn't work properly on Fort Benning.

"It's because of the Russians," Andrew had said when I'd mentioned this, and I'd laughed, but he'd only been half-joking. Even the addresses seemed designed to obscure: Everything was Building #5241 or #4394, and frequently, the numbers didn't follow any kind of logic or order, at least not one I could recognize. And there were so few buildings out here. I felt like I was driving into oblivion.

The directions I'd gotten were from a private Facebook group that a retiree had created in his spare time. His own son had been through the Ranger School process several years back, and he'd been frustrated by how scant the information was. Somehow, he had secured a direct channel to the cadre in charge and had become an oracle, spending his early retirement routinely updating the group with addresses, last-minute changes, information about required clothing that we needed to send to the soldiers, and rules on what care packages could include.

Our Family Readiness Group was well-funded and well-run, led by a paid staff member rather than a volunteer spouse. It was generally good at disseminating information, but I hadn't even gotten a schedule or information about pickup procedures. Ranger School was a "Big Army" school, and I was getting a taste of just how completely the Army left most families in the dark. All conventional units had once had a paid staff member leading the FRG, but the position had recently been phased out due to budget cuts. Only Special Operations retained this luxury. Andrew's unit was still regularly deploying and taking casualties. They needed a professional liaison between families and the Unit, someone to train key callers and treasurers, organize meal trains for spouses of soldiers wounded or killed in action, update extensive family rosters and order blankets with the unit crest for new babies. The old saying in the conventional Army was "if the Army wanted you to have a family, they would have issued you one." In the Unit, though, family seemed borderline essential, the gravitational force that allowed the guys to come and go at a breakneck pace and never lose their footing. *They can do what they do because of you,* a commanding officer had written in a mass email to the spouses right before the Unit had returned from deployment.

A compound of beige buildings came into view. Could this be it? The place, surrounded by a moat of overgrown weeds, had the air of an abandoned prison. And the parking lot across from it was nearly empty, which made me nervous. But I was early. As I got closer, I saw a sign in yellow letters against a brown background: *Camp Darby.* This was the place. A little sad and a little creepy, but definitely it.

The moment I stepped out of the car, the wind broke through my jacket, and I began to pace to get warm, my stomach in some lethal combination of butterflies and knots that was becoming the new baseline of my days. I had no idea what to expect of the eight hours ahead—I wasn't sure whom I'd be spending them with, how tired and hungry and broken Andrew might be. After Andrew left, Mira and Tyler had split up, and Mira had returned to Arizona. I thought of her often, though, what she had said about the training cycle, how the stress of it was worse than a deployment, for the guys and for us. I didn't know that any aspect of this life was more stressful than the other, but I could see what she meant, because deployment didn't exactly stand out. Everything was a variation of the same experience: waiting to see who Andrew would be when he came home.

Andrew had always been so steady. I was the flighty one. "He's holding on tight to your kite strings," a friend once told me. He was changing, though, chewing dip and leaving disgusting plastic bottles full of spit around the house, turning the car radio to the country station with surprising frequency, exchanging his bright button-downs for T-shirts. Sometimes, he came home from work ecstatic, wrapping his arms around me. Others, he arrived too worn out to speak. And more and more, he came back steeled, wearing invisible armor. The Sunday before he'd left for Ranger School, his team leaders had forced him to spend the day with them rather than me, taking him and the other private out drinking on the Chattahoochee in a motorboat they'd rented from base. When they spotted an alligator, they parked a hundred feet away from it, then took turns throwing the privates and each other into the water. He'd come home that night wet and angry and dispirited and readier to leave for Ranger School than he'd ever been. After he'd changed, he'd taken a beer out of the fridge and joined me at the dining room table, where I was drinking a glass of wine after dinner. I had just taken a sip when he said:

"When my contract ends in, like, three years, I think I'm getting out."

I almost spit out the wine.

"What?" I asked in a flat tone that didn't match the alarm sounding in my head.

"After this contract—"

"No, I heard you. But—what?" I asked again, this time bringing the incredulity into my voice.

"What's wrong? I thought you'd be happy."

In a sense, our life together had been a series of one-contract adventures—two years in Maryland, four months backpacking through Indonesia, a summer stint as forestry workers in Ontario, our return to New York for my graduate program. This one would be the longest, but what was one more? We were no longer twenty-four, though. We were twenty-nine. This was supposed to be his dream, a dream he was willing to leave me for, a dream I'd left my own life for, and now he was telling me that dream was just a dalliance.

"So, this thing that you would've left me for, you're done with it in, what?" I stopped, doing the math in my head. "Two years and eight months? That's it?" I asked. I looked at my glass of wine instead of him, hating how small my voice sounded.

"When I said that in the therapy session, I didn't mean it like that."

"Yes, you did," I said. "What else could you have meant?"

Andrew sighed and ran his hand over his face, like this conversation was already more than he had bargained for.

"I don't know," he said. "Maybe I'll stay." There was the slightest shakiness in his voice that made something inside of me wobble. "Maybe that's the only option anyway. Life before, it just feels . . . so far away. Like I couldn't imagine going back to any of it."

"Like New York?"

"Like, all of it?" he said, shrugging, and his face looked so boyish under the plastic light of the chandelier.

"I don't think any of those places would feel the same to me anymore," he went on. "Even Marin." There was a note of grief in his voice. Andrew loved our childhood home in a way I never had, knew the best taqueria, every winding back road and hidden beach at Point Reyes, the particular earthy smell of the trails around Phoenix Lake after a rain. Each time he returned, he experienced the kind of recognition that was so total and unquestioning, it felt like breathing. I'd never felt that way about Marin, or even New York. I'd felt that way about Andrew once, but I wasn't sure I did anymore. I loved him intensely. I still recognized his essence, but he'd become harder to read, more mercurial. He could just as easily finish this phase longing to get out or eager to deploy again. It was impossible for me to say.

More cars were beginning to arrive, and the weedy Ranger School parking lot was starting to crackle with anticipation as women stepped out and paced along with me. I returned to my own car to get the boxes of donuts and surveyed the women. Some looked remarkably young. One, with a shiny brown ponytail and a jean jacket, had come dressed for a pep rally, with ribbons in her hair and glitter on her face. Others held signs covered in stickers and streamers. I knew, from posts in our group, that some of them had driven through the night to be here, but they were all immaculate, the way I'd once imagined spouses would look at deployment goodbyes and homecomings. One rail-thin young woman was posing for what appeared to be a professional photographer. She was smiling for the camera in a blue dress and a cardigan, a string of pearls around her neck. She looked like she was playing dress-up, and, in a way, she was. She couldn't have been older than twenty-one, *maybe* twenty-two, but already she was training to be a company commander's wife. Some of these women were probably girlfriends still in college, or young fiancées with diamond engagement rings on their slim fingers, fresh-faced and bursting with the future. I looked down at the stack of donut boxes in my arms. *Bring food*, the wise man had told us. I didn't have the signs or the ribbons, but at least I had fried confections.

A tall soldier appeared from one of the buildings and we rushed toward the chain-link fence in a huddle, watching him walk at a frustratingly leisurely pace. Even from a distance, I could see that he had the air of someone in charge.

When he reached his side of the fence, he looked out in our direction, as if he were surveying the horizon rather than us. His face was wind-chapped, his eyes the color of the dry soil beneath his boots. He looked to be in his early thirties. "If you see your soldier, he's passed the first phase," he said as he opened the gate.

I waited for him to speak again, but instead came a rumbling, and then a torrent of T-shirts and jeans. I scrambled to the gate's exit, opened the donut box, and held it out toward the rush of soldiers, offering it like the platters I'd presented to wedding-goers in my catering days.

"I can have this?" a soldier asked, looking at me with a kind of pleading hope. His friends waited behind him. Their heads were shaven, their faces gaunt, and the color of their skin was wrong, somehow, ashen.

I nodded, and the soldier reached for one tentatively, as though some invisible hand were about to descend and slap it out of his grasp. His fingers were swollen and scratched.

He took a bite. "This is amazing. You're amazing," he said with his mouth full, looking like a six-year-old who'd just been given the world's sweetest cupcake. His unabashed appreciation shot through me like a drug, and as he scampered off, the guys behind him descended, and I got that hit again and again. I never wanted it to end.

The stampede was beginning to thin when I saw a guy with pale skin. *Andrew. Andrew! No, too short. Wait, that guy could be him. The right height and build. But no, his hair was too light. What about that soldier?* No, that wasn't Andrew's gait. They all looked the same. Any one of them could be him, and every time a soldier took a donut and smiled at me, I expected it to be my husband, and when it wasn't, I felt sad and desperate and giddy, all at the same time. It was so confusing, I had to keep myself from pulling each one in for a hug and kissing him.

When the donuts were gone, I closed the last empty box and placed it with the others on the ground. The stream of men had slowed to a trickle. Where was Andrew? I had to touch him, to inhale him. I was starting to feel queasy with worry when a gate opened at the other end of the fence, and a new herd of soldiers emerged, a cloud of dust surrounding them.

And then I saw him.

He was in the middle of the pack, lugging a green laundry bag over his shoulder. All of the guys were carrying them. They were in fatigues, which seemed strange. The other soldiers had been in T-shirts.

"Andrew!" I yelled, and ran toward him.

When I was just a few feet away from him, the expression on his face stopped me. It was sad and eerily silent. He looked a little afraid to speak, as if he thought his words might hurt me.

"I'm so sorry," he said.

"What do you mean?" I asked.

"I can't touch you."

"What?" The words didn't make any sense to me.

"I can't touch you."

"You can't touch me," I repeated back to him. While the rest of the group had moved on, two guys remained with Andrew, flanking him. One was short and stocky, no taller than I was, with dark skin and black hair. He looked like he might be Filipino, or maybe Hawaiian. The other was white, broad and tall, with an unsmiling expression that looked utterly immovable. It seemed they had stayed with Andrew out of loyalty.

"We're being recycled," said the short soldier. His voice was gentle, the kind a doctor used to deliver hard news.

"But that soldier said if I saw you, then you passed," I said, whimpering like a child, disappointed and betrayed and waiting for the world to make it up to me, right this minute. *Do something*, I thought, looking at Andrew, who was so uncharacteristically, maddeningly still.

Andrew sighed. His face was smudged with dirt, and his cheeks were the sallow color of someone who had been sick with something worse than flu, like cancer, or grief. I saw, suddenly, how loose his fatigues were on him. He looked like a kid in his big brother's clothing.

"They told us to do our laundry over there," he said, pointing to a low-lying beige concrete building that the rest of the guys he'd been traveling with had reached.

"They're parading us," the soft-spoken soldier said, though his voice had an edge now, like he wanted to spit in the dirt with disgust but was too polite to do so in front of me. "They're shaming us."

These last words finally broke through the static. Recycling was common. Making it straight through Ranger School without recycles was the outlier. But that didn't mean that the cadre were going to let a soldier or his loved one down softly.

"I want to scream at that man," I said, my eyes scanning the compound. "I want to give him hell." I looked at Andrew. His eyes widened.

"Don't worry," I said. "I won't."

"I'm so sorry," Andrew said. He touched his fingers to his lips like he was going to blow me a kiss, but he let them drop instead. Then he turned away, jogging with the two other guys toward the rest of the group. The soft-spoken soldier looked back at me, his bag of laundry hanging from his hand, and gave me a sad smile, which felt like an apology too.

My car was only a few meters away, but the walk was interminable. Andrew would have to sit around and wait, caged, for the first phase to begin again, and then do the three weeks over. This recycle would add at least five weeks to his absence, I realized, as I opened my car door and slumped into the driver's seat, staring out at the gate to the ugly compound where those women had jumped into their soldiers' arms. A handful of them were left. The girl in the pearls was one of them. I watched as she wiped her eyes and got into her sedan. We were the last women standing, and I felt a silent kinship with them, all of us sitting dazed, the expanse of parking lot as flat and empty as the moon.

As I turned the key in the ignition, my phone buzzed in my pocket. The sun coming through my windshield was bright, and I had to cup my hand around the screen to make out the text. It was a photo, a group of people at a dinner table strewn with dirty napkins and empty glasses, lighters and iPhones. My friend Reina sat at the center, a cigarette in her hand. I could almost smell the scent of her musky perfume mixing with the wisp of smoke that the camera had caught next to her face. I had sat at that table in Reina's apartment for dinner parties so many times. I missed New York, missed the renewing sensation of coming out from the dark of the subway tunnel underground to the sunlight above. I missed having a life that felt like mine.

And I missed Reina, my sensualist counterpart, who always dared me to get out of my head and live, for once, inside my body, dancing in Chinatown bars until 3 a.m. We were so different, but we'd always understood each other. When I told her I wasn't sure if I could marry Andrew, she'd looked at me and said, "You love the bones of that boy." Reina had never questioned or condemned Andrew's motivations, even when I had. She had only asked me if I was scared. And when I told her I was, she'd said, "I'm scared too." Reina had known that I was having to be genuinely brave in a way I'd never been before, and she wasn't going to let me do it alone.

Another text from Reina came in.

We missed you.

I started to weep. Softly at first, the salty tears running down my cheeks and landing on my lips. And then hard, harder than I'd cried in a long time, my body shaking with the sobs as some animal part of me overwhelmed my brain. Finally, my throat began to burn so fiercely it forced me to quiet down. My head was pounding. I fished my sunglasses out of my purse, and then I heard a tap at my window. I looked over and felt like my heart might fly out of my chest.

It was Andrew.

Why was he at my window? *How?* I rolled it down and he put his index finger to his lips. I grinned, despite the fact that I had just been howling insanely. He looked to his left, then his right, then stuck his head in the car and gave me a kiss. Then, he was gone.

It was a quick brush of the lips, unromantic and routine, the kind of peck you give your spouse when you leave for work in the morning. It was also the most gallant gesture in the world. If the cadre saw him kissing me, he'd be out of Ranger School, out of the Unit, out of this whole adventure he'd said he'd choose over me. In that moment, that kiss, he'd risked it all.

—

I was just minutes away from the turnoff into my neighborhood when Hailey called.

"Jack told me Andrew recycled," she said. "I'm sorry."

"Jack knows? Isn't he in Afghanistan?"

"News travels fast," she said. "I'm not doing anything. Come over. The door is unlocked."

If I kept going straight, the road would take me to Phenix City. I needed to go by Rachel's to feed her cat and water her damn petunias, because she was out of town. And I barely knew Hailey. Returning home, though, where I'd be all alone, felt as dangerous a prospect as walking into a bad neighborhood after dark.

I decided to keep going.

"Help yourself to a glass of water if you want," Hailey said when I walked into her house half an hour later. She was in her wooden rocking chair nursing Asher, her T-shirt drawn up above her chest. Even though she had invited me here, I had the odd feeling, as I sat down on her couch, that maybe I should come back at a better time. She was wearing sweatpants. There were no snacks or drinks on the coffee table. Her dishwasher was running. I looked down at the couch armrest, trying to avert my gaze from her chest. Pink and blue markings were scrawled all over it.

"Those are courtesy of Chloe," she said, and, when I looked up again, she was pulling her T-shirt back down, nestling Asher against her. He was fast asleep.

"I told you Ranger School is worse than a deployment," she said.

I smiled faintly. She looked tired. I'd seen myself in the rearview mirror, though, and I looked worse, a puffy, mascara-streaked mess. With the dishwasher whirring behind me, I told her bits of the story, leaving out the part about the text message, the howling, the tap on the window, and the fact that I cried the whole way home until she called, though the evidence was all over my face.

"Ranger School was hell on our marriage," Hailey said, and began to rock. Asher looked so peaceful in her arms. He was a small baby, with very little chub, his lashes impossibly long. "I got pregnant with Asher right before Jack went on his first deployment. Found out, like, five days after he'd left. We'd been living here two months. When he got home, he was here for a week, and then he went to Ranger School. By the time he got back, I was eight months pregnant. When Asher was three months old, he deployed again."

"That's insane," I said. Jack had only been in a year longer than Andrew, but he and Hailey both seemed so much more seasoned than us.

"That's the Unit," she said, pausing her rocking. She locked eyes with me, and the microscope of her gaze felt hot.

"That was the darkest time in my life, probably," she said. "I came this close to packing up with the kids and going back to Idaho." Her face and voice betrayed no emotion, making what she was saying all the more crushing. "Though there were a lot of dark times," she added with a dry laugh.

"You're from a pretty small town, right?"

"Yeah, three thousand people. So, when I got pregnant with Chloe, *everyone* knew. I was the dumb girl who went and got herself knocked up. We had no money. I took classes at the community college while

I waitressed at a Chinese place and the plan was to transfer to Boise State. I came close. Then all that changed."

"You had to grow up fast, I guess," I said. Jesus, I sounded like an after-school TV special.

"Oh, I have always been old," she said, laughing again, though there was more kindness in her laugh this time. She didn't look old. She looked like a kid with a baby in her arms, skinny and long-limbed and fresh-faced. But she did lack that defining buoyancy of youth.

I liked Hailey. She was smart in a way that felt watchful and wary, and she was utterly without pretense. She didn't sugarcoat or hew too closely to social conventions, and she was funny in that dark, knowing way people were when they'd been through something terrible. Despite all this, or maybe because of it, I couldn't quite figure out how to talk to her. When I'd told her the story about this morning, I felt so much of what I was trying to convey getting lost. Jack had gone straight through Ranger School, but it wasn't that. It was that we'd lived radically different timelines and trajectories up until now. We hadn't shared the cultural experiences that translated to everyday conversation. Talking to her was a little bit like yelling across the deck of a boat in a windstorm. She probably felt the same about me.

When I'd been at Columbia among children of Westchester bankers and Mumbai millionaires, my mother lived in a four-hundred-square-foot apartment, my father in a kitchenless studio in Indonesia where he washed his clothes by hand on the balcony. I was used to feeling outside whatever circle I was supposedly living within. I was used to the awkward, precipitous climb of the social ladder, of trying to compensate for the ways my background didn't measure up or make sense. But this was a new ladder altogether. Listening to Hailey talk about the daughter she'd had with so little support and the siblings she'd helped raise when she was young, I understood just how privileged my life had been, and what a gift my parents had given me by moving to Marin County, where I had access to bookstores and well-funded local scholarships. Maybe Hailey would have loved to spend her early twenties talking about "The Wasteland" in a dorm room hazy with pot smoke. Maybe she wouldn't have. But it seemed like it hadn't even been on her menu of options.

"Do you still want to go to college?" I asked.

"Like I said, I'm kind of old." She sighed, her face falling in a way that did make her look older than her years.

"How old are you exactly?"

"Twenty-five."

"That's young," I said.

She smiled and her face transformed. Under her tiredness, she was really pretty, luminous, even.

"It's just been so long since I've opened a textbook," she said. "It makes me nervous."

"You should go back," I said, feeling a surge of affection so strong it made my voice a little strident, almost coach-like. *Get back in the ring, girl.* What a relief to step out of my own life for a moment and try to manage someone else's. I hadn't been able to touch my husband today? So what? She'd sent her husband off to war with a new baby in her arms. She had watched an entire pregnancy and part of that first precious year of infancy become something she could only reference vaguely as "hell" with an acquaintance. For her other child, she had given up her dream of college.

Hailey stopped rocking. The dishwasher was done now, and the house was silent. "I feel bad for you, Simone," she said. Her face and voice were soft, even compassionate, but my whole body tensed at her words. I didn't know what I had been expecting her to say in response, but it wasn't that. I began to rub the arm of the couch with my fingertips in a soothing circular motion.

"The recycle?" I asked.

"Well, yeah, that sucks. But no, I was just thinking that you're all alone," she said.

She was alone too, wasn't she? Did she mean that I barely knew anyone yet? I looked at the sleeping baby in her arms, and suddenly, just as she spoke, I understood.

"You don't have any kids," she said.

She looked down at her baby, kissed his forehead, and then met my eyes.

But I'm free, I wanted to say. I came within a breath of actually saying it, but something almost steely had entered her gaze that told me I shouldn't. Did she pity me? Maybe she had felt me using her hardship to make myself feel better about my own, and she didn't like it. She was trying to tell me that the hell on her marriage, it wasn't the kids. She loved those kids; I had seen that the first time I walked into this house and watched her scoop Asher up into her arms, laugh adoringly at something Chloe said. They were her anchors. Without them, I sensed, she might drown or drift away.

Hell was the Unit. Hell was the kind of marriage it allowed you.

Andrew and I had been talking about children lately. We both wanted them, though I was nervous about just how unfree that might make me here. But I was also beginning to wonder about the value of the freedom I'd long had, which was starting to make me feel like I was careening, with nothing to keep me in place. There must be something so reassuring, so deeply satisfying, about being tethered in the way Hailey was to Asher. His eyelids fluttered in his sleep and I felt the strongest urge to walk over to Hailey and pick him up, to feel the heat of his warm, buttery skin. But he was hers, not mine, and so I stayed seated as he drew in and let out another breath, and felt my own slowing to match his.

CHAPTER 10

—

MASCAL

A month later, my phone dinged late in the evening. It was sitting on the chest we used as a coffee table, and from the couch I glimpsed Rachel's name. Dan, along with the rest of the Unit, was still deployed. Andrew was finishing up the first phase of Ranger School for a second time. If Rachel and I weren't together in the evenings, we were often texting, sometimes watching the same show from across the street, giving play-by-play commentary. But I wasn't in the mood for TV-texting tonight. I was bingeing *Modern Family* to distract myself.

The day had been fine. Since Andrew had restarted Ranger School, every day had been fine. In the mornings, I woke around seven, made a cup of a coffee, and wrote for a couple of hours at my desk. After that, I took a walk around the park, then returned home to edit an essay or column for the literary magazine or have a meeting with the other editors. In the afternoon, I'd work on a manuscript, or go to the gym on base and stop at the commissary for groceries. In the evenings, I drank wine with Rachel. Nothing felt funny or comforting or abundant, but, like life on *Modern Family*, nothing hurt very much either. Getting through each day was like skating on the surface of a deep lake. If I glided quickly enough, seamlessly enough, the ice wouldn't crack.

There had been one out-of-the-ordinary happening, though: The program director of a global media foundation for women journalists had emailed to invite me to apply for a two-week reporting fellowship in the Congo. I'd never even heard of the foundation, but an East Africa reporter who'd read a few of my published essays had recommended me for the fellowship. *Would you be interested in joining a reporting trip to cover untold stories in eastern Congo?* the director wrote. Me? I had never been to Africa, and had reported overseas only once, on a group fellowship to Israel and the West Bank in graduate school. I'd mostly accepted that the door to a life of on-the-ground reporting had closed for me. And maybe it really had, because, ultimately, I hadn't been chosen for the upcoming trip. But the director hoped that the organization could offer me a spot for a future one.

I leaned back and a ding came again. Maybe Rachel needed something.

Have you heard from your key caller yet? the text read.

No, I texted back.

You will, she said.

A minute later, my phone rang.

"I have a red message," my key caller said. There was a tremor in her voice that I could feel in my own throat. "On the morning of October 6, 2013, B-company conducted an offensive operation in Kandahar Province to capture a key insurgent cell leader. Two of our soldiers were killed in action, and nine were wounded. Two soldiers who were attached to the company were also killed," she said, delivering the script with admirable restraint. And then, she broke down.

"I'm so sorry," she said, blowing her nose on the end of the line. "I've just never seen a MASCAL like this." I didn't know that term, but its meaning was easy enough to figure out: mass casualty. I also didn't know my key caller, Lisa, and had never received a call like this, but I was pretty sure she wasn't supposed to start sobbing on the call. How could she not, though?

Andrew had introduced me to Lisa's husband at a company barbecue before he'd left. He was a seasoned platoon sergeant who'd joined in 2004 when the US was looking for weapons of mass destruction in Iraq ("They're still there," he'd told us confidently). This was his ninth deployment. Lisa had likely experienced the fallout of many of these, and this was the worst she'd seen. She blew her nose again, and a voice, unsolicited, crept into my head:

How could you be surprised? How could any of us be? Look at what our husbands signed up for. Look at what you signed up for.

Lisa's breath caught as she stifled a sob, and I felt a rush of guilt. "I'm sure you'll hear something from your husband soon," Lisa said. Calls from overseas went dark when something happened. Communication blackouts. Once the news had been disseminated, the phones began to ring.

"My husband's in Ranger School," I confessed, sheepish.

"Oh, good," she said. She sounded genuinely relieved for me. Or maybe she was just grateful that I was one less wife to worry about.

"I imagine you still have other wives to call?" I asked.

She exhaled heavily. "Ten. I don't know how I'm going to do it."

"They'll know their husbands are all right, at least," I said. The spouses of the killed and wounded had already been notified. That news was always delivered to you in person—at your front door, or your workplace. There was a confusing, heartbreaking relief in receiving a phone call like this.

"True," she said. "But not everyone's are."

—

The next morning, Rachel and I sat together in her living room. She was in her armchair, and I was next to her on the couch, surrounded by a sea of throw pillows. It was the weekend. Both of us were drinking to-go coffees she'd bought downtown, but the plate of blueberry muffins she'd made sat untouched between us on her end table.

"You're so calm," I said. Rachel was not a low-key gal. Where my emotions usually roiled beneath the surface, hers were impossible to hide. She looked eerily placid now, though, her face unreadable in the cloudy October light coming through the open blinds.

"I don't like that he's over there," she said. "I slept like shit last night after talking to my key caller. But I heard from Dan this morning. And he's in a different part of Afghanistan, which is sort of comforting."

I thought she was going to go on. Rachel usually did. But she stopped abruptly. I had the sense that she was withholding something—not information, per se, but whatever was happening inside of her right now.

The moment I'd woken up, I'd texted Maggie. Her husband was in Afghanistan and she was twelve weeks pregnant with her second child. All morning, I hadn't been able to stop thinking about the story she'd told me on our drive to the company party, couldn't get the image of that woman walking to her front door with the plastic grocery bags out of my mind. One of the soldiers who'd been killed had a wife. I didn't know her, had only seen a photo she'd posted of the two of them this morning in our Facebook group. It looked like a selfie, up close and intimate, their faces framed by light. Notification officers arrived at your door eight to twelve hours after your husband had been killed. For those eight to twelve hours, this woman had gone about her life, the world not quite rosy, but palatable, pleasurable even. There was laughter on the telephone with her mother, maybe, a song she liked on the radio as she drove home from work, a burger from one of the pubs downtown.

I was worried when I didn't hear from Mark, Maggie had texted back. *Then, as I talked to wives at a birthday party, it became clear that none of us had heard from our husbands, which meant sit back and hold your breath, because news is coming. And it did. It never knocks the wind out of you any less.*

This seems really bad, I wrote. *Like something went very wrong.*

It is, she said. *I've been through some rough deployments, but never any mass casualties like this.*

Do you know when it happened? How it happened? I asked. As the first sergeant's wife, I thought she might have more information than I did.

I don't, she wrote back. *The emails drafted from the forward operating base usually say "in a fire fight," which makes me wonder if there was a crash. I'd say watch the news in the next couple days.*

Rachel was quieter than I'd ever seen her. Usually, she was so expressive, wild when she was pissed off, affectionate when she was feeling sunny. But she was tentative now as she offered me the plate of muffins, her makeup-free face colorless. It was as though her volume had been turned down to the lowest possible decibel. The muffin, it felt like, was an offering, a replacement for whatever she couldn't, or didn't want to, share with me.

I picked one up and bit into it. It was still warm.

"I'm guessing you haven't heard anything from Andrew," she said.

I shook my head, listening to the sound of my own chewing and swallowing, the clacking of the dog's nails across the kitchen floor. "I'm angry," I said. I hadn't meant to say that, hadn't even realized until this moment that I felt that way.

She sat up straighter. "At Andrew? What did he do?" I could feel her hackles coming up. She was surprisingly scrappy, even fierce.

"No," I said. "Well, maybe. In some abstract sense. I'm angry at the Army. There's so much we don't know about their lives. One of the soldiers, he had a wife."

"I saw the photo," Rachel said softly.

"And she had to wait eight to twelve hours to learn about his death from some stranger at her door?"

Rachel nodded, the rest of her body utterly still, as though she was trying not to scare away a wild animal. The dog walked over and rested between our feet.

"We have no fucking power," I said. Rachel put her coffee cup down on the end table, and I could tell from the way it landed, wobbling for a moment like it might fall over, that it was empty. I hadn't seen her take a sip out of it in the last few minutes. She'd been clutching the already finished cup the whole time I'd been talking.

"Shit, I'm sorry," I said. "Andrew isn't even deployed. I have no right to go on like this."

"No, you do," Rachel said. "You can't even talk to Andrew. It was a huge relief to hear Dan's voice this morning."

"That's true," I said. Maybe it was Andrew I was angry at. In the past, he'd never once failed to show up or call me. But now that he didn't steer his own life, he was failing me all the time. He couldn't call, of course, but, somehow, this did not change the fact or the tenor of my anger. I just had nowhere to justifiably aim it. It lived in me now.

Five days later, I received a letter from Andrew. True to what Hailey had said, it was scrawled in pencil on a dirty lined note card, though it contained, at least, more than the list of candy bars Jack had sent her.

I heard from a very reliable source that my friend McCready was injured in the attack in Kandahar, Andrew wrote at the bottom of the first side of the card. *He lost both legs. . . . I still think there must be some mistake, but the source is good. McCready is such a sweet, innocent soul. Or he was. It's hard for me to imagine him being anything but bitter now.*

Sweet, gangly McCready? It did feel like some mistake. I'd only met him a couple of times, but, in his torn jeans and plaid button-downs, he'd looked to me like he should be skateboarding with friends in the loading lot of a grocery store, not going to war. He and Andrew had been through selection together. After Andrew had found our house, the two of them had spent the night in our empty living room in sleeping bags. In the morning, they'd gotten tattoos on Victory Drive. Andrew's was my name on a banner held by two sparrows. When we'd moved in, McCready had come by and given us a housewarming gift, a fridge magnet that said *Coffee, you're on the bench. Alcohol . . . suit up!*

The battalion commander was not releasing the names of the injured to us, so I couldn't fact-check Andrew's information. But he had sent out a letter about what exactly had happened. At an IED factory in Kandahar that the soldiers were raiding to stop a planned attack, a woman in a suicide vest had set off a "daisy chain of IEDs." The soldiers' actions had prevented a high-profile attack from taking place in Kandahar City, "saving countless innocent lives." This was, at least, the official message. The nine wounded soldiers, the commander said, had a significant recovery process ahead of them. These were not minor wounds; that much was clear. McCready had lost both of his legs? It was his second deployment. He was twenty-one years old.

—

The first thing Andrew did when he got home from Ranger School was sit down on our cement stoop and light a cigarette.

"Don't worry," he said. "I'm just having a few, enjoying every freedom available to me for a little while." Andrew had gone straight through after his recycle. When he'd left for pre–Ranger School training at Fort Benning four months before, he'd been a lean 175 pounds. Now he was a gaunt 145, his cheekbones jutting. In his class photo, he was asleep standing up.

It was the beginning of December, but the winter sun was strong enough that we only needed hoodies. His mostly hid the sores on his arms he'd shown me on the ride home from the graduation ceremony, though a few were still visible on his hands. His immune system had begun to shut down from lack of food and sleep, and any cut or abrasion he sustained only worsened instead of healed. I had expected the weight loss, the shorn hair, the strange pallor of his skin. But I had not expected those. I had also not expected him to be so enlivened, younger in spirit than when he'd left, as though the residue of everyday life had been wiped clean off of him.

Andrew took a deep, greedy pull of his cigarette. There were hungry Rangers and sleepy Rangers, he said, and he was a sleepy ranger, positively starving for sleep. In the mornings, after catching only two or three hours, the guys would have MREs for breakfast, and Andrew would trade most of his meal for the instant coffee that came with the highly preserved food and make himself a mega coffee.

"Then, after health checks for stuff like frostbite, we'd head out into the field, and I'd be firing on all cylinders."

"Kinda like you are now?" I said. He'd barely paused to take a breath since we'd sat down on the stoop.

"My mind has been moving a million miles an hour. Maybe because my only distractions have been conversation and fantasy. No NPR, no scrolling my phone, no TV. It's also so fucking miserable that if you don't bullshit and laugh all the time, you're liable to just off yourself," he said. "Talking has been the only fun thing to do these last few months. I've gotten pretty good at it."

Shut the fuck up, guys in his platoon would yell at him in the mornings after his daily concentrated dose of caffeine. He'd found his fellow conversationalists, though, guys who talked through the night with him while pulling security, sitting around the fire to stay warm. Andrew loved the spare beauty of these nights, the way life got stripped down to its barest essentials.

"I told some of those guys things I never told anyone," he said. *Not even me*, I thought.

I wanted to share my own rare and beautiful thing with Andrew, but what? I'd lost a few pounds working off my anxious energy at the gym, edited a couple of manuscripts, eaten spaghetti with Hailey and her kids, dropped off soup for Maggie when her pregnancy nausea refused to abate. I wrote Andrew an obscene number of letters, sometimes one a day. I'd spent two weeks in a little cabin in the Blue Ridge Mountains at a writing residency, and one night, I had stayed up into the wee hours talking with a couple of other writers. That pocket of time had felt meaningful then, but now, it didn't even seem worth mentioning. There had been no great confessions. I had not pressed my body in a huddle with theirs to create a "manferno" on the coldest nights, the way Andrew had with his classmates. I had not returned physically broken and psychically renewed.

Andrew stubbed out the cigarette on the stoop. "Hey, that's amazing about that Congo fellowship," he said.

"Well, I didn't get it," I said.

"But they invited you to apply for the next one, right?"

I nodded. We were both quiet for a minute, blinking against the brightness. Now seemed as good a time as any. "McCready . . ." I started.

"Oh, he's okay."

"Oh my god, really? You're just now telling me this?"

"Sorry, I . . . kind of forgot I wrote that in my letter. A lot of that time is a blur. Yeah, McCready's fine. It was a different guy who lost his legs."

"Who?"

"Another guy I went through selection with. He bunked next to me. I didn't really know him. Someone else lost both his legs, too. He has a baby due in a few months."

"Fuck," I said. "Were they all major injuries like that?"

"Most of them were, yeah." He shook his head, like it was hard to believe. "Another guy I went through selection with, he was standing next to someone who got blown up. Pieces of bone stuck like shrapnel in his face."

"Did you know the guys who were killed?" I asked. We had once shared everything, but this question, which I now realized I'd been working up to for the last twenty minutes, felt strangely invasive.

"They were in a different company, but I knew Rory, the one who wasn't married. Met him during the selection process too, actually; he was quiet," he said. It was dizzying, the number of these guys who had been on the exact same timeline as Andrew. He could've easily been assigned to B-company and gone on that mission. It was all so random. I hugged my arms around my chest, suddenly feeling cold. I'd seen the picture of Rory online, his eyes in a squint and his cheeks ruddy with youth. This was his "hero photo," as the guys referred to it. When I'd seen Andrew's, I chided him for not smiling, and he'd looked at me like I was a little slow.

"Yeah, you don't smile in Army photos."

The obvious reason for this didn't hit me until I was looking at Rory's face on my laptop screen: You weren't supposed to smile because this was the photo that newspapers would print if you were killed.

"The news said it was a roadside bomb, but that's not the information we got in an email from the battalion commander," I said.

"Yeah, don't read the news. More often than not, it's wrong."

"Really?" I asked.

He looked at me. "So far, that's been my experience."

I knew Andrew wasn't saying the news lied, exactly. Unlike some of the guys he worked with, he trusted reliable news sources. But the press-averse military made it difficult for reporters to do their job. The letter the commander had sent us could be a half-truth as well, though. The only people who knew the facts of what had happened were the ones who'd been on the ground.

Later, after Andrew had rested, he lit a candle in the bathroom and we got into a shallow bath. I usually lay with my back against his chest, but this time he leaned against me, and I was careful to be gentle as I wrapped my legs around his sides. I looked down at his body, the candle flickering in the corner of my eye. Sores covered his calves and his sides, hid in the dark hair on his thighs. His hips had been rubbed raw by his rucksack. Andrew's physical strength had always felt to me like a protective shield against the world. It was disorienting, seeing him like this.

"Simone, your pants are on fire," he said suddenly.

"Hm?"

He pointed at the toilet. "They are on fire."

I looked over to see a hole burning its way through my jeans that I'd thrown absentmindedly in the direction of the toilet. They'd landed right up against the candle Andrew had lit.

"Oh shit," I said, leaping out of the bath, grabbing the pants, and stomping on them hard. If Andrew were his fully operational self, he'd have been out of the bath the moment he saw the fire. He probably would have caught them midair when I'd flung them.

"Guess I'm not the only one who needs supervision right now," he said. We both laughed, and the laughter was like a release valve letting out all the pressure of the last four months.

—

CHAPTER 11

A PROFESSION OF ARMS

The next day, we threw a party for the Ranger School graduates. The guys from Andrew's company were still deployed, but the friends he'd made at Ranger School all came, and they were the easiest guests in the world. They ate greasy pizza like it was the first time they'd ever tasted the delicacy, talked incessantly like childhood friends reunited, filled the house with an infectious enthusiasm for everything—the softness of the couch, the coldness of the Budweiser, the winter light coming through the window and warming us all at the dining table. "This guy got *letters*," one of them told me. "I think you sent the most of all the wives." Their presence gave our home a new luster. Even the American flag that Andrew had hung looked beautiful through the front window, blowing in the wind.

It was a week later, a few days after we went to a barbecue at Rich's, a friend of Jack's from another team in the company, that I suggested we finally go to the shooting range. Rich lived in a little prefab house on six acres of land in a rural area outside of Columbus, so the guys liked to go there to shoot. When we'd arrived, Jack, Wes, and a couple of new privates I didn't know were huddled around the dining table, where Rich was opening a long, violin-like case. Inside it was an assault rifle, a civilian version of the kind the guys used at work and overseas. The type often used in mass shootings.

The sight of it set me on edge, but the moment it was in Rich's hands, I felt myself relax. He handled it with a kind of familiar care, as though it were a beloved instrument, and the guys passed it around like they were engaging in some kind of ritual. Jack recalled deer hunting in the Idaho autumn, and another guy talked about stalking wild boar in the Texas prairie land where he grew up. These places of origin were the only they had really known outside of the cities and countries the Army had sent them to, and these were still the spots in the world that felt most right to them. I knew this because I'd heard all them say so, but I hadn't really understood until I watched the way the gun stirred their memory. Learning to shoot had been a rite of passage for them. It had been one for Andrew too. We'd been living in Georgia for over a year now, and I'd known for most of that time that I needed, for safety's sake, to learn how to operate a gun. But I hadn't wanted to. In that moment around the table, though, a quiet but strong desire clicked into place for me.

"Are you sure?" Andrew had asked when I brought it up, and I'd nodded. But now that we were standing at the gun rental counter at Shooters, the guy behind it looking right through me, I felt much less certain.

"You military?" the guy asked Andrew. He wore a camo cap and an American flag in the shape of a crucifix around his neck. On the wall behind him was a wrinkled flyer advertising Ladies' Night: *Monday night, 6–8pm, all ladies time is free. Bring your wife, your girlfriend, or your daughter.*

Andrew nodded, sliding his California ID across the glass counter. Beneath it were rows of handguns, gleaming like wedding bands.

"The left coast, huh?" the man asked skeptically as he studied the ID. "I'm from Minnesota originally," he said. "The communists live there too."

Andrew gave him a weak smile. We'd gotten used to hearing this kind of thing from some of the guys in his unit. *Communists, Yankees, traitors.* They were half-joking, but, of course, that meant they were half-serious, too. Andrew chose a silver revolver, the lowest-caliber weapon they had, and the man behind the counter gave us some "eyes and ears," as he called them—two pairs of protective goggles and ear-muffs. We signed a few waivers and bought some overpriced ammo. It was almost time to start shooting. There was just one more thing.

"Pick a target," said the man, nodding toward the area behind us.

We turned around. Neatly stacked in a wire rack were typical targets for a buck apiece, and just above those were goblins and bloody zombie brides for twice as much. A man in wire-rimmed glasses approached and grabbed a target from a stack I couldn't see clearly on the highest shelf. As he walked away, I caught a glimpse of it in his hand: a bearded cartoon in a keffiyeh sneering and clutching a Kalashnikov.

"Is that—?"

"Yep," Andrew said with a finality that meant *let's not talk about this here*, then grabbed one of the standard targets and steered me quickly toward the range. More and more, being in public with him felt like talking on one of our monitored phone calls. Nearly everywhere I was tempted to go in conversation was a wrong turn.

Andrew opened a heavy door that led to a vestibule. It was empty and quiet and I wanted to stay, at least for a moment, but Andrew was leading me through the next door and the sound of gunfire was hitting me. The range was narrow and windowless and stiflingly humid and it smelled like a teenager's bedroom. Men were scattered among the shooting stands and all of them looked, from the back, like suburban dads, their bodies and T-shirts softened by age, as they aimed pistols at targets that hung at a range of distances, from ten to twenty-five feet away, their shoulders barely moving with each shot. Mine were jumping, though, and I wasn't even in the room yet. I was the only woman here.

"These aren't working!" I yelled, pointing to my earmuffs.

"It's the sensation!" Andrew yelled back as I followed him to a shooting stand, empty bullet casings rolling under my feet. "You'll get used to it." It *was* a sensation more than a sound, as strange and disorienting as the minor earthquakes I'd experienced growing up in California.

"Shooting is athletic!" he yelled. "How you hold your body matters." He demonstrated: left foot forward, arms taut but slightly bent, the way a batter might ready himself at home plate, except forward-facing. I tried my best to mimic him, but I could never match his physical ease. I was all thought, no instinct.

"All right, tell me three of the four basic rules of gun safety," he said. He had drilled these into me on the ride over. I wanted to ace this.

"Treat every weapon as if it is loaded," I began dutifully, then paused, thinking. "Never point the weapon at anything you don't intend to destroy. That seems like an important one." I was stalling, hoping for a laugh, but the teacher was not going to crack.

"And . . . keep your finger straight and off the trigger until you're ready to fire," I finished.

"Good. Now line your eye up with the sight, and make sure that red dot you see is just below where you're aiming." He paused. "Release the safety," he said, doing it for me. "Take a breath. Exhale. Then pull."

"What if it goes spinning out of my hands?" I yelled. I was dead serious, but that got Andrew to laugh.

"Keep your eyes open," Andrew said just as I closed my eyes and pulled the trigger.

Nothing. I opened my eyes and pulled again. And again.

"What am I doing wrong?" I asked.

He took the revolver and I stepped back as he fired off a few quick rounds. I'd seen Andrew shoot a rifle in Jack's backyard, but I had always been watching at a distance. Here, I was so close, I could see the sweat at the nape of his neck.

Andrew turned back to me and handed me the revolver.

"You're afraid," he said gently. "Don't be."

I paused, regained my stance, and tried again. Nothing.

"Pull a little harder," Andrew said.

I pulled again, and then, because my finger was starting to cramp, I let the gun slip gently out of my hands and onto the counter with the barrel pointing straight at us.

Andrew scooped it up instantly. "Never point a gun, loaded or un-loaded, toward anyone," he said sternly.

"Sorry," I said, feeling my cheeks go hot. Maybe the fact that I was unable to shoot meant we could abandon our mission, go home, and do something I was good at, like reading books.

I watched as Andrew turned the gun over, studying it as though it were a puzzle he could solve for me. I hadn't entirely recognized him when he was shooting, but his hands were still his, with the scar on the knuckle of his left thumb and the ever deepening calluses across the pads. I had always loved his hands.

"Revolvers can be tough," Andrew said. "Give me a second."

The gun he returned with was black and heavy-looking. It was a Glock .45. By comparison, the silver revolver seemed like a prop out of an old western. Andrew showed me how to load the magazine, then shot off a few rounds, each bullet casing hitting the side of the stand. As he handed it to me, I felt like he was giving me the leash to an angry rottweiler.

I stepped up to the stand. I could just barely make out the target's bull's-eye as I brought up the gun and pointed toward it, squinting through the sight and locating the floating white dot. *Pull the trigger*, I told myself. Then, after a moment's hesitation, I went for it.

The force of the shot hit me instantly, the gun kicking back against my hands, through my arms, and into my shoulders.

"Keep shooting," Andrew said.

I adjusted my feet and pulled the trigger again. The same bone-rattling surge. I took a breath.

"There's no need to pause," he said.

"There is definitely a need to pause," I said, then took one more shot before putting down the .45 and looking at the target. I was suddenly so tired, its edges blurred in my vision.

"I'm going to take a breather!" I yelled over the noise.

"That's it?" Andrew asked.

I nodded and retreated to the vestibule, my shoulders falling with relief the moment the door closed behind me. Through a porthole, I watched Andrew shoot at the target. I didn't want to touch that gun again today, which meant I was going to leave here about as ignorant as I came. Maybe I'd never really been interested in safety and responsibility. Maybe coming here had been less about learning guns and more about learning Andrew, catching a glint of that part of him that shot guns for fun and went not just willingly, but excitedly, into combat. I wanted to feel close to him. I wanted to share in some experience that no words could sufficiently explain, like what he'd just had with the Ranger School guys. And yet, here I was, still watching him from a distance, the hugeness of the space between us only growing.

—

At the end of December, I was sitting on our bed reading a book in the low winter light when Andrew walked in and drew out a black handgun from a crumpled brown bag.

"That was scary easy," he said, setting it down on our comforter, which was cream and baby blue, pale-colored like everything else in the room—the blond-stained wardrobe, the beige carpet, my white nightstand. The gun looked ominously out of place in here.

Andrew first mentioned buying a handgun right after we went to the range. *No way*, I'd told him. About a month later, we were cleaning the kitchen after dinner when he told me a guy at work was selling a Glock. I'd found a way to change the subject. Not long after that, we were walking downtown when Andrew stopped in front of a pawn shop.

"I want to check out their handguns," he'd said, his fingers around the door handle.

"Why?" I asked, stopping on the sidewalk.

"Why not?" He dropped his hand and turned to me.

I stared at him like he should know the answer by now.

"Why don't you want a gun?" he asked.

"It's dangerous," I said.

"You don't trust me with it?"

"I don't trust myself," I said.

I had pushed to understand his motives, the same way I had pushed to understand why he'd wanted to enlist: *Tell me what you like about guns. Tell me why you think we need one.* He'd answered patiently: 1) Home defense: Since we got here, there had been two break-ins on our block. Shotguns were taken from both homes. Did we really want to be the one house on the street without a gun? 2) Work: His was a profession of arms, military leaders always said. During deployment, Andrew carried a loaded gun wherever he went, and had one on him for most trainings, though it wasn't always loaded with live rounds. A gun had begun to feel like another appendage to him. 3) As for why he liked them? *I just do. I like shooting. I like how they look and feel. Some of them are even beautiful.*

Finally, I'd capitulated. I couldn't even remember what I'd said, how we'd come to an agreement. I'd just resigned myself, much in the way I'd resigned myself to the Army. A gun was coming to our home. That was that. I was tired. Tired of pushing so hard to understand Andrew that I wound up pushing him away. My throat was raw from all the arguing, and I didn't want my marriage to be one intractable fight like my parents' had been. But looking at the gun, I understood what a long way resignation was from acceptance.

"Did you register it?" I asked Andrew, looking up at him from our bed.

"Nope," he said. "You're not required to in Georgia. Dealers keep a record of who they sold it to, but I bought it from Dan." This meant there was no traceable connection between Andrew and the Glock. It was free-floating in the Georgia atmosphere.

"Rachel will be happy you took it off his hands," I said. Dan collected guns, and it was an understatement to say that Rachel was not a fan of this expensive obsession.

"Do you want to get a feel for it?" Andrew asked, picking up the Glock and handing it to me. He looked hopeful. He wanted this to be something we shared in, just like books.

I turned the gun over in my hands. It was cool and had a weight to it that was strangely comforting. The metal slide looked heavy, like it would be difficult to pull back.

"I think I'll stay away from it," I said, handing it back to him. I wanted to say more. *This is a part of your world, not mine.* But who was I kidding? Our lives and livelihoods were intertwined. Violence put food on *our* table. The real questions were the ones I had for myself:

Tell me why you're letting a gun into your home.
Tell me why you allow violence to put food on your table.

—

Early in the new year, a pounding on the front door woke us up at 2 a.m.

"Stay here," Andrew said, grabbing the gun from his nightstand and disappearing from the room in what felt like one swift motion.

I lay there waiting, suddenly so alert that even my skin felt awake. After a long silence, I finally heard voices, and I crept out of bed and down the hallway, glimpsing the dining table, which was still strewn with empty beer bottles from a barbecue we'd hosted that evening. The front door was open and Andrew was standing at the threshold. A slurred voice came tumbling out of the night and into our house.

"What are you doing here, man?" Andrew asked. I couldn't see where Andrew had placed the gun, if it was still in his hand or if he'd put it down. I hoped he was still holding it.

"I'm here for the barbecue!" the voice said. Andrew began to laugh and my chest unclenched.

It was McCready. He had intended to come by hours earlier but had gotten sidelined at the bars downtown.

"I thought, isn't D having a barbecue? Then I just started walking, but I couldn't remember how to get here, so it took a while."

Andrew turned on the living room light. A huge smear of blood covered McCready's cheek.

"What happened?" Andrew asked. McCready brought his hand to his face, then drew it away, looked at his palm.

"Shit, that's a lot of blood. I fell somewhere. Under a bridge. It was really fucking dark."

When we woke the next morning, McCready was gone, leaving

behind a smear of dried blood on the sheets I'd laid out for him. Andrew pulled them from the couch while I sat in the dining room drinking coffee. I could smell the foul sharpness of hungover sweat.

"Maybe we should incinerate those," I said. I thought of Andrew's quick motion to grab the gun the night before. He'd promised me he'd install a safe as soon as possible, but I imagined he wouldn't have been able to get to it with quite the same speed had it been locked away.

"You know, I didn't exactly hate seeing that gun in your hands last night," I said.

"Oh yeah?"

"What were you thinking when you grabbed it?" I asked.

He paused. "I wasn't thinking," he admitted.

"Trained to defend," I said in the voice of a speech-giving commander.

"To kill, actually," Andrew said, then turned away from me to open the door to the mudroom to put the sheets in the wash. I was glad he couldn't see me, because there was, I was pretty sure, a look of disgust on my face. I didn't know if it was the word itself, *kill*, or the laconic way he'd spat it out, but I hated it. I wished he could just say *defend* the way politicians did.

"Why do you have to use that word?" I called, irritated.

"It's the word we use at work," he called back.

Kill. The Army didn't just casually talk about killing. It celebrated the act and the skill. Many of the most violent and derogatory boot camp cadences had been banned in recent years, but killing was still all over them. *Left right left right left right kill*. During the year I'd spent reading about the Army and the war in Afghanistan, I'd stumbled on a famous World War II study that determined fewer than 25 percent of soldiers aimed and fired their weapons with the intent to kill. Though some researchers have called into question the original study's methods of inquiry, its findings had a huge impact on the military's approach to training. After World War II, the Army began training soldiers to overcome any hesitations through muscle memory-building "kill drills" that simulated combat as closely as possible. These kill drills raised shooting rates to around 90 percent during the Vietnam War.

I could hear the tumult of the washer starting as Andrew returned to the living room with an expectant look on his face, like he was waiting for me to respond. There was so much I wanted to ask this man I loved. I wondered how much hesitation Andrew had come into boot camp with. I wondered if, only one deployment and so many trainings and schools in, he had built any real muscle memory yet. How did he perform on those kill drills? I didn't know how to ask these questions, though. And I wasn't even sure I wanted the answers.

CHAPTER 12

—

HEROINE TO THE INFANTRY

January 2014

The woman standing behind the register was likely around forty, but she was pretty in the unadorned, un-self-conscious way of someone much younger, with apple cheeks that had a natural blush and walnut-colored hair pulled back into a loose ponytail. A faded floral apron hugged her petite frame. It looked like it had spent a lifetime hanging in a sunlit kitchen.

"Welcome to Midtown Coffee," she said. The oddly formal greeting sounded effortless coming out of her mouth.

"This is such a great place," I said, taking in the chalkboards advertising Rwandan fair trade coffee, the patrons at mismatched wooden tables, the pop-folk playing softly beneath their conversation. I couldn't believe it. I'd been yearning for a nearby café ever since we'd arrived in Georgia more than a year before.

"Oh, thank you," she said, smiling. "We're so happy to be up and running finally. We had some stops and starts. Are you in the neighborhood?"

"Just up the hill," I said. Andrew was gone for a two-week training in Tennessee. He'd left three days before, and, sitting at my desk this morning, I realized I hadn't showered since he left. The new coffee shop was the perfect excuse to get out. I had also used it to entice Maggie to come meet me. She was very pregnant now. "This stage of pregnancy is pretty much like being under house arrest," she'd told me. But I knew she'd have to break away from home to drop Emmie at Mother's Morning Out. I had to see her. She was leaving Georgia soon. After fifteen years, her husband was officially done with his time in the Unit, and was heading to Fort Bragg in North Carolina to do a selection for a different Special Operations group.

"He just up and told me this is what he was doing," she'd said. She had hoped for a slower pace in the conventional Army, an assignment in Hawaii, or maybe Italy. Instead, the intensity in their everyday lives was about to go up a notch.

The woman at the register came out from behind the counter to shake my hand. "I'm Abby," she said. This was a surprise. Strangers in Columbus occasionally cornered me in grocery aisles to talk over toilet paper options. Bank tellers could be extremely chatty, and the first time I'd sent Andrew a care package at the post office, it had taken forty-five minutes to get through a five-person line because the clerk knew someone's mother and someone else's husband. But the city had a wariness about it. There were always military transients passing through, families and young infantry soldiers coming for boot camp and airborne training and Ranger School. Locals rarely took the time to get to know you because they expected you to move on soon. "Southern hospitality is real, just not in Columbus," a wife in Andrew's unit had told me.

"I'm Simone," I said, taking Abby's hand in mine. It was small and soft, but her handshake was reassuringly firm.

"Are you military?" Abby asked after I ordered a cappuccino. "We have a 10 percent discount."

"I am. I mean, my husband is," I said, taking my ID out of my wallet.

"My husband was active duty for years. He's reserve now," she said, nodding toward a man with salt-and-pepper hair who was standing at the kitchen pass window. A preteen girl glided past him, stopping when she reached Abby. She had Abby's tidy ponytail and big brown eyes, and was, of all things, on roller skates.

"Which table, Mom?" she asked. Abby pointed and she sailed away.

"I homeschool our girls in the back of the café," Abby said. Behind me, someone cleared her throat, and I realized I was holding up the line.

"She seems lovely," I said, and moved aside to let the next customer order. The scene was so wholesome I could cry. When I'd first moved to New York, there had been a genuine café culture. I'd fallen in love with a place in the East Village called Cinema Classics, where old movies played in the back behind a red velvet curtain. My friends and I would spend whole afternoons there, chain-smoking and refilling our coffee mugs. Later, Cinema Classics became a bar with bone-white walls and ghostly lighting, and, by the time we left for Georgia, the cafés that hadn't turned into night spots had begun to feel like corporate offices with low morale, the owners flitting in and out like apparitions, the patrons sitting silently in front of laptops with headphones shoved in their ears. The tables were always occupied, and customers would loiter impatiently by the door, waiting to swoop in on the next open seat. Here, a few tables sat empty, and the rest were full of colleagues sharing a slow lunch, mothers with their babies, and even a group of young men in surprisingly earnest conversation having what appeared to be some kind of book club. They were clean-shaven and Army-age, but I'd learned to spot a soldier, and these guys weren't it. They were too thin-limbed, too goofy, too at ease. Soldiers were so tightly wound. As the tallest of the men leaned back from the table, I glimpsed one of the books more closely. It was thick, open at its middle, with a ribbon down the center.

It was a Bible. They were all Bibles.

I sat down at a table toward the back and Abby's daughter brought me the cappuccino I'd ordered. I thanked her, and as she skated away, I looked at the laminated black card clipped to a paperweight sitting at the table's center:

But he said to me, "My grace is sufficient for you, for my power is made perfect in weakness." 2 Corinthians 12:9.

I looked more closely, then, at the chalkboards hanging around the café and realized they weren't all advertising the day's soups. Many were covered in psalms. And the soft background music—it wasn't standard folk pop. This was the Christian pop Rachel sometimes played in her car. The singer, who always seemed to be a man, was reliably emotive, going on about redemption or love or both.

I took a sip of my cappuccino. *Fuck.* It was good. Rich but not overwhelmingly strong, smooth and a little bit sweet. I looked over at the counter, and Abby caught my eye and smiled. This café would work. It had to.

It was the start of a new year, 2014, and I was on a mission to make Georgia as livable as possible. Andrew's life had improved vastly since he'd graduated from Ranger School the month before. Wes, the sociopathic team leader, had left the company and the whole team had solidified: Andrew had been promoted to team leader, with privates of his own, and Jack had become the section leader. Jack had grown noticeably in size over the last year and had honed a cutting wit. Both of these qualities made people keep their distance from him, but we had bonded over books: He had been the one in his household reading *The Power Broker*, it turned out.

Under Jack were Andrew and Emmett, Andrew's co–team leader. Emmet was twenty-one and six-foot-four. He was capable of drinking an entire bottle of whiskey in one night, but, somehow, he always remained sweet and polite, with a constant look of boyish surprise on his face and a lumbering gait. It was impossible not to like Emmett, whose charming innocence was so incongruous with the facts of his life.

I was feeling more hopeful about my own career than I had in quite a while. I'd recently landed an essay in the *New York Times*, and I'd also just heard back, miraculously, from the program director of the Congo fellowship, who'd told me that if I secured one more letter from an assigning editor, they'd love to have me on the next trip. But I hadn't found a place here, or had not yet figured out how to fit into the place I had made, at least not like Andrew had. And now I was losing Maggie.

"Sorry I'm late."

I looked up to see Maggie standing above me in a flowing blouse. Her hair was still damp, falling in curls around her face. There was a slight sheen of perspiration above her upper lip and a trail of acne along her jawline.

"I'm just happy I persuaded you to come out," I said, getting up to give her an awkward hug. She was the kind of pregnant now that was impossible to properly wrap your arms around.

"The coffee is fancy fair-trade stuff from Rwanda," I said. "And it's very good."

"You're talking to a Starbucks macchiato drive-through girl. Your tactics are not effective," she said. "I ordered something filled with hazelnut syrup."

We sat down across from each other, and her stomach pressed into the edge of the table in a way that looked painful. A new Christian pop song had come on. I'd heard this one in Rachel's car. *No matter the hurt, the cross has made you flawless.* Rachel was my only Christian friend here who knew I wasn't religious. I'd even told her about the abortion. Maggie's pro-life march photos were still seared into my mind, and I tried to avoid the topic of God with her as much as possible. And even though Maggie always got what I was saying, more than anyone else I knew here, I wasn't as tight with her as I was with Rachel. The guys who went through preliminary trainings and deployments and hazings together were in lockstep with one another, and it was the same for the wives.

"You are getting closer," I said, nodding at her stomach. "But you look lighter, somehow, than the last time I saw you."

"Yeah, that's because a two-and-a-half-year-old isn't currently running circles around me," she said.

"You have, like, ten weeks to go?" I asked.

"Don't remind me," she said. "I can barely fit into this chair as it is. Or my car. Or my skin. I don't even want to think about all those beautiful post–Weight Watchers clothes hanging in my closet."

Abby's daughter placed Maggie's drink in front of her and glided away.

Maggie did a double take. "Is she . . . on roller skates?"

"She is."

"Good god, the agility of the young," she said.

"It must be impossible to even begin to pack, especially with the guys gone," I said.

Maggie took a sip of her coffee. "Oh, like Mark's a huge help." Since Maggie's husband was the first sergeant of Andrew's company, even when he was here, his schedule was grueling. While Andrew left the house at 5:30 a.m., Mark was out the door at 4 a.m., the sky still black. "When the man decides to clean once a year, he just takes everything and puts it into garbage bags and shoves it all into the garage."

"So, you're saying you're already halfway packed, then?" I said, trying to make her laugh, but she just rolled her eyes.

"Honestly, it's easier when they're gone," she said. I'd heard her say that before. The FRG made T-shirts and coffee mugs with phrases like

You were given this life because you're strong enough to live it emblazoned on them, but Maggie had her own set of axioms. *I can't wait for him to deploy* would probably look wrong on a tank top, but generally, her sayings felt far more dead-on. A year earlier, I would have balked at what she'd just said, but I now knew exactly what she meant.

During the last local night-training I'd woken around 7 a.m. to find Andrew drinking a beer and eating a frozen pizza on the couch, watching, of all things, *Generation Kill*, the shades drawn, no lights on. I'd thought living the Army 24/7 would suppress his appetite for war movies and shows, but he loved them more than ever, only now he corrected everything they got wrong, as frustrated and unhinged as a Georgia State fan barking at the TV.

He'd looked up at me and nodded, then gone back to the television, and I'd felt an irrational surge of annoyance. I'd always been a morning person, and he was not, and once upon a time, this had seemed like our biggest problem. This was *my* morning in my house, and he was ruining it already. I'd gone to shower and put on makeup and found him walking down the hall, headed to bed as I was leaving to run an errand before meeting Rachel for breakfast. He'd given me a kiss and as he'd pulled back, I'd made a face.

"What?"

"You stink of beer," I'd said.

"I've been up for thirty hours," he said. "I had a beer."

I looked down at Maggie's hands curled around her ceramic mug. There was something naked about them. It was her wedding ring, I realized. It was gone. It must've been that it was no longer fitting at this point in the pregnancy.

"At least when they're away, I have my house," I said. "*Our* house, I mean." I'd been doing that lately, stumbling, then hastening to correct myself.

"*My* house, for sure," Maggie said, nodding. And then her face changed. It didn't fall exactly, but it did look a little sad. "Though he's the landlord, right? My financier."

I gave her a rueful smile. I didn't feel like Andrew was my financier. He was still my partner. Wasn't he? He did pay the lion's share of the bills these days. When I was a teenager, my father had advised me to never rely on a man for my income. He doled out all kinds of advice when I was growing up, most of it a shade inappropriate, like "Never try heroin, it feels like heaven" or "Always hitchhike with a friend." He dispensed these nuggets of wisdom so often I came to ignore them, but this one had stayed with me. I could even remember where we were when he told me, driving south on Highway 101 along San Francisco Bay, the water shimmering in the sun. And here I was now, fifteen years later, wholly dependent on a man and yet also alone. When I'd left for New York at seventeen, eager to crack open the world, I could never have envisioned this. I would never have wanted to.

"Do you know how long they'll be back before they leave again?" I asked Maggie. The training cycle was in full swing, which entailed a packed schedule I knew little about. Maggie's husband helped the company commander put together training schedules, and luckily, she had a steel-trap mind. Some wives were fine with being in the dark—preferred it, even. But Maggie wanted to know all. She was my guide. Losing her meant losing my key to the castle. In this very practical sense, I wasn't sure what I was going to do without her when she was gone.

"Maybe three weeks?" she said. "I'll ask Mark. I know they're going to Fort Campbell." She paused, as though she'd just thought of something. "Hey, remember that English paper I basically wrote for Mark?"

I nodded and took a sip of my coffee. "Um-hm," I said in a disapproving tone from behind my cup.

Maggie grinned widely. "He got an A."

"Maggie," I said, putting down my coffee. I didn't need to say more, because I'd already said it all in the past: Mark was a grown man who'd been on eleven combat deployments; surely he could write his own papers. It was becoming a near requirement for higher-ranking enlisted men in the Unit to complete college degrees online—or, as the guys put it, "do college," as though it were a task on the day's list after "clean weapons." Mark, of course, had zero time to do college. As the first sergeant, Mark practically lived at work. So, like paying the electricity bill, going grocery shopping, and fixing the leak in the sink, helping Mark with his schoolwork became one more item on Maggie's to-do list.

"Still got it, if I do say so myself," she said, flipping her curls back over her shoulder. I laughed, but I was shaking my head. Maggie was quick-witted and fast-thinking in a way that I envied. But the confidence she had when it came to passing Mark's exams didn't extend to her own pursuits.

"I'm telling you, start that blog," I said.

Maggie shrugged. "I do not have the time. And who's going to read it?"

I had no idea what it was like to raise a toddler with a husband who was never home, and Maggie had mentioned the idea of starting a blog only once, but I felt like reaching across the table and taking her by the shoulders. I knew my emotional investment was a little intense. But it wasn't just about Maggie. She was far from the only wife who did her husband's homework. Some made flash cards for their spouses to study for information-heavy tests they had to pass at work, and many helped them prepare for promotion boards, where all of the first sergeants grilled them about their short- and long-term goals as a soldier, quizzed them on Unit history, and asked them questions about current events to make sure they had at least a loose grasp on what was going on in the world. Once, when Andrew was up for sergeant and Jack was up for staff sergeant, Hailey had even conducted mock boards for the team, with a whiteboard and everything. Hailey wanted to be a teacher, but she often said it was probably too late, too far out of her reach, too stressful with Jack's job. Looking at Maggie now, I felt just as I did every time Hailey said that. *Why don't you believe in yourself?*

"Start it, and they will come," I said to Maggie. "*I* will come."

She looked wistfully out the front window of the café for a moment before returning her gaze to mine, her eyes dreamy. They looked more green than brown in this light. "It is nice to be recognized. The battalion commander gave me two medals at Mark's change-of-responsibility ceremony. One of them said *Heroine to the infantry*. Isn't that great? I mean, come on, who wouldn't want to be a heroine?"

The naked astonishment in her voice stung. Two medals didn't seem even close to enough, given all she'd sacrificed over the last decade. I knew it wouldn't feel like enough for me.

Maggie looked down at at her phone sitting on the table. "Shit, I've gotta get Emmie in twenty-five minutes."

"Really?" I said. "Wow, that sped by."

"It always does when someone else is watching them," she said. "You'll see."

You'll see was becoming something of a refrain in my life. All the wives, and all the men too, assumed that kids would be coming along for me any minute. And I did have an itch. Not quite a fever. But a longing. Andrew and I had been talking more seriously about kids. But I still worried about just how much I'd have to give up when I became a parent. After college, I'd supplemented my income with evening babysitting, watching two toddlers, a boy and a girl. I loved those kids, their warm little bodies and grins full of mischief, but I often found my hours with them tedious and isolating, one eternal snow day. I worried that this would be what motherhood was like, especially when Andrew was gone—crushingly boring, terrifyingly lonely.

"When Emmie's older, will you go back to reporting?" I asked Maggie.

She burst out in laughter. "Me? I'm so far behind now, I can't imagine it."

I was surprised, though I tried not to show it. Maggie was thirty-four. She was behind, but not *that* far.

"Plus," she said, after a pause, "this was always my dream."

"What was?" I asked, confused.

"Being a mother."

Maggie had struggled to get pregnant with her first, pining for a child while she attended one baby shower after another. I understood how the longer you wanted something, the more single-minded the desire became. I understood the way, once you got it, you felt like you had to devote all of your energies to it or you might fuck it up. That's how I'd felt when I'd landed my job as an editor in New York. And then, of course, I'd given it up.

"I mean, a career is great and all," she said. "But your career won't love you, your career won't curl up in your lap and make your heart burst, will it? A career won't be there for you when you're old."

"Well, no, you can't cuddle with a career," I said. "But maybe it could make your heart burst." She looked at me skeptically, like she was considering, for the briefest of moments, what I'd just said, and then shook her head.

Did that mean ambition was a cold, hard thing belonging only to cold, hard women? In New York, at least the New York I'd lived in, a woman without ambition was a woman without a compass. But Maggie was trying to tell me that motherhood *was* the ambition. The ultimate prize. While the go-to dinner party question in New York was, "What do you do?" here, at company functions and barbecues, it was, "Do you have any little ones yet?" and when I said no, the woman usually moved on to a wife she had more in common with. Motherhood, in this world, allowed you to take up space, stake your spot in the sand. It made you matter. You weren't just a wife in the Unit, but a leader of a brood, the person who picked up all the pieces your husband left behind. Everyone got "through this" because of you. Maggie and Hailey were often halfway present and in a constant state of housework. Juggling too much. But maybe these women had unlocked something I hadn't. A burst of the heart, a leap, a life, the quiet, burning secret of motherhood.

—

It was late February when I got word that I would be going to Congo.

"You are always upping the ante," Andrew said, clinking his glass of wine against mine at dinner. It was Friday night, the end of the week, and I'd just told him the general itinerary. In early May, I'd be flying to Kenya for a safety training before leaving for Kinshasa, the capital of the Democratic Republic of the Congo. After five days in the city, a group of women reporters would fly to Rwanda, then drive over the border to Goma in eastern Congo, where we'd spend ten days reporting a story. For a while now, it had seemed like Andrew was the only one in this relationship raising the stakes. It felt good to be joining him. When he'd told me he wanted to be at the beating heart of the world, I hadn't said what I'd been thinking: *So do I.*

"Are you nervous?" I asked Andrew.

"No, you'll be fine," he said. "You'll be great. I'll make you a first aid kit. Tourniquets, gauze for packing bullet wounds—"

"Bullet wounds?!"

"Oh yeah, this isn't gonna be some bullshit first aid kit," he said. Then he broke into a grin. "Maybe I could come be your personal security?"

I was nervous, but not about the prospect of danger. I had done very little reporting in the last few years, and now I was going to drop into a country—a continent—I'd never even visited, that I knew only from the books I'd scoured in order to prepare my application. I was exceedingly fortunate to have the support of a foundation and local fixers who knew Goma and Kinshasa. What gave me pause were the other reporters going on the trip.

Trying to fall asleep later that night, I scrolled through the mass email the director had sent us, poring over the details of the other journalists' careers.

The bios of the other five women going on the trip are so intimidating, I texted Hailey. All of them were seasoned freelancers who'd reported overseas extensively.

Well, maybe the story you report will be your Pulitzer, she wrote back. *Stop dicking yourself down.*

Dicking myself down, huh?

That's what Jack's always telling me. Stop dicking yourself down, Hailey.

Maybe that's what I should've said to Maggie: *Stop dicking yourself down.*

—

The next week, I scrambled to prepare, sending away for visas and ordering a new tape recorder for interviews. After lunch on Wednesday, I headed to the hospital on base to get my yellow fever vaccine. The afternoon was blustery and gray, and as I drove down Victory Drive, I had the feeling that I was sailing across a bay. Thank god Andrew and I hadn't made any solid plans for babies. If I had a newborn right now, I wouldn't be heading off to Congo. I wouldn't even be walking down to the café to work.

I turned onto Fort Benning Road, stopping at the Yield sign to let the oncoming traffic pass. To my right, a mattress delivery truck sat parked in the near empty parking lot of Main Gate Plaza. Maybe the place had once resembled a halfway respectable strip mall, but now it was home only to an Ace Furniture store and the Victory barbershop. It was a depressing corner, and I was beginning to get restless and worried that I might be late for my appointment, when I felt a rumbling.

I glanced up to see a set of wheels in my rearview mirror barreling toward me. They were so high, I could barely make out the vehicle on top of them.

That jeep is going to hit me, I thought.

And then it did, hard and quick, the crunching sound of metal on metal so loud my ears ached.

Automatically, I drove off the road and into a parking lot and got out. The wind was biting, breaking through my jacket and chilling me instantly. I looked down at my hands. They were shaking. Out of the corner of my eye, I saw a uniformed soldier running toward me.

"Ohmygodareyouokay?" he said, his words running together. I spotted a lifted jeep parked about twenty feet away and understood that this was the man who'd just hit me. And to my horror, he was extending his arms in my direction. Was he going to hug me? Who hugged a person after smashing into her car? I backed away.

"I was just coming back from lunch," he said, thankfully bringing his arms down to his sides. "I was in a hurry, I didn't see you." Was he drunk? He didn't smell of alcohol, but his words sounded loose and wrong.

I walked to the back of my car to survey the damage. The hatchback door of the trunk was pushed in, the lights shattered, the license plate warped and hanging at an angle.

"Jesus fucking Christ," I said, but the wind was so loud, it swallowed my words whole.

—

CHAPTER 13

INTESTINAL FORTITUDE

After surgery two days later, Andrew fed me chocolate pudding, the spoon hard and cold against my tongue. My throat burned as I swallowed, and I reached my hand instinctively to the bandage on my neck. The neurosurgeon had gone through the front, near my thyroid, to reach my cervical spine. It was such a vulnerable place to be cut. I was a doll held together with tape. Take it away and my head might fall off.

I'd gone straight to the ER as a precaution after the accident. Whiplash, I thought, when I felt the slightest twinge in my neck. Andrew had been training somewhere remote on base, but I'd called Hailey, and she had gotten through the grapevine to the company commander, who had let Andrew come meet me at the hospital. Twelve hours, an X-ray, CAT scan, and MRI later, the pain kicked in: slowly at first, in foreshocks down my neck and back, until all at once, it took me down. Just to bear it, minute by minute, required tremendous mental focus. "You've lost 75 percent of your neck strength," the neurologist on call told me. I had sustained a traumatic fracture in my cervical spine and torn several ligaments surrounding my vertebrae. The surgery had repaired the spinal fracture, and the rest, the surgeon said, would heal in time.

While a nurse was pushing me around the hospital in a wheelchair, other journalists were packing their bags for the Africa fellowship. This fact was scalding in its disappointment, but for two whole weeks, Andrew wasn't going to work. The morning after we returned from the hospital, he helped me out of bed, brushed my hair, dressed me, even hooked earrings into my ears, though of course I wasn't going anywhere. My pain was loud and unruly, and its only match was Vicodin. I dozed on the couch in the living room while Andrew sat at my feet, drinking coffee and reading books, logging the hour each time I took a Vicodin, bringing me bowls of soup.

The FRG set up a meal train, and over the next week, wives I'd never even met dropped off lasagna, barbecue pulled pork, taco makings. A blond Tinkerbell of a woman showed up with brownies and pizza she'd made from scratch.

"Even the dough?" I asked, astounded. "You're like a fairy godmother."

She waved me away.

Hailey brought me the *Divergent* series and a batch of her famous blondies. Rachel dropped by with magazines and a stew that she let simmer in her Crockpot for a full day. Andrew, my mother, and my father all chalked up the crash to shitty luck, but Rachel was angry. "That asshole should have never been on the road," she said, her thin frame practically shaking with rage. According to the injury lawyer she'd helped me find, the soldier who crashed into me had bottom-of-the-barrel insurance; we weren't going to get anything out of him unless we took him to court, which I had no desire to do.

In the mornings after breakfast, Andrew laced his arm around my waist as I shuffled slowly, painfully, around the block. Since Andrew had joined the Army, time had the quality, always, of sand running through the hourglass. There was never enough. We were on a constant countdown to the next training or deployment. Now, though, we were suspended in a kind of unreality, and I wondered how I'd ever gone a day without him.

"Thank you for being with me," I said to him one morning as we rounded the block. Already, the chill of winter had burned off and the azaleas were in bloom. The sight of them returning was a comfort. I'd lost Africa. I'd lost more than I really understood yet, but I had Andrew here next to me. I had spring.

"That's what this life is about, isn't it?" he said.

"What's that?" I asked. My voice was still hoarse from the surgery.

"Loving you."

After two weeks, my pain had dimmed only slightly. Its one match was Vicodin, and I was almost out.

"I need more," I told Andrew, who was just about to leave for a month-long training in Yuma, Arizona. He called the doctor, and the prescription was refilled. The pill transformed me when it hit my bloodstream, blotting out the pain and making me quietly happy— hopeful, even. But as the drug's effect waned, the pain came rushing back, rocking my body, and then my mood, with bone-rattling force.

"She needs to take the next one before the effect of the first runs out," the doctor told Andrew. I followed his instructions. It worked. I stopped crashing into darkness, most of the time. But that hopeful feeling disappeared, too.

—

The air-conditioning in the neurologist's office was on full blast, making the hairs on my arms stand up. It had been a month since the surgery, two weeks since Andrew had left for Yuma, and my surgeon was looking at my X-ray on his computer screen. I had been in so much pain the few times I'd seen him before, I hadn't really taken him in. He looked to be in his late thirties, lean and symmetrical, handsome in a sterile way, like a model from an advertisement for prescription glasses.

"The fusion looks good," he said finally, swiveling toward me on his stool. "I can't let you drive yet, especially since you're still on Vicodin. But keep up your walks." Rachel had wanted to drive me here, but I'd told her that was absurd. The office was just a quarter mile away. And Rachel's company and affection, anyone's really, felt like an intrusion right now. Andrew had left me alone, and now I wanted the whole world to leave me alone too.

"I need the exercise," I'd told Rachel, which was true. I was supposed to walk daily, and I did, making a loop around the park at the bottom of our hill every morning. These early morning walks were easily the best part of my day, the air not yet stifling, the world still wrapped in the silk of sunrise. I loved feeling the reliable presence of others around me, the power walkers and runners, the men doing pull-ups on the metal park equipment. The first time I set eyes on Lakebottom Park, I'd known that it would become my refuge, but I had never imagined that, a year and a half into living here, it would become my entire reason for getting out of bed in the morning.

"How is your pain?" the surgeon asked.

"Sharp," I said. "And it's not just in my neck; it moves down my back, my arms."

"I'll prescribe you another month of Vicodin. That's hopefully all you should need to recover," he said.

"My fingers tingle," I said. "My limbs just go numb sometimes. Is that normal?"

He paused, choosing his words. "It's not *ab*normal," he said.

"Will it go away?" I asked.

"Maybe."

"Maybe?"

"Maybe not. This was a life-altering injury. You're going to get arthritis in your neck, probably early. You're never going to be the same." He said this plainly but carefully. Surgically. He smiled stiffly then, got up from his seat, and shook my hand, leaving me alone in the cold little room, his words still whirring in the air.

What if I tried very hard, though? I thought on my way home. Nearly every morning on my walks, the same woman was there, running past me, broad-shouldered and strong, her gaze focused on some predetermined goal only she could see. I wasn't a runner, but I recalled having that kind of focus, the drive that a goal in the distance can give you. Maybe I'd get back there one day. There were guys in Andrew's unit who'd sustained multiple wounds from machine guns or lost limbs to IEDs and were back in the fight. One of the guys who'd lost both legs in the mass casualty was training to be in the Paralympics for sled hockey. I didn't have their "intestinal fortitude," but couldn't I return to my personal baseline, which, let's face it, wasn't terribly impressive to start with?

By the time I reached my door, I was exhausted. The house smelled like something in it had turned. Since Andrew had left, I had stopped cleaning, resorting to doing the dishes only when I ran out of every utensil in the house. As I retreated to my room, I tried to ignore the disaster of the kitchen, where a line of ants had taken up marching orders along the back of the counter.

When I got to the back of the house, I stopped at the threshold of my office for a moment. My desk sat covered in a mess of notebooks. It looked untouchable, like a display in a museum. I thought of Africa, of the book I'd imagined writing when I'd first gotten here. Maybe that's not who I was anymore. But then, who was I?

Andrew called late in the day, when the sky was just beginning to darken. I was sitting on the toilet, watching hot water run into a bath I was drawing. The house was dim, not a single light on.

"You sound like you're in rough shape," he said. His phone was on speaker and I was having a hard time hearing what he was saying. He was driving back to the hotel from the gym. This Arizona training was of the cushy variety, with a queen-sized bed in an air-conditioned private room rather than a thin cot in a warehouse crowded with sixty guys.

"You sound weird," I said, wanting to punish him for some reason I didn't entirely understand. "Like you're following a script or something."

He paused, inhaling sharply. "I'm going to call you back in half an hour." His voice was tight. He was trying not to get mad. He hung up, and I hated him and I hated myself.

Before the accident, I'd been feeling like I had finally begun to chart a path here. But I'd literally been knocked off course, and I could not see a way back. I thought again of that runner at the park, the steeliness of her gaze. Had I ever really possessed a gaze like that? Had I ever had true ambition, or was I only driven by a messy heap of desire and need? Those were the faulty rudders that had steered me here. Not ambition. Ambition belonged to Andrew.

My phone rang on the edge of the tub.

"I would do anything to take away the pain you're in," Andrew said. "You know that."

"I know," I said. "I'm sorry." I didn't hate him anymore. I felt only indescribably sad. His voice was velvety and close against the speaker, but he was many states away. This was the only way I'd ever been married, and yet, I didn't know how to be married like this.

I shifted my weight slightly and sat up. The water was so hot my thighs were the searing red color of the sores that had covered Andrew's body after Ranger School. I'd had to be so tender with him then. I wanted that kind of consideration now. Without him here, I felt like I might actually be disappearing. I needed him to make me feel real, to alchemize two voices on a telephone into a marriage, to spin straw from gold. I needed to hear him say what he'd just said again.

"Anything? Really?" I asked.

"I'd do anything," he said.

—

The next morning, I opened my front door to find Hailey on the stoop. She was wearing white capris and holding two to-go cups in her hands, the scent of fresh coffee wafting from them.

I'm in the neighborhood, she'd texted five minutes before. *You home?*

I hadn't replied. I didn't want to lie, but I also didn't want anyone seeing how I was living right now.

"Sorry, the house is a mess," I said as she walked inside. My blinds were down, and I hadn't realized how cloudless and bright it was outside, birdsong in the air. The fresh sunlight felt exposing. I rushed to shut the door behind her.

In the past, whenever I apologized for the state of my house, Hailey would say, "You've seen my place, right?" When Rachel's got chaotic, she called it "Simone-level clean." We joked about the absurd fullness of our sinks when the guys were gone, the lint and crumbs on our floors that stuck to our bare feet. Alone, you grew a little feral, let the house slip. I'd stopped apologizing. But this was different. I'd let it go too far this time.

Hailey handed me one of the coffees and looked me up and down. "No offense, Simone, but you don't look good," she said. "Do I need to put you in the shower?"

She walked into the dining room, and I followed her like a puppy, desperate to shield the house from her. There was a look of wariness in her eyes as she surveyed it all: the dining table covered in congealed, half-full mugs of old coffee, the fresh coat of cracker crumbs on the couch, the dirty laundry strewn down the hallway.

She moved, then, on to the kitchen with the assurance of a realtor checking out a house, and my stomach tightened as I saw her take in the counter. The marching ants, the caked coffee grounds, the half-eaten, rotten banana.

"I'm sorry, my house really is a wreck," I said, ineffectually picking up magazines from the dining table.

Hailey turned from her spot in the kitchen to where I stood in the dining room and looked at me. I met her eyes, trying to appear casual, lighthearted, even, but her gaze was so soft, almost sad, that I had to look away. Out of the corner of my eye, I saw her walk toward me and I thought, for a moment, that she was going to hug me, which would have been something Rachel would do, but not Hailey. Hailey was a dispenser of food, not affection.

Instead, she took the stack of magazines from my arms.

"This isn't okay, Simone," she said. I locked eyes with her again, and I could see that this wasn't an admonishment. It was recognition. *I see you*, she was saying. *And what I'm seeing isn't good.*

"Let me help you," she said, and put the magazines in the rack that sat at the end of the couch. She picked up a few of the mugs from the table and brought them into the kitchen, then grabbed a dish rag that was hanging from the oven and started to wipe down the counter.

"No, no, it's okay, really," I said. "I'm going to take care of it. Today. You have enough on your plate." It was torturous to stand in the dining room a few feet away and watch, knowing how much grime must be coming up on that rag.

There was so much I wanted to say.

I'm slipping into a dark place.

I need help.

I was profoundly depressed. I'd known that. But, watching Hailey pick up a sponge, I understood that the Vicodin wasn't carrying me through the depression. It was drowning me. I was the frog and the water was boiling at full pitch.

I don't know how to stop, I thought as I watched Hailey decimate the trail of ants, her arm moving in one quick, confident motion.

I willed myself to say it aloud. But I couldn't get out the words.

CHAPTER 14

—

GREEN ON BLUE

A ndrew was shaving in the bathroom mirror when I noticed him eyeing me in his reflection. I was standing next to him, opening my orange bottle of Vicodin.

"Maybe it's time to stop those pills," he said.

"I am," I told him, taking one out and breaking it in two. "I'm weaning myself, starting today."

Andrew had been back from Yuma for a week, and every night of that week, I'd promised myself that my bedtime pill would be my last. Then I'd wake in a fog and reach for one without hesitation. It always gave me the lift I needed. *Today is the day I'll turn things around*, I'd think during my morning walk. By the time I was back at home, doing tedious TA work for an English professor in Los Angeles a friend had connected me with, my neck would begin to stiffen, and I would take another pill. Advil would've dulled the pain a bit, but I could feel the shift in my internal weather beginning, and only Vicodin would steady that for me. As the day turned to evening, though, the third pill gave me only a short-lived boost before taking me down. And wherever I landed, I was locked there until the next morning pill.

I'd been in that frozen, gray state when Andrew returned from Yuma. We'd lain next to each other on our bed as I talked in stops and starts, feeling nothing except for the hot tears streaming sideways from my eyes. He told me he loved me but felt out of his depth, that I needed a therapist, like I'd had for a time in New York. I said I'd look for one, but there were so many hoops to jump through with Army insurance, and navigating all that right now felt somehow insurmountable.

Around lunchtime, I took another half of a pill. The day was moving forward without any highs or lows. Then, bedtime hit. All night, I twisted and turned, wanting out of my body, writhing like I was trying to shed my own skin. When I got up in the morning, I felt like I hadn't slept at all. I opened the little orange bottle and hungered for the delicious wholeness of one big, white pill. But I forced myself to swallow just the leftover half sitting at the top of the pile.

After two days of this, my head had partially cleared. I liked having my mind back. Editing and writing were much easier. But my skin felt too tight, every sound painfully loud. When Andrew got home and put his hand against my cheek, it actually hurt. "How was your day?" he asked, his voice like the screeching of tires. I wanted to throw a plate at the wall.

I hate it here, I thought one night, almost two weeks after Andrew's return, when I'd been completely off the Vicodin for three days. The thought appeared in my mind like a bomb dropped with no advance notification. We were sitting on the couch, watching a movie in the dark, and the cushions felt itchy and rough against my thighs. Hate what? The South, this couch, my marriage? Maybe all three. I thought of what Hailey had said. *Hell on my marriage.* Such hell she'd even

briefly considered returning to Idaho pregnant with a four-year-old
in tow. Then, I remembered how, when Andrew was a private, he'd
said, "Maybe I shouldn't have come." Maybe *I* shouldn't have come.
Maybe I should leave. But I couldn't imagine returning to New York.
After the mass casualty, I'd written friends there about it, and many
hadn't even responded. Reina and I had remained in loose touch, and
our emails and texts were always intimate and easy, but it was apparent
how different our lives were. She was working a stint at Dow Jones in
Hong Kong, traveling to Myanmar and Thailand, going to dinner parties
at lofts belonging to absurdly wealthy men. On Facebook, I scrolled
through old acquaintances' updates and photos out at bars or work
conferences, but I'd stopped commenting. Talking to my old friends
felt like talking to Hailey had when we first met, like yelling across that
deck in a storm. I couldn't tell if I missed the city so much the sight of it
stung or if I didn't miss it anymore, and that was what hurt. Whatever
the case, leaving the city and coming here, changing my life so radically,
had been like cauterizing a wound. There was no undoing it.

I hate it here I hate it here I hate it here.

As the TV blared, the thought cycled through my mind, again and
again, wash, rinse, repeat.

Andrew had put on *We Were Soldiers,* a Mel Gibson movie based
on a book about Ia Drang, a famously brutal Vietnam battle that lasted
three days. Andrew had watched it at least twenty times since he was
a kid. Ever since he'd enlisted and made me sit through *Black Hawk
Down,* I'd been unable to stomach war movies, and this one was basically
a relentless firefight, with moments on the home front that had been
filmed in Fort Benning's White Elephants. The neighborhood looked
just as it did now. Even the wooden screen doors were unchanged. I'd
managed to avoid watching a lot of it by washing the dishes, putting
away the food, and cleaning up the table and kitchen floor with pains-

taking care, but it wasn't over yet, and I didn't want to be alone with my thoughts. Plus, Andrew would be gone training again soon, and then he would deploy. I wanted time with him, even if we didn't spend that time in the way I wanted to.

"I wonder what was going through Custer's mind when he realized that he'd led his men into a slaughter?" Mel Gibson, who was playing Lieutenant Colonel Hal Moore, asked his sergeant major. It was dark on the screen, the glow of explosives and gunfire intermittently illuminating their faces.

The gray-haired sergeant major looked at him sternly. "Sir, Custer was a pussy. You ain't." Mel Gibson laughed, his face filling with pain.

"The war we're fighting now is similar to Vietnam, isn't it?" I asked. My voice sounded strange and far away. What I meant was, America was weeding out terrorists the Taliban had given safe harbor to, and, supposedly, nation-building. "Like, you're fighting some Afghans, and you're fighting alongside others. So, a whole people is not just the enemy?"

"Some of the guys hate all the Afghans," Andrew said. "Especially the ones they're training." He took a sip of his beer, his eyes on the screen.

"Especially?"

"Yeah, there has been no small number of green-on-blue attacks."

"Green on blue?" I asked.

"Afghan soldiers killing US ones."

"No small number? You got any stats on that, Sergeant?" Andrew had gotten promoted to sergeant before he left for Yuma, and I had been using the title affectionately, but there was bite in my voice this time.

Andrew cracked a smile. "Let's just say it's not always clear who the enemy is. So, sometimes guys decide it's everyone you didn't train with back home."

"What do you mean, decide? What do they do?"

"They don't *do* anything," Andrew said. "It's just talk."

I stared at him until he broke away from the screen and met my eyes. Quick, automatic gunfire filled the room. I could see that he wanted to end it here.

"Talk?" I asked, an edge creeping into my voice.

Andrew took a breath, hesitating as if he were making a decision.

"Like I said, it's just talk. Stuff like 'let's nuke the whole country,' or 'burn the place to the ground,' or remember that T-shirt we saw at Ranger Joe's by base that freaked you out?"

"What T-shirt?"

"The one with that quote from the Crusades on the back? KILL THEM ALL, LET GOD SORT THEM OUT?"

"All of that is *sick*," I said. I knew I'd just nearly yelled, but I didn't really care, and besides, the TV was loud. Why did Andrew play the television so goddamn loud? Had he always done this? It seemed like he'd played television and music at a reasonable decibel once upon a time, but the guys' penchant for blaring volume had clearly rubbed off on him, just like so many other customs of the Unit—the dip, the energy drinks and caffeine pills to get through long trainings, the swearing peppered throughout every sentence like filler words: *I'll just go down to the fucking store and get some chicken.*

Before we got here, I had thought about how war might change Andrew, but I had never even paused to consider how the culture of a storied institution might mold him, alter the way he spoke and walked and saw the world. Sometimes, when he came home, he'd bark in my direction and I'd have to remind him I wasn't one of his privates. More and more, the Andrew who returned at the end of the day was Andrew the soldier, the sergeant, not Andrew my husband. The problem with this was that Andrew the husband *was* Andrew the soldier. We'd married nine days before he left for boot camp. But I wanted to separate out the two, take the part of him that chewed tobacco and shot guns and traded in dark jokes with his coworkers and remove it, put it on a shelf like a lunch box, then hand it back to him when he went to work in the morning. "Have a good day, honey! Remember to leave this at work this time!" I wanted Andrew. I also wanted him, in this moment, to be anything other than what he was.

We both got up from the couch at the same time. His body was tense with frustration. On the screen a gunfight was raging, blasting into our living room.

"Simone, people make really fucking dark jokes because that's the way you live with this job, if you're going to keep doing it," he said, his face serious in a way I wasn't sure I'd ever seen. "You can't get soft about it. You can't go be Tim O'Brien and ruminate on its senselessness. You'd lose your mind, and you really can't lose your fucking mind. Some of these guys who've been doing this job for a decade were so close to their friends when they were killed that their blood got on their uniforms. When people try to kill you again and again, people you see use kids as human shields, people who celebrate or even had something to do with 9/11, your perspective changes. And it's not wrong or right, it's just different. And then, the guy you're training turns around and shoots your friend in the back? Yeah, you've got some rage after that. Still, you do everything in your power not to kill civilians. But the rage has to go somewhere, so you say some shit."

I sighed. I got what he was saying, more than I wanted to admit. But I didn't want to get it, didn't want to be having this argument at all, longed to go back to when I'd never thought about any of this.

"You know what, I'm done talking about this shit."

"Why do you always do this?" he said. "Just leave the conversation because you can't handle it. Do you want to be like those couples who don't talk about anything? We used to talk, Simone. I miss it."

Had we stopped? Now that he said this, I realized I missed talking with Andrew so much it hurt, and the pain was so intense I'd rather turn to stone than feel it. Maybe that's what I'd just been doing with the Vicodin.

"You won't talk to me about anything," I said. "Everything is OPSEC this, OPSEC that." Operational security. The phrase had become as inevitable and commonplace in my life as the sweaty PT uniform at the bottom of our hamper. The FRG had even once sent us a *Green Eggs and Ham* riff to really drive home the message: *You CAN say it in the shower, but do NOT go sharing at happy hour. DON'T make the Army Public Affairs sweat. DON'T post about it on the internet.*

"That's not true," he said. "I tell you things. I come home every night with stories from work."

"You never tell me how you feel," I said.

"I don't talk like that," he said.

"Yes, you do. You did." Did he? I thought he did. I couldn't remember anymore. I did remember talking on the floor of his New York sublet late into the night. I remembered thinking at the Manhattan courthouse that even a marriage like this would be worth it, if it meant I could talk to Andrew forever.

"I don't want any part of this," I said, walking briskly to our bedroom and closing the door, hard. I knew I was being childish and mean. But it felt good to behave badly, to throw my weight around. I lay back on the bed, wondering what I had even meant. Any part of what? My marriage, his unit, this endless tug-of-war between us?

After Andrew made it through the selection process, a sergeant first class had given his group of soldiers a talk on what they were in for. Andrew had called me in New York afterward. One of the guys who'd just made it through months of training and part of the selection process had quit after the talk.

"He just said, 'I want no part of this,' a third of the way through selection, six weeks away from graduating, if he made it," Andrew had said in disbelief. When I pressed him for more details about the talk, he said, "It was just really dark shit. Stories about shooting people in their sleep. Sociopath stuff. Who knows if any of it was even true." I stopped pressing after that, unsure if I wanted any more details. Later, that sergeant first class was kicked out of the Unit. There were rumors of mental health issues and domestic abuse, but nothing was ever confirmed. Who knew? I only knew that whatever he'd said had driven that young man away. What was in Andrew that had allowed him to stay?

I had lived with this question, just sitting in my chest, ever since.

Maybe Andrew did still talk to me, or at least tried. But I was so scared to find out the answer to this question that I had stopped listening. "How was your day, honey?" would be a much simpler query if he were a techie, a lawyer, a farmer who sold lettuce at the weekend farmers' market.

I took my phone out of my back pocket. Shit. Rachel had texted earlier in the day asking if I wanted to get lunch at Abby's café, and I'd completely forgotten to reply. *Sorry I've been so withdrawn*, I wrote. *I hate it here. I hate the Army*. Then I picked up Andrew's pillow from the bed and threw it against the wall.

I shifted onto my side and looked at the wedding photo on my nightstand. When I'd decorated, one of the first things I'd done was frame the shot Reina had taken at the courthouse. In it, Andrew and I were both laughing. I looked particularly excited, still floating from the way the officiant had bid me goodbye with, "Have a beautiful life, doll," in his thick Brooklyn accent.

Andrew had called me after the talk that sergeant first class had given because he needed to hear my voice. There had been palpable fear in his.

"I want to grow old with you," he'd said. "I want to have children with you. I don't want to die." His fear was my fear, and it had overwhelmed me to hear him articulate it, but I had stayed on the phone and I had listened.

—

The next morning, Rachel brought me coffee from Abby's. It was muggy and gray out. "Abby says she misses you. Also, you never texted me back." She stuck out her tongue and I laughed.

"You spoil me," I said.

"I wanted to come see how you are after last night," she said, walking into the living room and closing the door behind her. "You didn't sound so great on text."

"Thanks for listening to me rant. And sorry I disappeared at the end there. I passed out." I tried for a laugh, but it caught in my throat and I had to cough to keep from letting out something that felt worryingly like a sob.

"Good, I'm glad you got some sleep," she said. "And say no more— you have talked me off the ledge many times. We gotta take turns being the sane one in this friendship, and more often than not, that's you."

I did not feel like we took turns. I felt like we were both a little bit nutty all of the time. Over text the night before, I'd told Rachel that Andrew and I were fighting. *Girl, I used the D-word the other night*, she had texted back. *Divorce.* I couldn't imagine saying such a thing, even in the worst of fights. It wasn't that my marriage was more titanium than hers. That word just felt terrifyingly explosive to me. You couldn't take it back. At least, not in my marriage. That was the thing no one told you when you got married. Most of the marital advice offered up in half-drunk wedding speeches was useless because Tolstoy was wrong. Happy or unhappy, every family, every marriage, had its own rules and values.

We sat down on the couch. The cushions felt soft again and my mind was clearer than it had been in a long time.

"Did you and Andrew make up last night?" she asked.

"Sort of," I said, and there it was again, that catch in my voice.

We hadn't made up, not really. Andrew had come to bed after I'd fallen asleep. Somewhere in the middle of the night, he had reached out and held my hand. After a moment, he let go, then traveled up beneath my shirt, pressing his body against mine. I thought we might start having sex, but then he'd fallen back to sleep. In the morning, he was gone.

"Just as soon as things felt like they were coming together for me, they fell apart," I said.

Rachel shook her head. "The fucker," she said. I knew she was thinking about the soldier who'd hit me. But this sensation of unraveling felt so much bigger than the crash, bigger than the surgery or the Vicodin. Bigger than the Army. Bigger than my marriage, even. Something foundational in me was fracturing, or maybe it already had.

"How did I end up here?" I asked, looking out the living room window. From here, I could see just the bottom corner of the flag. It had become a kind of steadying landmark over these last months, and the sight of it was oddly comforting. The street outside was dead, just as it had been the winter I'd arrived. I'd asked myself this same question then. I wasn't so alone anymore—I had Rachel to ask now—but the question remained, and it had become so much more complicated. How, after two years, had I ended up *here*? My young marriage profoundly strained, my mind in such disarray it felt like a neighborhood I wanted out of, my career—well, I liked to think that I had sustained a career since I'd left New York, but who was I kidding? Maybe what I was doing was the equivalent of passing the time, no more than crocheting.

"Honestly, I wonder that myself all the time," Rachel said, putting her arm around me. I let myself fall into her, and finally, the sob came. Somehow, I knew her question was as big as mine. The contours of it were different, but its breadth, its depth—it was the same. She hadn't gotten the wedding she'd dreamed of, and this life wasn't what she'd dreamed of either. People told us, from time to time, that we knew what we were "signing up for." But who really knows what she is signing up for?

CHAPTER 15

—

POLITICS

In July, Rachel took a dollar-store pregnancy test. She was only one day late. And she and Dan hadn't been trying. There hadn't really been time to try. Dan had finished Ranger School in June, returned home for two weeks, and then deployed to Afghanistan to join his company, which had already been there for two months. He'd been gone for five days. But Rachel had a feeling. Her breasts hurt. She felt like she was getting sick. And this was how so many of the women got pregnant, whether they were trying to or not. There was even a term for it: "deployment babies." These babies were conceived in the sliver of time the soldier had leave, either before or after deployment. Practically speaking, the first was preferable. Deployments generally lasted four months, so the father was likely to be home when the baby was due.

Rachel called me after she took the test. We were supposed to be getting burgers downtown in an hour. "Can you come meet me in my driveway?" she asked. She wanted clear and honest daylight.

"That's positive, right?" she asked me, holding it between us. We were standing by the bumper of her car.

There were two distinct pink lines. The second wasn't even faint.

"Very," I said, then looked at her, smiling. "Congratulations."

"Fuck," she said, but a smile was spreading across her face too. She'd always wanted to have a family. It just seemed like there was never what you might call a good time. There was only the sensation, a hand pressing gently but insistently, saying, *It's time.*

"Fuck," I said, and laughed out of an excited but uncomfortable giddiness. I was happy for her. I was also about to be the last childless woman standing.

Rachel told Dan over Skype, on her laptop, pressing the cheap test against the screen. The connection was terrible. "What the hell is that?" he kept asking. Andrew was gone too, but he was at Marine Corps Mountain Warfare School in California instead of Afghanistan, missing another deployment. The war had recently undergone a major shift: Obama had lowered the troop count in Afghanistan, and the US military was trying to transition responsibility of the country to the Afghan National Army. This meant that for the first time since 9/11, only half of the Unit had deployed on this year's rotation. Andrew was disappointed that his company hadn't been selected this time.

Two weeks after Rachel showed me the test, she called in the afternoon. I'd been at my desk grading papers for the professor in LA for hours, and my eyes were burning from the screen. "You want to come look at a house with me?" she asked. From almost the moment Rachel and Dan knew they were expecting, he was emailing her links to houses for sale and she was calling realtors. They didn't have much of a nest egg, but they had the VA loan. They needed more space, and this seemed the smartest way to get it.

"It's a little out of our price range, but it's just a mile away and it looks perfect," she said.

Twenty minutes later, Rachel and I were walking up the front steps of a single-story brick home, trailing behind a realtor's cloud of perfume. Rachel didn't like her. She was always trying to show her places in neighborhoods Rachel wasn't interested in—new homes in tidy subdivisions in North Columbus. Safe neighborhoods. White neighborhoods. "I swear she won't show me houses in this older part of Columbus because Black people live here," Rachel had told me on the drive over.

It was a beautiful house, the same 1930s era as our bungalows, but much bigger, somewhere between a Colonial and a Cape Cod. Its condition wasn't pristine. The window frames outside were chipped, the walls needed new paint, and there weren't any appliances. But it had good bones and old-house charm, with original oak floors, lattice windows, and french doors off the living room that led to a formal dining room filled with afternoon light. It was on the register of historic homes in the neighborhood. The list price was $135,000. The same house where I'd grown up would easily sell for a million dollars.

"The sellers don't want to go under asking," the realtor said, planting herself in front of the fireplace with her arms across her chest. The brown dye in her hair was growing out, revealing gray roots. She kept fidgeting, crossing and recrossing her arms, like she was jonesing for something. Maybe a smoke. Rachel ignored her, heading into the den, and I followed. It was darker in this room, but cozy.

"It's nice to have this room right off the kitchen," I said. She nodded, quiet as she looked around. I trailed behind her as she walked into the hallway, then stopped short when she leaned, suddenly, against the wall, her hand to her stomach.

"Nauseous?" I asked. It had hit her hard in the last week.

She nodded.

"Let's get some air," I said, gesturing toward the door just ahead of us.

The hallway door opened onto a huge, wooden deck in full sunlight, an addition a previous owner must have made. It was weathered and old but looked solid, like the house itself. We sat down on the steps that led to the backyard. In the back corner was a southern sugar maple that nearly reached the roof. Branches hung over from the trees in the lots next door, shading the rest of the yard. There was a breeze in the air cutting the summer heat.

"I like this place for you guys," I said. I could see Rachel and Dan hosting a barbecue on the deck, Rachel planting flowers in the empty bed along the back of the house, pregnant and on all fours.

Rachel sighed. "I don't like this realtor, but she is right. $135,000 is out of our range. It's been on the market for three months already, though. If it stays on for another month or two, I bet the price will come down."

"I'd miss you," I said.

"I'd only be a mile away."

"I know, I'm kind of kidding," I said, though I wasn't, really. A mile felt far. Would she forget me if she didn't see me rolling my trash can out in the evenings? Would I lose her to motherhood? She was my ballast. She was, I suddenly felt sure, the entire reason I'd been able to stay.

"I get it," she said. "You being across the street is the only reason I've survived the last two years." It was as though she were reading my mind. She was always reading my mind.

She looked at me, her eyes suddenly bright, like she'd just gotten a brilliant idea. "Why don't you guys buy a house? There's gotta be another one right around here."

"I don't know. Who knows if we'll stay in Columbus? It feels complicated." Complicated was an understatement. Still, at her suggestion, a pleasant clarity came over me, the same sensation I felt lately every time I thought about having a baby.

"You're not allowed to leave," she said. The brightness in her face was gone, but her voice was light. She knew just as well as I did that one day we were all leaving. Eventually, the Army would move us. Guys would get out and head back to their home states. None of us wanted to live here, anyway. All of us were half-drowning in our lives most of the time. But there was something oddly comforting, even necessary, about pretending that we were stuck here together, forever.

"Same for you," I said.

—

A week later, I called Hailey. "What if I started a book club? Would you join?"

There was a cry in the background, then the stamping of feet. "Go to your room!" she yelled.

The night before, I'd been on the phone with Andrew, lamenting how much I missed my old writers' group in New York. "Well, you can't have a writers' group with these women, but what about a book club?" he'd said. This felt like the kind of thing moms who talked about their latest kitchen renovation did, which wasn't exactly the wives. But they were moms. And Hailey was a reader. I knew I could count on her. Maybe this would be my golden ticket to belonging that I'd been looking for ever since I'd arrived.

Hailey deftly switched her volume and tone. "Sorry, I'm raising animals. Obviously, I'll join. What the hell else am I doing?" She paused for a moment. I heard a door slam. "Who should we invite?"

I could feel her getting excited, the gears of her mind turning. Hailey loved a reason to put together a gathering. We decided on Rachel, Jo, and Sadie.

Sadie and Jo were close friends of Hailey's. I'd met both of them but didn't know either well. Sadie was an esthetician who cooked a delicious gumbo and was always impeccably put together. Jo never wore makeup and ascribed to a practical dress code of T-shirts and jeans.

"Let's invite Julia, too," Hailey said after a moment. Julia was the wife of Jack's new officer counterpart, and I'd met her recently at a barbecue we'd had at our place. She had rosy cheeks, a tight bun of thick hair, and a graceful poise she'd cultivated in a career in small-city ballet. At twenty-six, she'd already chosen to retire so she could marry her high school sweetheart and join him at Fort Benning. She'd been quiet at the barbecue, but I got the sense there was quite a bit she was refraining from saying.

"An officer wife?" I asked. I'd never once had a casual coffee with an officer wife. It just wasn't done. Often, I had more in common with them than with the enlisted wives. An obvious shared cultural experience was college, but it wasn't just education. We'd grown up, most of us, in leafy suburbs and midsized cities with bookstores and a decent collection of restaurants, not small towns like Hailey's. We'd been raised with access or expectations, or both.

Once, at the restaurant where I'd worked in Sausalito the year I'd returned to California at twenty-one, I'd thanked a regular for always treating me as a human being. "Of course," he'd said. "I knew from the moment you started that this was an interim gig. You're way too smart." It had struck me as a strange thing to say. What about the evening bartender who'd raised two kids and sent them to college working behind San Francisco's bars? Did the customer think less of him because he wasn't just passing through? Sometimes, I wondered if the officer wives looked at me the same way. *The wife of an enlisted man? Must be an interim gig. Way too smart.*

Despite our commonalities, I felt as distant from them as I did from that patron who paid me the backhanded compliment, or the

PTA-curated crowd at my high school. I'd grown up surrounded by privilege, and that was an enormous privilege in and of itself, but nearly every officer wife I'd met so far seemed well-bred in the way those kids from my high school had, like they'd probably grown up with dance lessons and summer camps and sweet notes in their lunch boxes. All these years later, I still felt caught in some liminal space between crowds, most at ease spending lunch hour by myself.

"I don't think Julia cares about any of that crap," Hailey said.

"You're probably right," I said. "When I met her, she complained to me that it was all politics with the officer wives. Army politics, of course. Since actual political talk would likely end in blood." I got in political arguments with the guys sometimes, after we'd all had too much to drink, because that territory felt low stakes with them. Friendship between the spouses was a more fragile but vital arrangement that could easily collapse under the weight of such fraught discussions.

Hailey laughed. "Dude, people would pay good money to watch an officer-wife gladiator match."

I laughed too, but I was suddenly feeling a little nervous about Andrew's brilliant golden-ticket idea. How would I pick a book that would please all of these women and mortally offend none of them?

—

It was September when we finally gathered at Hailey's for the first meeting. Her place was filled with the scent of butter and sugar and fresh-from-the-oven heat. We had all been assigned to bring cookies. *Bookies and cookies*, Hailey was calling it, which worried me a little, but I told myself it was just a name. I placed my store-bought box of snickerdoodles on the kitchen bar and watched Hailey whisk around the kitchen, plating still more cookies.

"You baked most of what's here, didn't you?" I said.

She stopped and shrug-smiled at me in her nonchalant way. Confections weren't just Hailey's preferred form of affection. They were also her way of showing up everyone else. I knew she was secretly pleased that no one had outdone her.

I turned toward the group in the living room. It was an unusually gray day for the weird, still-warm time in the South between summer and fall, and the house was lit by lamps. Kids were scampering across the carpet, Asher toddling after them, alternately laughing and whining. Rachel, who was nearing the end of her first trimester, had decided at the last minute to stay home. She was nauseous, she'd told me over the phone. Dan was still deployed, but due home soon. "Of course he goes and knocks me up in the two weeks he's here in seven months," she'd groaned.

Everyone else was here, though, sitting on the carpet and in chairs, with the tumult of their lives spread out across the house as though they'd all decided to move in. Diaper bags were thrown across the couch, strollers sat in a group by the door, and tablets for kids were scattered on the kitchen table. Sadie, who lived just around the corner from Hailey, had brought a full-on mechanical swing set for her three-month-old. Most of the men were either deployed or training right now, and babysitters were a rare indulgence. Kids were just part of the fabric of life, not quite belonging to any one woman, but rather, to the group.

By the time I left my editing job in New York, sitting around and dissecting a book had begun to seem like a basic life skill to me. But I had been out of that world long enough now to understand that it wasn't. I'd considered this when I chose Paula Hawkins's *The Girl on the Train*—a quick, engaging thriller, substantial enough to hold everyone's attention, but light enough to feel approachable. I hoped the other wives would like it, or would at least find it easy to talk about. I'd read it in a couple of days. Its time and perspective shifts felt like a heavy-handed way to keep the reader in the dark, but it was an addictive read. I had a feeling that the group was going to hate every single flawed character in the book. The wives were not a particularly forgiving bunch. Looking around the room, I didn't see copies of it anywhere. I glanced down at my own in my hands. Its edge was crowded with Post-it notes. I shoved it under my arm before I sat down on the carpet across from Julia and Sadie.

"I'm getting mine tailored right now," Sadie was saying. She had a Cajun accent, her words running together and curling in on themselves. She was sitting with her hands on her thighs, her legs tucked under her in a position that would have made my knees ache. Her fingernails were painted fuchsia to match her lipstick, and her posture was just slightly forward leaning, like she was ready to pounce. It was clear to me that Sadie was pretty, but there was something about her face that I couldn't quite take in. If I'd had to paint her from memory, I would've been stumped. Her nose was . . . buttonish? Her mouth was . . . nice? Her sharp little canines did give her face a point of interest, at least.

"Mine is done, fortunately," Hailey called to the group from the kitchen.

"What are you guys talking about? Are you in a wedding?" I asked.

Sadie, Hailey, Jo, and Julia all stopped and looked at me. Their collective gaze felt like the heat of a spotlight. I wished I'd kept my mouth shut.

"The Ball," Sadie said, her tone on the sharp side. The heat ratcheted up a notch, burning my cheeks.

Right. But I'd thought that wasn't until January. It was only September. When Andrew had first mentioned the Ball, I thought it was just one more mandatory event where we'd have to make an appearance, but I had learned from Hailey that it wasn't just any event. It was *the* event, a formal celebratory gathering that happened only every two years. This one was the thirtieth anniversary of the Unit, too. Couples made a night of it, hiring babysitters or flying in family to watch their kids while they spent the night at a hotel downtown. Hailey had shown me her dress one afternoon, a slinky red piece hanging in a plastic sheath in her dark closet that I knew would look dynamite on her slim frame. But Hailey did everything months ahead of time.

"Isn't that at the end of January?" I asked Sadie.

"Yes." I could have sworn she had to keep herself from rolling her eyes. Before today, I had suspected that, under different circumstances, Sadie and I would do little more than exchange an obligatory handshake. I felt sure of it now. And despite the fact that we didn't discuss politics, I knew her leanings from Facebook. There were a lot of memes about freedom and the second amendment.

"Don't listen to her, Simone," Jo said from the couch. "I haven't found anything yet." She was, as always, in an oversized T-shirt, her long brown hair up in a ponytail. I gave her an appreciative smile. She was a seasoned spouse, but she didn't wear her husband's deployments like badges as some women did. Instead, she carried the experiences in the way she moved and talked, straight-backed and straightforward, without pretense. I'd talked with her at a couple of gatherings, and she had a gift for gab, so I'd learned a bit about her. She was thirty, had grown up in Michigan, and never wanted to have to dig her car out of the snow again in her life. She was an atheist who attended the chaplain's religious talks at marriage retreats to show her support, a college graduate who would happily take a part-time job as a grocery cashier, a woman charmingly devoid of hang-ups. Her closest friends were both die-hard conservatives and down-to-the-marrow liberals, and she genuinely did not seem to care which camp you fell into. I liked her. She also intimidated me. It had something to do with her ease—in her body, in the physical world, in our tight-knit little universe.

Hailey put down some chips and dips on the coffee table, and then sat at the edge of her rocking chair, crossing her legs, setting her book on her lap. It was strange, almost wrong, to see her actually sitting down at one of her gatherings. She rubbed the back of her neck. I gave her ten minutes tops.

"Maybe we should actually talk about the book," she said, picking up her copy. I took my own out from under my arm, and Jo summoned hers from somewhere in the couch cushions.

"We were supposed to bring it?" Sadie said. "Sorry, I didn't finish. The main woman drove me nuts," she said.

"The drunk?" Jo asked.

"Yes, I couldn't stand her," Sadie said. "Actually, I need a beer for this. Anyone want one?"

Jo and I raised our hands.

"It was engrossing enough, I guess," said Hailey as Sadie got up from the carpet. "What do I know, but I feel like the writing was kind of choppy, right? All the going back and forth in time."

Jo nodded. "Yes. And the main character, the drunk—what was her name? Rachel? A lot of what she did just didn't add up. Okay, I get it, she's a drunk. She's troubled. But still . . ." Jo trailed off, shaking her head.

"Like, you didn't understand her motivations?" I asked Jo. I had felt this way too, at least in parts.

"Right," Jo said, with more vigor. "Like, who gets on the same damn train every day and just goes nowhere? I don't care how drunk you are. It's not realistic." Sadie nodded quietly, inspecting her nails. I had a feeling she hadn't made it very far into the book. She got a pass, though. She had a new baby and a three-year-old boy who was an agent of chaos.

"It was weird," Julia agreed. She was by far the newest wife of the bunch, and this was the first I'd heard her speak since I'd arrived. She had a soft but elegant voice, as assured as her dancer's posture. I was glad we'd invited her. Her presence was calming, like a slow-moving river, and I had the sense that she would say more down the line. Maybe I should have chosen something more substantial. I should've learned by now not to underestimate these women.

"Where's Colton today?" Julia asked Sadie. "That's your boy's name, right?"

"Oh, he's with Tommy," she said. "They're having a boys' day."

"Tommy's so good. Jack can't really handle Asher at all, or maybe I just don't trust him," Hailey said, getting up to merely hover, it seemed, at the edge of the kitchen. Asher ran to her, whining. She sighed but picked him up and gave him a kiss on the cheek.

These men managed to stay cool under enemy fire. You'd think they could handle a single three-year-old. But I'd seen them in their own homes. Most of them didn't even know where the diapers were. The men loved their kids. Sadie's husband was especially tender with his son, always comforting him when he cried, pushing him on his trike, coming in from the backyard to see him because he missed him. But the men were used to the women doing it all, and the women were used to it too. At one weekend barbecue at Hailey's, I'd watched as Jack vacuumed up some crumbs. "That was easy as hell," he said, baiting her. "I could totally be a housewife." Half-serious public fighting was one of their favorite forms of intimacy, but Hailey had looked like she might actually flay him alive. Jack's words had too much real bite.

"I got lucky with Tommy," Sadie said. "I was nineteen when we got pregnant with Colton, and Tommy wasn't much older."

"Wow," I said dumbly, wondering how I'd manage to steer the conversation back to the book from here.

"But I knew right when I met him he'd be a good father."

Jo put down the chocolate chip cookie she was eating. "Wait, how old are you, Sadie?"

"Twenty-three."

"No wonder you bounced back so quickly," Jo said. There was resentment in her voice, but also relief. *Ah, so you're just young, not perfect.*

"Tommy's from your hometown?" Jo asked. This was a common conversation piece: How You Met Your Husband. One of the first story lines you usually learned about another wife.

"Well, from a nearby one. He was home on leave when I met him."

"So, he's been in a while," she said.

"Since the end of high school."

"Will he reenlist? Have you guys talked about it?" We were all watching their conversation intently now. It was rare for a wife to ask another wife this many questions in a row, but I was starting to see that Jo was like me, at least in this way. She was not just curious. She was investigative.

"I'm sure he'll re-up," Sadie said. "I have no voice."

Hailey and Jo nodded, as though that settled the conversation, and then the women moved on to other topics—the upcoming deployment, where to get manicures for the Ball, the state of the war, that strange but easy mix of the serious and frivolous that made up the meat of our conversations. The book club conversation was over, it seemed. Its brevity was disappointing, but I was stuck on what Sadie had just said, the way the room had so readily accepted it, how small her voice had been.

In the past, I probably would have spoken up. "You *should* have a voice," I would have said, softly or stridently, depending on my mood. But now, I sat silent. Something had passed between Sadie and Hailey and Jo just now, an unspoken intimacy, a shared experience, a place where, oddly, they all seemed to have a voice, for a moment. I hadn't nodded with them because I'd felt sure that I was the exception. I had a voice in my marriage. We ran everything by each other. We made decisions together. Didn't we?

By the end of the meeting, the sun was starting to break through the clouds, filling the living room with a gentle light. Hailey let in their new black Lab from the backyard, and she leaped around the room, jumping on the kids. Everyone was gathered around Julia, dispensing advice to her. Even Hailey was sitting on the couch, eating a brownie. Hailey loved a good advice session.

"Just go ahead and eat dinner without him," I said to Julia, surprised by the tone of authority in my voice. "Don't expect him to show up." Everyone in the room nodded in agreement.

CHAPTER 16

—

THE MAKING OF THE GROG

January 2015

The evening of the Ball, I found Rachel at her en suite bathroom mirror, leaning over a spread of glittery eye shadows and discarded tissues, her bump pushing against the counter's edge as she applied mascara. We were supposed to be leaving in twenty minutes and she was still in sweatpants. Andrew and I had arrived fully dressed, him in his formal uniform and me in a long blue gown with a sequined bust. Dan was ready to go, pacing around the dining room with a beer in his hand. After he'd gotten back from deployment, the beautiful brick house had gone into foreclosure, and the price had dropped into their range. They'd been living here now for a month.

"Are you sure we have time for my makeup?" I asked her reflection. "I can just slap on some mascara and blush."

Rachel put the mascara wand back in its sheath and blinked. "I didn't work at the Clinique counter for nothing. Sit down." She turned toward me and pointed at the closed toilet seat.

I did as I was told and she took a seat on a wooden stool across from me, studying my face. It was a strange, almost nerve-racking sensation, to have her inspect me so closely. We spent so much time together, but how often did we really look at each other?

"I don't have anything as olive as your tone, but I'll figure it out," she said, going to work, turning around and grabbing different pots and tubes and brushes from the counter. I had no idea what she was doing; it was all Greek to me. But I loved the feeling of the soft bristles against my cheek, and now that she had a task, her fine-tuned attention was soothing.

"So, the new neighbors, huh?" she said.

I sighed. "Yep." That's all it took to make her laugh. After she and Dan had moved, their house had sat empty for a month before a new family moved in. *I miss you guys*, I'd texted Rachel, along with a photo of their pickup truck parked on the front lawn.

Oh they're legit Georgia, she'd written back. Parking on your lawn ten feet away from a perfectly good driveway was a neighborhood tradition that Andrew, Dan, Rachel, and I had never been able to make sense of. The family across the street appeared to be multigenerational: a man and woman, their daughter, I guessed, and their daughter's baby. The daughter looked like a teenager, and the man and woman, though weathered, were still fairly young. I guessed they'd probably had the girl when they were teenagers themselves.

About a quarter of the houses on our block were occupied by Black families; the majority of the rest, white. These new neighbors were white. I'd seen the girl sitting on the porch smoking a cigarette with the baby in her lap, looking bored as hell, her straight dark hair hanging in her face. Yesterday, when I'd pulled into my driveway, she'd been sitting there while her father was out working on his car. As I got out of mine, he waved to me. And then, to my surprise, he started to cross the street, stopping midway.

"We're having a barbecue tonight," he said with a hint of a Georgia accent. "Probably around 5 p.m." He ran his hand through his hair, which was the color of parched dirt. His skin was red and blistered-looking, like someone had left him cooking for too long.

Was he inviting me? I shielded my eyes from the glaring light and tried to think of excuses to get out of this. I wasn't sure what it was exactly, but this guy didn't give me the best feeling, and I still didn't even know his name. He finished crossing the street so that we stood, more or less, face to face.

"We'll try to keep it down," he finally said, and I felt myself relax.

"I'm Simone, by the way," I said, putting out my hand. I could afford to be neighborly now that I was off the hook.

"I'm Joe," my new neighbor said. He hesitated for a moment, like he wasn't sure about this custom, then reached back and shook my hand. His palm was rough but sweaty, and his arms were meaty, covered in tattoos, most of them words written in cursive script. As I pumped his hand up and down, I read one of them on the inside of his forearm. I looked back at his face and he smiled, showing his teeth. My whole body went cold. I dropped his hand and backed away, getting a better look at the tattoo.

That couldn't be what it said.

But it was.

Pure race.

I focused, now, on Rachel's freckles as she dabbed at my chin with a makeup sponge. "They are a subpar replacement," I said, because that's all we really had time for.

"We need to do your eyes still, but look at that skin color I created with three different foundations," she said, standing up and handing me a mirror from the counter. "I am a genius, I tell you. A genius."

I held up the mirror to my face. I could hardly believe it. I went to touch my cheek to confirm that this was, in fact, my face, but she gently swatted my hand away.

"Don't fuck it up," she said.

"You *are* a genius," I said.

"I told you," she said.

I put the mirror down on my lap. "Now go get your ass dressed."

—

A single red rose sat at the center of our table, stark against the bleached white tablecloth. Andrew and I, Jack and Hailey, and Emmett and his wife, Kayla, were seated together near the front of the space, beautifully dressed couples and caterers weaving their way around us. The Unit Ball was at a restored grain mill with exposed brick walls and tall beamed ceilings. I could have imagined we were at a wedding if it weren't for the stage in front of us, where a general flanked by American and Unit flags was finishing a short speech.

"You look like Snow White," I said to Hailey, leaning over Jack next to me so that she could hear. The general was leaving the stage and the room had erupted into applause, some of the more inebriated attendees getting up and hollering. Hailey had swept her dark waves into an updo and chosen a black stone pendant for her neck that accentuated the milkiness of her skin. Emmett was seated across from me, taking over a solid quarter of the table with his enormous size. Next to him was his wife, who was so quiet and young, I still hadn't figured out how to carry on a decent conversation with her.

"More like the wicked queen," Hailey said, and Jack nodded, smiling wryly. I looked out at the room, trying and failing to spot Rachel, who was on the other side with Dan's company. All of the women here had clearly prepared for this night as though it were their wedding, or at least their senior prom, with professionally done hair and makeup and beaded gowns that went to the floor. I had thankfully found my blue gown a few days before, at Macy's. I pointed out to Hailey the five other women I'd spotted wearing the exact same one.

"You look better in it," she said loyally.

Andrew put his hand on my leg and I turned to him. There really was something about a man in uniform, or at least this uniform, and this man. I rarely even saw Andrew in his fatigues—like all the guys, he left and came home in his workout clothes. "Your husband a physical trainer or something?" neighbors would ask us. It was still a novelty to see Andrew in uniform, especially his dress one, with its navy fabric and yellow piping. Ever since I'd brought him in for a kiss at boot camp graduation, I'd loved not just the look but the rough wooly feel of it. "That's a 1.4-second kiss, soldiers. Nothing pornographic," Drill Sergeant Brown had told the graduates, and he hadn't been joking. I should have known then just how completely the Army would own Andrew.

That had been three years ago. Andrew filled out the dress blues now in a way he hadn't then. He looked older, too, not just around his eyes, but in his body, in the way he moved, waking some mornings with legs so stiff he walked like the Tin Man. This job kept you young but made you old, Andrew had recently said to me, and, in this room of every imaginable rank, there was evidence of that phenomenon. Each sergeant and captain and major here was far fitter than your average civilian, but you could see, as they patted each other on the back or reached to pour a bottle of wine at their table, that they carried pain in their bodies. The oldest men in the room, like the general who'd just talked and the battalion commander who'd introduced him, were trim and strong, giving them the appearance, from a distance, of younger men. But up close, their faces were weathered and strangely bloodless-looking.

The room began to quiet, and I turned toward the stage to see a line of soldiers filing silently onto it. Each one of them was holding a bottle or container of some sort. The first in line, who was holding a microphone, stopped at a deep, wide silver bowl sitting at the center of a long folding table.

"Is this the part where we find out you're actually in a cult?" I whispered to Andrew.

"It's the making of the grog," he said.

"The what?"

He put his finger to his lips.

The first soldier poured in a bottle of dark liquor. "Cognac for the men who stormed the beach at Normandy," his voice boomed across the ballroom, eerily toneless, and behind him on a screen a black-and-white image appeared of soldiers traipsing through waves toward a shore hazy with rain.

The next soldier poured a tall, green bottle. "Soju for the men who died in Korea," he said before taking a long gulp. The crowd cheered.

Another stepped up to the podium. "For the sweat our soldiers poured in Vietnam, a Budweiser," he said, tipping the bottle over as the screen transitioned to a photo of two Vietnam-era soldiers carrying a wounded comrade through the tall grass.

"Rum for the men who were killed in Panama," the next one said, pouring out most of it before flinging his head back and chugging the rest. This time, nearly everyone in the room got out of their seats and cheered.

The following soldier was carrying what looked like an urn. "Sand from the desert of Iraq," he said, and lifted it up for the audience before pouring it into the bowl. Behind him, a shot of fresh-faced soldiers packed inside a C-17 filled the screen. The nervous excitement on their faces spilled into the room.

I leaned into Andrew again. "Sand?"

His mouth twitched. He was trying not to laugh.

This ceremony was utterly bizarre. But it had a music that was hard to resist. Andrew had told me once that he'd joined the Unit because he wanted to be part of history. He'd only ever said that to me, no one else, and so I understood it was a facet of this experience that was sacred to him. I didn't really get it. In moments, I judged it. Why did men always need to leave their mark? But as the battalion commander took a tremendous gulp from the silver bowl, and liquid dripped down the sides of his face and onto his dress uniform, over the badges and cords that he had spent hours pinning and stitching with painstaking care, and the men and women started chanting and stomping with a thunderous kind of joy, and the grog began to move from one table to the next, and the images behind the stage kept coming, what Andrew had tried to tell me finally clicked. Andrew wasn't just a member of the Army or the Unit. He was part of a greater lineage, and that lineage, I could see, as he watched the images on the screen with an appreciative but sad smile, was deeply meaningful to him.

By the time the grog reached our table, I was feeling pretty good. The bowl was just a quarter full.

"You first," Jack said to Hailey.

"Hell no," she said.

Jack turned to me, his eyes twinkling with mischief. "Come on, Simone," he said. "If there's any wife who's gonna go for it, it's you." I peered into the bowl. It was brown and cloudy, with a dark smudge in the center where the sand had settled. I looked at Jack, and then at Hailey next to him. She was picking at her cuticles. I was starting to get a bit of a reputation. It wasn't a bad one, exactly. But it was different. I liked to drink with the guys and listen to them talk shop. Most of the wives were deeply uninterested in these conversations, but I always wanted to know what nit-picky policy the first sergeant had started enforcing, which private had gotten fired, who had been an absolute stud on the most recent deployment. Most of the other wives didn't drink much. They rarely had the luxury. They had kids to put to bed at 8 p.m. while their husbands were doing the drinking.

I looked at Jack again and grabbed the bowl from him, bringing my lips to the cold metal rim and taking a gulp. It was gritty and acidic. My chest burned.

"Gross," Hailey said, visibly disgusted, and I coughed.

Jack put his arm around me. "You're an amazing wife," he said, and the fire in my chest spread through my arms and legs. I felt like I had won a prize. *An amazing wife.*

These days, *Wife* was my entire identity. At times, the title sounded like a nag to me. "It's your wife on the phone, Sergeant," Andrew's private would call to him when I called him at work, and I'd feel myself cringe. I chafed so fiercely against the title's constraints that I'd even written an essay at one point about my frustration called "The Writer and the Army Wife." No one here knew me as a writer. Everyone knew me as a wife.

"Wife" could be worn as a badge of honor or thrown around as casually and affectionately as a phrase like "you guys." *It'll just be the wives.* "Just" could be used differently, though, said with a twist of a knife. "She's just a wife," I'd heard guys say, which meant: She didn't wear a combat infantry badge or a Ranger tab. She hadn't done anything deserving recognition. This felt different from any of those, though. This was confirmation, acceptance. I had drunk the Kool-Aid, and now I was in, stamped, sealed, and approved by a soldier. It was a reward I hadn't even known I'd sought. I wondered, though, if it came at the expense of my friendship with Hailey, in some quiet way. She still wasn't looking me in the eye.

"Want to dance?" Andrew whispered in my ear, and I followed him to the empty floor. The DJ was playing John Legend's "All of Me," a song with lyrics so sappy Andrew immediately changed the station when it came on the radio.

Maybe it was the cocktails I'd had, or how handsome he looked. Maybe it was seeing the men together, free of rank now that the formal portion of the evening was over. Team leaders had their arms around first sergeants and, a few tables down from ours, Emmett was even getting the speech-giving general to take a double shot of Jack Daniel's with him. Whatever it was, it felt to me as though the whole room was glowing with love—the love the guys had for each other, but also for something bigger, for the Unit itself, for history and the privilege of being part of it. The glow of belonging.

"That boy can dance like the devil," Reina used to say of Andrew. I had never felt comfortable being in a spotlight of any kind, except for when I danced with him. He was lit up and alive then, all id, no self-consciousness, and so I was too. In Harlem, we'd gone dancing at the historic Cotton Club on the weekends, gliding across the floor while the swing band played under black and gold streamers that made the whole thing feel like a show in a retirement home. The two of us had our own show, and I felt amazed that I got to be part of it. "You dance great together," the host said to us one night in his cheesy game-show-announcer voice, and I beamed. One evening, Andrew spun me around my second-floor Brooklyn apartment, and a couple stopped beneath a streetlamp to watch through our windows. Andrew didn't see. He would have stopped immediately had he known. But I knew, and I loved it. I didn't know if anyone was watching us now, and I didn't care. It just felt so good to dance with him again. He'd channeled all the electricity in his veins into his work, and there hadn't been much left over for anything else. Dancing was just one of the parts of him that he had set aside. So often these days it felt like I was leaving behind the past in order to make peace with my present. But dancing with Andrew, our hands entwined, I could feel that it hadn't left me, or him.

"No one dances at these things, do they?" I yelled to Andrew.

"Jack and Hailey!" Andrew said, and I looked over to see them next to us.

"Nice moves," Jack said.

Two couples was it all it took to open the floodgates. Suddenly, from every corner of the room, soldiers and their dates were approaching the dance floor, and I felt a drunk affection for all of them as Andrew dipped me, the lights blurring in my vision. When he brought me back up, he leaned in and gave me a long kiss.

"Get a room," Hailey said, and I laughed, putting my cheek against Andrew's chest. The fabric of his uniform was stiff, but he was warm. *It's time.* The thought appeared, then went out, like an ember in the dark of my mind.

"I think I'm ready," I said to Andrew, lifting my head so that my lips were within an inch of his ear.

"For what?" he asked, but I could feel him grinning. He knew what I meant.

PART III

"Combat isn't where you might die—though that does happen—it's where you find out whether you get to keep on living. Don't underestimate the power of that revelation. Don't underestimate the things young men will wager in order to play that game one more time."

—Sebastian Junger, *War*

CHAPTER 17

—

FIGHTING SEASON

One year later
Valentine's Day 2016

I was only one day late. But I was too impatient to endure the not-knowing for even the duration of the drive home from the commissary, so, after purchasing the test with my groceries, I left the cart outside the restroom and shut myself in a stall. The heat was on so high, I was sweating by the time I peed on the stick and placed it on the lid of the waste bin.

Three minutes.

In the last few months, tracking my ovulation had become the central focus of my days. Worried that I hadn't gotten pregnant yet, I'd even gone to see a gynecologist at the hospital on base.

"Give it another three months before you start worrying," he'd said gently. But we didn't have another three months. Andrew was deploying in six weeks. We were on a timeline. I needed to get pregnant before he left so that he could return home in time for the birth and be around for the newborn stage. We had wanted to start trying earlier, but the last year had waylaid our plans. I'd spent months in physical therapy learning to live with the new inflexibility in my neck only to discover that the crash had also torn my rotator cuff. Then, after six months in physical therapy, I had surrendered to surgery in November. My shoulder sling had been off for only a few weeks.

Rachel's baby girl had arrived on April Fools' Day 2015, two weeks past her due date and three days after I had walked the stairs with her along the Chattahoochee river walk, again and again, trying to get labor going. Violet was now, it was hard to believe, ten months old, already lifting up to standing and crawling so efficiently Rachel couldn't keep track of her in the house. Andrew and I had visited them in the hospital the day after the birth. Violet had been a serene newborn, her brown eyes wide and searching. Holding her, Andrew had smiled in that goofy way he had when he'd gotten off the bus after his first deployment. "You're a natural," Rachel told him. And he was.

Andrew was taking on more responsibility at work and his hours had become longer. He missed dinner more often. Whenever Jack was gone or on leave, Andrew was in charge, which mostly meant he dealt with the team's mishaps. The night Emmett drank so much his wife had to take him to the ER to get his stomach pumped, it was Andrew she'd called crying from a parking lot. Andrew's enlistment contract of four and a half years, which had started counting down the day he'd shipped out to boot camp, was ending in a few months. In theory, Andrew was being groomed to move up and take over for Jack—but only if he re-upped. The Army wanted to know whether it was keeping you, vetting you to step up the ladder, or releasing you back to the civilian world. We'd weighed the pros and cons of another four-year commitment as we walked around the park, washed the dishes together, talked on the phone during separations. But reenlistment had seemed so far off, almost theoretical. Suddenly, now, it was upon us. We had to decide before Andrew deployed.

Time was ticking. I looked down at my phone. A minute and a half to go.

While Andrew had been in and out all year, I had moved deeper into the network of the wives. The book club had not been my golden ticket, after all—the meetings were rarely about the book. Mostly, they were about the quotidian stuff of our lives, though, occasionally, we veered into the verboten territory of politics, which had become increasingly difficult to avoid. Trump was, somehow, our Republican nominee and Sadie loved the man. She wasn't holding her nose and voting for him, didn't think he had questionable morals and great business acumen. She thought he was kind and goodhearted and posted on Facebook about him on a near-weekly basis, sometimes even including photos of him and Melania together, holding them up as an example of a romantic, loving partnership. It was strange. It was also a sticking point in her friendship with Hailey, who was a Bernie Bro to her core.

The book club had been *a* ticket for me, though—it had given me a real place in this group of women, and a new kind of visibility among the greater community. I was even the company FRG treasurer now.

"A treasurer? Like for student council?" I'd asked Audrey, the outgoing company commander's wife, when she called me to ask if I was interested. I hadn't really understood the FRG's primary purpose when I'd first arrived, with its locker-decorating parties at the end of deployments and "find your spark" workshops and mass emails to spouses that seemed intended for a different audience entirely (*Ladies: All hunters who harvest a deer on the Georgia side of the installation are required to check their harvest at Building 5883 in Harmony Church*). Then, after the mass casualty in Afghanistan in 2013, I'd watched them organize meal trains for the spouses of the wounded and the woman whose husband had been killed. They did the same for a wife who lost her pregnancy at six months while her husband was deployed, made blankets for every new baby, organized Easter egg hunts for the kids. And they had been there for me after the accident. I felt, on some level, that I owed them. Plus,

Audrey had buttered me up. "We just really need someone competent and responsible, and I thought of you," she'd said. It hadn't even felt like a request. It had been more of a gentle, well-calculated command. *I need someone to do this. And you are that someone.*

A minute left to go.

This was the one reliable feature of our lives: Someone always needed someone to do something. After rotator cuff surgery, when Andrew immediately left for training, I needed Hailey to take me to base to get a Christmas tree and tie it to the top of my new-to-me Subaru. I needed Rachel to go grocery shopping for me, bringing in the bags and filling up my fridge. And Hailey needed me to watch her kids when she had a dental appointment; Rachel needed me to accompany her to the OB when Dan was gone; Hailey's kids needed me to show up as their mom's plus-one for school shows and ceremonies. Rachel needed me to talk her down from the ledge when the Army's change of plans forced her to cancel a beach vacation to Destin, Florida, and Hailey needed me to come over after she told her kids their dad wouldn't be home in time for trick-or-treating. I moved meetings for Rachel and Hailey, put aside writing to answer their calls or knocks on the door, and, for me, they rearranged schedules, sacrificed sleep, gave up the slivers of time they had to themselves.

The restroom door squeaked on its hinges as someone entered. I heard their steps across the tile, and then the alarm on my phone went off, quiet but insistent. I picked up the test.

And there it was, just as I somehow knew it would be: a second pink line.

—

When Andrew walked in that evening, he was carrying a bouquet of roses. They were wrapped in red cellophane, like the heart-shaped

Russell Stover boxes of chocolates I'd seen a group of young soldiers picking through earlier at the commissary. Andrew had long seemed like a full-blown man to me, even when he was younger, but, standing here in the dining room, his arm outstretched holding the roses, he reminded me of those boys, earnest and hopeful and searching.

"I have a present for you too," I said, taking the roses from Andrew and dropping them on the kitchen counter before disappearing down the hall. I felt like I might burst into laughter. I'd had that sensation all afternoon, ever since I'd seen that pink line and stuffed the test into my purse, like there was a secret thrumming just beneath the surface of my skin that was trying to get out.

"A present for me? Good thing I remembered flowers," Andrew called.

I felt an unexpected rush of sadness as I took down the silly mug from the top shelf of my office closet. I couldn't believe how long it had been up here. I'd impulsively ordered it for Andrew when we had first talked about trying. The accident had put so much on hold, and in that limbo time we fought more than we'd ever had. I was usually the one starting the fights; I'd learned well from my parents. It was as if the accident had flipped a switch in me and I couldn't turn it off.

Our biggest one had been six months before, on a weekday evening in August. While Andrew was at work that day, I'd gone to see the first women graduate from Ranger School at Fort Benning. The place had been packed with soldiers taking a moment from work, reporters from local and national news outlets, and students from Columbus State. Everyone was there to see the two young women making history. They were, like many of the graduates, in their early twenties, white, their hair buzzed short. But they stood out—not because of their gender, but because they wore the biggest smiles of everyone there.

"We're gonna open it all up," I overheard a general tell a group of female soldiers at the graduation. He meant that soon, women were going to be allowed into combat arms and Special Operations. The guys in Andrew's unit had reservations about this. They worried, for one thing, about women not being physically able to do what needed to be done in an emergency. Many of the wives shared in this worry, and some felt threatened by the idea of women being around. They had enough to worry about when it came to their husbands' jobs and had no desire to add "work wife" to that list. But I wasn't sure exactly where Andrew stood on the matter. So, the evening after the graduation, I pushed him to tell me.

"It's going to change the culture drastically, and the higher-ups don't want to talk honestly about that," Andrew said, wading slowly into the conversation. The culture was intimate. The guys showered together. It was also foul. They made disgusting jokes. Privates sat and openly watched porn in the zoo.

"Can you imagine women coming into this environment?" he asked.

"Well, the environment needs to change," I said.

"It is changing," he'd replied, and he'd sounded disappointed by this fact. Every new generation said that the Army was getting "softer," and Andrew was no different.

"I'm not saying women shouldn't be allowed. It's inevitable, really, and we might as well embrace it. But leadership isn't looking at the raw facts of the situation. The transition is going to be complicated, to the say the least. I mean, you read that article," Andrew said, referring to a piece I'd shared with him detailing the results of a Rand Corp survey of Special Operations soldiers. Eighty-five percent of the respondents said they opposed opening Special Operations to women.

Do we expect men to bleed out because a female soldier could not drag him to cover? one respondent had asked. *Gender equality is not an option when the bullets are flying*, another had said. *Most males in the area of the world I work in would rather backhand a female than listen to her speak. There is a reason we send men to do these jobs.* The article had described their responses as "blunt, and, at times, profanity-laced." I had laughed with recognition at that. I had even understood where the respondents were coming from. But it was so much harder to give Andrew that same grace.

Are you in or are you out?

"They're asking us to go out there and do uncivilized things, and then telling us to watch our language," Andrew said. "They're so fucking out of touch."

"It seems like a small price to pay for equality," I'd said.

"Well, the higher-ups agree with you," he said.

"And you don't?" I asked, even though I knew he wasn't going to give me a straight answer. "It's bigoted to keep women out. Your whole argument is bigoted." I wasn't even sure what I meant by that, but the word *bigoted* sure felt great to say.

The blood rushed to his face, and I knew I had pushed a button. It was, I suddenly realized, exactly what I'd been trying to do.

"Don't call me a bigot," he'd said, standing up from the couch. He walked swiftly to the bookcase by the front door and picked up his keys from the dish sitting on it.

"Where are you going?" I asked, the anger suddenly gone from my voice.

"I don't know, away from you," he said, and slammed the door behind him. Moments later, his tires screeched across the asphalt. Neither one of us had ever left in the midst of an argument like that. I had pushed him past his edge, the way I had done in our early days. It wasn't an easy thing to do.

When he got home two hours later, I was sitting on our bed.

"I went to a bar. It was depressing as hell," he said, putting his back to our bedroom door and sinking to the floor. We both sat silent for a few minutes until he said, "We need to go back to couples therapy."

I'd agreed, but six months later, we still hadn't gone. Andrew was away so much, it was hard to find the time. But we hadn't had an argument like that since, and our kinks had smoothed themselves out, mostly. Deployment was coming down the pike in six weeks, though, and we'd started bickering. Every day that we got closer to the departure window, each moment we had left mattered that much more. I could feel the sand rushing through the hourglass with alarming speed.

I would finally find us a therapist, I decided as I shut the closet door and looked down at the mug. It was a ridiculous gift that I was sure Andrew would love. He was always bringing ugly mugs back from every airport he traveled through.

"#1 DAD," Andrew read, when I thrust it toward him in the dining room. "#1 DAD?" he repeated, the phrase a question this time. He looked at me, then looked at the mug, then looked back at me again. "Does this mean what I think it means?" he asked, the smile on his face filling his voice.

I nodded, and the laughter I'd been holding in all day erupted.

"Oh my god, you're pregnant," he said. He kissed me. The secret coming to the surface made me feel like all my nerve endings were exposed, and the sensation was overwhelming. I felt like I might explode into a thousand little bits.

Andrew peered into the mug. "There's a dead earwig in here," he said.

"It was in the closet for a solid year," I acknowledged.

This past year, the accident had been our defining landmark in time. Now, a new, more joyous one would take its place. A baby. I was excited. More excited than I had ever been for anything, maybe. Underneath that excitement, though, I could feel that sand moving faster than ever before.

—

Bring a package of diapers and enter to win a dinner for two at a fabulous restaurant which hasn't been determined yet! today's evite to the Indianhead Village Community Center read. I dropped the Huggies I'd brought into the pile by the door and joined Hailey at a table near the back of the room. Officially, the FRG was holding the lunch to celebrate its volunteers, but it always welcomed new babies at spouse functions with diapers and personally embroidered baby blankets.

All of the company spouses had been invited today, but there were only thirty or so people milling across the floor, grabbing red Solo cups of punch, gathering in small groups by the tall windows to talk. It was a Wednesday at noon and some women had to work, others had to stay home with sick kids, and a good chunk of wives never came to these things. It was the kind of event I would have skipped in my first couple of years here. But I was the company FRG treasurer now. I had to show.

"Sorry I'm late," I said, sitting down across from Hailey. "I could not find this damn building."

"Dude, I was going in circles for twenty minutes," Hailey said. "I cannot function when the Maps stop working." Her freshly done hair smelled fruity and I had the distinct urge to take a shock of it in my hand and inhale. She looked beautiful. Since I'd found out about the pregnancy, everyone looked beautiful to me. It had been only a week, but already, I felt different. It was all I could think about.

"So, what happens at these FRG appreciation lunches?" I asked, looking toward the front of the room. The new company commander was up there, standing next to a soldier whose face seemed oddly frozen, like he'd recently had a Botox appointment with an overzealous dermatologist. A tall, freckled woman was Velcroed to his side. I didn't recognize her. She was probably the new FRG leader, Bianca, the one who'd put together this lunch. She'd recently replaced Audrey. The soldier she was clinging to had to be her husband, the new first sergeant.

"Well, I think we eat lunch," Hailey said.

"Shut up."

"I don't know, this is my first time volunteering to be a key caller. Maybe they call our names and give us little plaques. Wouldn't that be mortifying?"

"Jo should be here too, right? Isn't she a key caller?" I asked, looking around the room before spotting her at the end of the banquet table in conversation with a petite red-haired woman. Jo was pregnant with her second, and she was really showing now, her boxy, bright green T-shirt hugging her middle in a way that looked uncomfortable.

"How far along is she?" I asked Hailey.

"I think about six months," she said.

"She looks great," I said.

"So do you," Hailey said.

I looked back at her. "I'm barely pregnant, Hailey," I said. I had texted both her and Rachel the day after I found out, and Hailey had called me immediately from the speakerphone in her car, shouting, "Simone's having a baby!" to her disinterested three- and eight-year-old in the back.

"Well, you're already glowing," Hailey said. The joy on her face was so unrestrained it looked almost like pride.

"Who's that short woman with the red hair Jo's talking to?" I asked Hailey. "Do you know her?"

"Oh yeah, that's Mallory, Eddie's wife. You know Eddie, right?"

"Of course." Eddie was a platoon sergeant Andrew would be working closely with on this upcoming deployment. He was six foot seven, with a tremendous wingspan and a goofy, joke-cracking personality as big as his physical size. Andrew adored him, and he adored Andrew. "This guy just crushes books," Eddie said affectionately of Andrew when I first met him.

"That's Eddie's wife? She's, like, five feet tall."

"I know, it's hilarious," Hailey said.

Jo caught sight of us and headed in our direction.

"Well, you look suspiciously happy," she said to me when she reached the table.

I stood up and gave her a hug. "I have a secret," I said in her ear. *Shit.* What was I doing? I wasn't supposed to be telling everyone yet. I was only five weeks along. The pregnancy could disappear tomorrow, for all I knew.

"Hold on, I need to sit down," Jo said. She collapsed onto the chair next to mine. I could see sweat at the edge of her hairline. "So, what's your secret?" she asked, looking over at me. She seemed, at best, mildly intrigued.

I sat back down and Hailey smiled at me, as if to give me permission.

"I'm five weeks pregnant," I blurted out.

"Congratulations," Jo said. The expression on her face was tender and slightly patronizing, a "bless your heart" kind of look. Jo was one year younger than I was, but I always felt like a grade schooler around her.

"Also, good luck," she added dryly.

"Oh, come on, Jo, let her enjoy it," Hailey said. She turned toward me. "Pregnancy does suck. But it's better when they're on the outside. Babies are the very best. Of humanity. It's all downhill from there."

The room around us quieted suddenly. The commander was introducing the new first sergeant and the two new FRG leaders: the first sergeant's wife, Bianca, and Mallory, the woman Jo had been talking to a few minutes before.

"There are two FRG leaders?" I asked in a voice just above a whisper.

"They're both enlisted wives," Jo said. "I guess they figure, if it takes one officer wife to screw in a light bulb, it probably takes two of us."

"What about the new commander's wife?"

"I guess she didn't want to do it," Jo said.

"Huh," I said. That was a surprise. I'd asked Maggie once whether the commander's wife turning down the role of FRG leader would hurt the commander's career. "Not necessarily," she'd said. "But saying yes definitely doesn't hurt."

"Good for her," Hailey said. "I'm really regretting this whole decision to sign up as a key caller, right before deployment. I don't think I can handle those red message phone calls."

"Well, let's just hope there aren't any," Jo said.

"Why *did* you sign up, Hailey?" I asked.

"Why did you become the treasurer, Simone? Peer fucking pressure."

"Audrey got to you too?"

"She's very persuasive. And now she's gone, and we're still here, chugging along."

"Funny how that works," Jo said. Andrew called what officers did in the Unit a sprint. After their time here, they often went on to promotion schools or graduate programs at prestigious institutions like Stanford and Harvard. The wives got their husbands back for a while, and the chance to live in quaint college towns on the Army's dime. For our enlisted husbands, and for us, the Unit wasn't a sprint, or a 10K, or even a marathon. It was just life.

"I think there's part of me that wants to be of service," Hailey admitted. She made a face like she'd caught a whiff of something rank. "Yuck, I know. I'm such a Girl Scout."

"You are," I said, locking eyes with her before she averted her gaze. She was always doing that, scurrying away from loving recognition.

"The new first sergeant looks like a Ken doll," she said, nodding toward the soldier standing next to the commander at the front of the room. He was tall and blond and chiseled and, with that frozen face, did kind of look like he belonged in a plastic display case.

"Do you think he's got private parts under that uniform?" Jo said under her breath.

"Jo," Hailey said admonishingly, but she looked like she was trying not to laugh.

"Well, he's got his Barbie," Jo said, nodding toward the Velcro woman holding his hand. She did look like she might have been fashioned on an assembly line, too, with impressively perky breasts, a tiny waist and long, shapely legs encased in skin-tight jeans.

"Sorry, I don't want to be mean, but just wait until you meet Bianca," Jo said. "She's . . . a lot."

"Is she for real with the hand-holding?" Hailey said. Displays of affection at an event like this were frowned upon, especially if you were in charge.

"I mean, the man is in uniform," I said, the words coming out of my mouth before I even realized what I was saying. Yikes. I'd sounded like I actually cared about Army propriety.

"Most spouses aren't built for this life," the first sergeant was saying, finishing with a line we'd all heard before. "We are so grateful to have you on our team, supporting our guys. We could not do what we do without you." I was sure this man had no idea who I was, or what any of us really did for the FRG—how many Excel spreadsheets I'd made, the number of spouses Hailey had called, and called again, then texted when she couldn't reach them, to confirm their address and phone number, how many of the women in here had had to call other spouses with a red message late at night. He walked off to a quiet corner with his wife, and the room grew louder again. As people around us began rising from their seats to grab food from the buffet, I looked at Jo's belly pushing against her T-shirt and did the math. She'd be giving birth during the deployment.

I didn't know where exactly the guys would be going, but it seemed probable they'd be at Bagram Air Base, the largest US facility in Afghanistan. Many of the smaller bases had either closed down or the Afghan National Army had taken over manning them, so Bagram had become the main deployment destination for the entire US military. When Andrew joined in 2012, troop numbers in Afghanistan had been near their highest. Obama promised that year that he would steadily winnow down the number and end the war in 2014. He tried to make good on that promise, declaring an end to US combat operations in Afghanistan at the end of 2014. The US and NATO even held a ceremony to mark the occasion, though it was oddly anticlimactic, with Obama teleconferencing in from Hawaii. Obama kept 10,800 troops in the country, saying that they would stay out of the fight, acting only as trainers and advisors.

But, from what I could see, there were plenty of soldiers, primarily those in Andrew's unit, who were still very much in the fight. Obama had promised a full withdrawal by 2016, but here we were, in the early spring of 2016, and our husbands were heading to Afghanistan. The American government was relying heavily on a small pool of highly professional soldiers to fight the war now, some of whom had been fighting overseas for almost half their lives. To the small percentage of the public that was still paying attention, this shift in approach made it look like the war might finally be winding down. To us, it felt like a fragile and dangerous situation to which there was no end in sight.

To most guys in the Unit, it felt like exactly what they'd signed up for. By this point, some of them had become functional addicts of war, and, after fourteen deployments, still hadn't gotten their fill. They were gunslingers, as Andrew said, and went on missions like they were heading out for a night of blackjack. A little bit of war only made them want more war, and when they came home, after the initial pleasures of sex and beer and burgers on the grill, they got antsy and ill at ease, because nothing could quite compete with combat. Even the bond they had with their guys at home wasn't as good, as ironclad and unquestioning, as it was overseas. War was terrible, but it was also beautiful, with its sunsets and peals of laughter and near-misses. And it was exhausting and dirty and horrific, but it was also comfortable because the stakes were so clear and the tasks were so limited in scope. As the FRG memo from Andrew's first deployment had said: When they came home, their vision was narrow because all they did overseas was train, plan, and execute the mission, rest, then do it all over again. Suddenly, they had to widen their lens, take in and deal with electricity bills and credit card statements and broken water heaters and kids' stomach viruses. They had to contend with their spouses' frustration, the stress of the training cycle, the pressure to constantly earn their keep. War was so much more straightforward.

Some of the older ones were getting tired of the routine, in the way that people get tired of any job. It was a young man's game, after all. And others, after years of maintaining such a breakneck pace, were struggling, or so I'd heard. There were stories of NCOs getting drunk and waving loaded guns at friends' faces or putting them to their wives' heads, and Andrew heard about "domestic disputes" from time to time. But all of this was so well hidden that many of these anecdotes had the outsized, unconfirmed quality of combat stories—details shifted with each retelling, and who really knew the entire truth of what had happened in the first place, amid the fog of war? A year after we arrived, a soldier in Andrew's unit had killed himself in the barracks, but he had been a private, had never even deployed. No one knew his story, it seemed, and so, he got no story at all. I couldn't even recall his name.

"Will Blake be coming back for the birth?" I asked Jo.

"Yeah, much to his chagrin," she said. "I'm having a C-section because Bryce broke my tailbone with his ten-pound body last time."

"Holy shit," Hailey said.

"Blake will come back for two weeks, and then leave again," Jo said, sounding resigned. I knew what she was thinking: *I'm lucky, even if I don't feel like it.* Most deployed spouses watched their children come into this world over Skype, if they were able to watch at all. We were fortunate that the Unit did everything in its power to bring the fathers home.

"What do you mean, 'much to his chagrin'?" I asked. I knew the guys in Andrew's company were ravenous to deploy the same way I was ravenous for time with my husband. Fighting season was just about to begin in Afghanistan, which usually ran from April, when opium was planted, to October, when it was harvested. At that point, many insurgents turned their attention to the opium trade, and then the harsh winter socked everyone in, making routes to and from Pakistan, a primary provider of weapons and recruits, impossible to traverse. The snow was melting now, though, and Andrew's company was going at just the right time for a "kinetic" deployment—a "good time," as the guys called it.

Jo sighed heavily. "Let's just say baby number two was a bit of a surprise, and he did not have the best reaction."

Hailey raised her eyebrows.

"I think his exact words were, 'This isn't a good time for a second kid.' The deployment cycle slowed down right when he became a platoon sergeant, so he hasn't deployed with his guys yet. He's excited for this one, doesn't want anything to fuck it up."

"I'm seriously ready to push Jack out the door," Hailey said. "We've been at each other's throats. That's when I know it's time for him to leave."

Jo nodded. "I'm ready to rip off the damn Band-Aid now. But I was pissed. I told him, 'You can just stay in Afghanistan for the birth,' and I meant it."

"*This isn't a good time?* Did Blake really say that?" I asked.

"I mean, he's obviously on board now. But yeah. He said that." Jo shrugged. "This is who I married." She lifted herself out of her chair with a soft grunt and looked toward the buffet, then back at us. "I'm gonna go get some lunch. Who catered it?"

"Moe's," Hailey said in an apologetic tone.

Jo made a face. "I've eaten way too much queso since I got pregnant."

I watched as she made her way over to the food, straight-backed and efficient, despite her front-heavy load. *That* was who Blake had married—a woman who mastered independence and acquiescence in the very same instant. Had Jo come "built for this life"? Or had this life made her like this, heated and baked her in a kind of oven, molded her, made her? If Andrew re-upped, would I someday be like Jo? And would Andrew someday be like Blake? Andrew was overjoyed that I was pregnant. But he did not have to return mid-deployment for the birth. And while I was already obsessing over how much Andrew would miss in these next months, the thought hadn't even seemed to occur to him.

I turned to Hailey. "So, you're really feeling ready for Jack to leave?"

Hailey nodded. "Jo is right. Just rip off the damn Band-Aid already."

That hourglass lodged in my heart *was* getting uncomfortable. It would be a sad kind of relief when all the sand reached the bottom. At least when they were gone, you weren't waiting for departure timelines to change and plans to be canceled. Living in limbo like this gave all of us a little edge of madness. And yet, I wanted so badly to hold on to this sliver of time with Andrew. I wanted to turn the hourglass on its side.

"I hate this war, though," Hailey said, her voice wavering just slightly. Hailey could do that sometimes, shift like a breeze. It was so abrupt, it always caught me off guard. "I mean, I don't know where we'd be without the Army. Chloe was two when Jack joined. I was making nothing at that Chinese restaurant. I'd gone to the recruiting office with him and everything, but when he called me to say he was definitely gonna do it, I cried in my car."

"You were scared," I said.

"No. Well, I was. But I was more worried. Like, about who he would become. What he would do. It's just horrible, isn't it?"

"What is?"

"I believe that quote about rough men standing ready," she said. "You know the one."

I nodded. Certain wives in the Unit shared memes with that quote on Facebook sometimes, occasionally using it to jab passive-aggressively at friends who liked to equate their husbands' work trips with deployments. *People sleep peacefully in their beds at night only because rough men stand ready to do violence on their behalf.*

"But do people ever think about what it's like to be married to those rough men? That these guys we've hitched ourselves to are killers? Maybe they do. Maybe they think we're heartless." At the front of the room, the first sergeant and commander were laughing, slapping each other on the back.

"I think about that a lot," I said. "I didn't know you did." I had talked around the ethics of war with both Hailey and Rachel before, but never this overtly, and I could feel something shift in the air between me and Hailey, a closing of distance.

"I'm proud of Jack. But also, he kills people, and my life is better for it. I don't know. Do you think we're heartless?"

She wasn't looking at me as she asked this, and I sensed she didn't even want an answer. This was a relief, because I wasn't sure I had one.

"It's just a terrible thing to reconcile," she said.

"How do you?" I asked. This would be Jack's fourth deployment. I genuinely hoped that Hailey might have an answer.

"You can't," she said, meeting my eyes. "Trust me, I've tried."

CHAPTER 18

—

REENLISTMENT

A week later, a scan at Martin Army Hospital confirmed it: I was six weeks and two days along. Andrew came over from work, taking my hand and squeezing it as we listened to the *whoosh, whoosh, whoosh* of the heartbeat together, as strong and galloping as a horse. I was stunned something so small could make such a sound.

The nausea hit a few days later, and I was lying on the couch drinking a ginger ale and feeling hot and uneasy, when Andrew walked in the door from work.

"You want some light in here?" Andrew asked, reaching toward the switch by the door.

"Please don't," I said.

He picked up my legs and laid them across his lap as he sat down at the end of the couch.

"I called a couples therapist," I said. "We have an appointment next Friday at five. Can you get off early enough?"

He nodded. "Thanks for doing that," he said. Then, he cleared his throat. I felt the ginger ale slosh around my stomach. A throat-clearing meant something was coming. Was deployment being moved up?

"Jack asked me today about reenlistment."

I groaned with a mix of frustration and relief.

"We gotta decide before I leave. I'd be signing the paperwork in Afghanistan." Guys tried to reenlist overseas so that their bonus, like all deployment pay, would be tax-free.

"Why didn't we make this decision before I got pregnant, when I could actually think clearly?" I asked. Seemingly overnight, I had become allergic to even the most minor marital spats. If either one of us began to raise our voice, I'd shut down the conversation. This was a problem, because every time we tried to talk about reenlistment, I raised my voice.

"We can't argue," I'd said the last time Andrew had tried to bring it up. "It's not good for the baby." We'd been talking through—or maybe around—it for months.

"Jack ideally wants me to take over for him," Andrew said slowly. "But I talked to him about the possibility of transferring to Fort Lewis in Washington. And he said he could make that happen."

"Really?" I sat up straighter.

"That's what he said. It would be harder for me career-wise. I'd have to earn my place all over again. I wouldn't get to take over the section I came up in. It's honestly nerve-racking to think about."

"Yeah, but, the West Coast. We'd be closer to our moms. There would be more jobs for me. Maybe I'd even meet some writer friends."

"But you'd be leaving your friends here, right after having a baby," he said. "It would be hard. The baby would be, like, three months old when we moved. I might deploy the moment we get there, just like I did when we got here."

I inhaled sharply. If Andrew reenlisted, I would have to mother through multiple deployments. How would I manage that without the women who'd taught me everything I knew about parenthood? The thought of it made me feel like the kite my friend had said I was, but with absolutely no one holding on to my strings.

"On the other hand, who knows how long my friends will even be here?" I said. "And we don't want to raise kids in Columbus."

He shook his head. "No, we don't." His voice sounded almost sad. We wanted to raise our children in a more progressive place with better schools. I felt an ease come over me as I pictured what our life could be out in Washington: a temperate summer breeze, evergreens, greater proximity to family, more like-minded friends.

But also: raising a child, often alone. Would my life look just like Hailey's and Rachel's, but with more rain and higher housing prices?

"You could get out and I could land a good job somewhere," I said, though I knew starting a brand-new position with a brand-new baby was easier said than done.

"But what job could you get that will give us the kind of security the military offers? There isn't one."

The heat rose up my neck instantly. "That isn't fair," I said.

"How it is not fair?" he said. "It's true! What editing job will give you a pension?"

"That isn't fucking fair," I repeated. Tears filled my eyes, those goddamn tears, as involuntary and sudden as perspiration on a humid day. I didn't want Andrew to think I was sad, because I wasn't. I was angry. But maybe he couldn't properly see me. It was so dark in here. His face was in profile, toward the door, and I could make out little more than its contours.

"You don't need to yell," he said.

Was I yelling? Well, at least I'd gotten my point across about the anger.

"You don't need to back me into a corner," I said. "And really? Security? That's why you chose to sign up to be in a dangerous Special Operations unit?"

"Hasn't our move in some ways been a good thing? You've been able to write, go to a residency."

"Yes," I admitted. "That's been a gift. But it's also been hard. And I'm pregnant now. The freedoms I do have are about to disappear."

He nodded, considering. "It's just that I'm not done with this." He said the words slowly, carefully, his eyes still trained ahead. "My contract ends when we're in Afghanistan. I thought I would have had a lot more deployment time in this contract. But that's only two deployments. Time is running out."

"That's what you said when you joined," I said. Four years later, time was still running out on the forever war.

Andrew met my eyes and the look on his face was unbelievably open and willing, like he wasn't sure if I was about to hug him or slap him, but either way, he would take it. "If you don't want this, I'll get out," he said.

I had not expected this. Where were the arguments about all the benefits a career could confer? The VA loan that would allow us to buy a house, the ability to transfer the 9/11 GI Bill to our future children? Where was the resistance for me to fight against? He was offering me freedom, and it felt like a pair of handcuffs.

"If I say no, you'll resent me forever," I said.

Andrew's body went slack and he listed toward me awkwardly, his hands clasped, as if he were about to beg, or pray.

"I'd hope I wouldn't," he said. "But I worry about that too."

His face was close enough to mine now that I could see it well. He looked a little lost, like he didn't know the right way to turn either. Maybe he felt handcuffed too. Maybe everyone felt this way in marriage sometimes.

"I don't want to be one of the wives," I said.

"But you are one."

"I am and I'm not. It's different once you have kids," I said, thinking of how Hailey was always dealing with one virus or another and every time I saw Rachel these days she seemed spaced out and on edge.

"You won't be alone," he said, taking my hand. "I am your partner, every step of the way."

He looked me square in the eyes, and I could feel the last remnants of anger leaving my body. I willed it to stay. Anger was cold, but it was clarity. Did I even want to say no? The thought of leaving the Army was strangely scary. It would be like ripping away a security blanket. Maybe the fact that I felt this way meant I *was* a wife, after all, because I'd seen it a few times now: spouses who kicked and screamed against the Army, but when the time for reenlistment came, they backed off. It looked, sometimes, like they were acquiescing to their husbands. But maybe it was more complicated than that. They had "grown up" in the Army too. To exist outside of it was to struggle to learn how to live in a different world, with a different set of rules. And who wanted to grow up all over again?

"We don't have to decide right now about which battalion," he said. "But we do need to give Jack a general yes or no."

"Okay," I said into the darkness.

"Okay?" He looked at me, took my hand. His wedding ring felt cool against my skin.

"Okay," I repeated, because I didn't know how to say yes. But I knew I couldn't say no.

—

Through the slats of the blinds, the last bits of daylight were fading from the sky. Gary, our new therapist, sat in front of the window in a leather armchair. He had a great head of silver hair and a wall of diplomas behind him. A gold wedding band glinted on his left hand. Andrew and I sat across from him in our own leather chairs, a round marble table wedged between us. It was a fancy office. I wondered how many military families he saw.

"Tell me why you're here," Gary said to neither one of us in particular. I forced myself to meet his eyes for a moment before straying to the mahogany desk to his right. On it was a photo of two smiling teenage girls.

"I'm seven weeks pregnant," I said to the girls before looking back at Gary. His face lit up.

"Congratulations," he said.

"Thanks," I said, then pointed to the photos. "Are those your daughters?" Andrew let out an almost imperceptible sigh. A breath, really, with just a little extra muscle behind it. *Simone, this is a therapy appointment, not a dinner party*, I could hear him thinking. But the therapist had put his personal life on display. Maybe he wanted to be asked.

"They are," he said, smiling warmly. "Is the pregnancy one of the reasons you're here?"

"We've been fighting a lot," Andrew said.

"We *were* fighting a lot," I said, looking over at Andrew. His face was freshly shaven and looked so smooth, I felt the urge to reach out and touch it. "It's been better. Wouldn't you say it's been better?"

"It has," Andrew admitted. "Or it was," he said. "But there's more . . . friction lately. We're fighting over little things."

"Or big things," I cut in. "Like the fact that he's about to deploy and going to miss most of my pregnancy."

"But I'll be home for the birth," Andrew said, and I felt my hands clench involuntarily with frustration. Lately, his penchant for looking on the bright side felt like willful blindness in the face of reality. My reality, in particular.

"When are you deploying?" the therapist asked Andrew.

Andrew concentrated for a moment, doing the math in his head. "Five weeks."

The therapist raised his eyebrows. I could have sworn he wanted to whistle. "That's soon," he said with admirable restraint.

I looked over at Andrew. The dimple on his right cheek was showing. He was smiling, ever so slightly. Andrew enjoyed this man. This was a relief. We could have gone to the Unit's family counselor. But, when it came to showing weakness of any kind, the guys in Andrew's unit were like sharks in the water. "They can smell blood," he'd told me. He wasn't going anywhere near that therapist's office, which was nestled inside Battalion Headquarters. I understood. I couldn't imagine getting therapy at Battalion Headquarters either. So, I had looked for a civilian therapist in town who took military insurance. Few did, probably because Tricare reimbursed practitioners so little, but I'd stumbled on Gary and booked an appointment under my name so that Andrew could accomplish his own version of leaving *no trace behind*. Andrew measured therapists exactly. He wanted someone seasoned and wise, but not soft. Smart and incisive, but not too cerebral. Gary, with his thick, silver hair and leather-filled office that made me feel like I should be sipping whiskey, was perfect.

"It's always soon," I said to Gary. "He's never around."

"I've been around a lot," Andrew said to me. He turned toward the therapist and added, "Our company got skipped over for the last deployment."

"They still sent you to every Army school known to man," I said to Andrew.

"We wanted the pregnancy to happen now," Andrew told Gary. "It lines up well with the deployment. I'll be back in plenty of time for the birth." I hated how calm and collected he sounded. Easy peasy, lemon squeezy. I didn't have a retort for that, though, because it was true. Andrew's options were either miss the first months of our child's life or miss the pregnancy. This was how we'd planned it, and it had worked out perfectly. So, why didn't it feel that way?

Every day my pregnancy progressed, I became a little bit more paralyzed with fear for Andrew's safety, and a little more terrified of doing this pregnancy alone. I was scared in a way I hadn't been before Andrew's first deployment. Maybe it was because I now knew what it was like to get a red message late at night. Maybe it was because when he left I'd be only eleven weeks along, not yet done with the first trimester. What if I lost the baby while he was gone?

"He doesn't get it," I said to Gary, who was now leaning forward slightly in his chair. "He's always telling me lots of civilian spouses travel for work—"

"They do—" Andrew interjected.

I pushed out a long, aggravated sigh. "It is not the same. Stop acting like it's the same."

"Well, this is my job," he said. "I have to go."

"You *want* to go," I said, and my voice sounded much sadder than I'd intended it to be. Of course he wanted to deploy. I understood that. He had not signed up to spend his life in training. But it still hurt, to be left. To know he wanted to leave. And it was terrifying to know that a baby was coming and there was a chance he might not come home. I hadn't said this to him. It felt too dangerous to speak those words out loud, like I might make it happen if I did. But I thought about it constantly. If Andrew were killed, I would be left not just a widow, but a single mother.

"And you'll keep going," I continued. I looked at Gary now. "He's going to reenlist while he's in Afghanistan."

"But you agreed to that," Andrew said.

I had. Fuck, why had I agreed to that?

Gary nodded.

"You really want to change the decision now, when we have a baby coming?" Andrew asked, looking at me, incredulous. "We don't have a backup plan."

I sighed. "No, I'm not saying that. It's just . . ." I trailed off, looking down at my feet. The only sound in the room was the ticking of the clock on Gary's wall.

When I finally spoke again, my voice came out small. "You won't be here when I need you most." I was thinking of the pregnancy, but I was also thinking about later on, after the baby arrived. There was something Maggie had said about how children change the experience of deployments. *You become acutely aware that each day is a day they missed and will never get back.* I wouldn't get it back either, at least not the way it could have been. Because it was different, loving a child with someone else. The love expanded, changed shape.

"Haven't I always found a way to be with you? Calling, texting, sending you photos? I've been doing this longer. It won't be like that first deployment. I will call you every chance I get."

"It's not the same," I said. "It's not just that you'll be gone. It's that you won't let me in."

"You want in?" he asked. "Well, I'm scared too. I mean, I want to deploy, but it does feel different now that you're pregnant. I want to come back in one piece to meet my kid."

I shook my head, as if trying to dislodge what he'd just said. "I don't know if I can carry your fear too," I said. It was unfair of me to open a door and then shut it in his face, but I hadn't known he was going to say that, or understood how overwhelming it would be to hear.

Andrew looked at me. It was hard to read the expression on his face. Was it confusion? Anger?

"So, you don't actually want in," he said, and, in his voice, I heard what that look had been. Hurt.

"Why don't we slow down for a minute," the therapist said softly but firmly. We both quieted and looked at him. The man already had command over us.

"We have limited time," he said, bringing his hands together beneath his chin. "We can work with that. But let's take a step back. When you go home tonight, I want you both to think about objectives, what it is you want to work on."

Objectives. If only I could tell Gary what I wished for from these coming weeks. I wanted to turn back time, to change the decision Andrew and I had made together about reenlistment. Why had I said yes? And why had I thought it was a good idea to get pregnant now? When we were trying, I'd felt like I was safeguarding something, preserving a piece of Andrew if anything happened to him. How foolish. I'd made a grievous error.

Andrew was quiet, thinking. I looked at Gary, with his calm, blue eyes and that incredible head of silver hair, and considered what to say.

Gary, could you wave a wand and change the facts of our life?

Gary, I can't end this forever war, but maybe you could, with your wisdom and gravitas and office of dark hues.

Or: *Gary, could you convince my husband to go AWOL, cross the border to Canada? Because I've done some research, and I think it's doable.*

Or maybe just: *Gary, you seem like quite a guy. Could you ensure, somehow, that my husband doesn't die?*

I settled on this: "Gary, can you fix our problems in five weeks?"

Gary's whole face lit up in surprise and he laughed, a real belly laugh, the crow's-feet deepening around his eyes. I pictured him and his wife sharing an after-dinner drink at their dining table, her making him laugh like that, their home a mix of his dark mahogany and whatever she preferred, maybe something a little lighter, like teak and pine, plush, colorful throw pillows across the couch. All of it enduring and sturdy, comfortably worn-in. I wanted to ask him how they'd gotten there, how they'd made their marriage work.

Gary picked up his agenda from the side table next to him. "Can you come back at the end of this week?"

I looked at Andrew. His face was tight. Negotiating the Tetris of his schedule stressed him out.

"Can you do evenings?" Andrew asked.

Gary nodded.

"Then, yes, let's do it," Andrew said, and he reached for my hand, squeezing it with urgency, like he had during my scan.

Gary looked at us. "I can already tell you're extraordinarily well-matched," he said. "But you're under a lot of stress. Our greatest challenge will be squeezing in enough sessions. We'll figure it out, though." He flashed us a Cheshire cat smile. "It'll even be fun."

—

The next morning after a late breakfast, Andrew and I went down to Lakebottom Park. It was Saturday and sunny. We usually stayed on the gravel loop, but we decided to cut into the grass and walk along the creek that ran down the park's middle instead. Both of us were quiet.

The evening before, Andrew had stood across from me on the front steps of the therapist's building. "Friends?" he'd asked, as he did after every argument or difficult conversation. The parking lot lamps had lit his face as he'd searched mine, and I saw in his just how much he wanted to leave it all behind.

"Friends," I'd agreed.

But we hadn't left the session behind. We carried it with us, through the night and into the morning, in the slightly timid way we spoke to each other now, in the gentleness of our touch. We were handling the relationship with a new kind of caution, as though it were something fragile.

"Can you believe what Gary said about enjoying watching us fight?" I said.

"Sicko," Andrew said, but he was smiling.

"Because we're smart!" I protested. "'Smart as hell,' actually. Isn't that what he said?"

Andrew laughed.

"You love him," I said.

"The whole park looks different from here," Andrew said, pausing as he looked out at the creek.

"I was thinking that too," I said. The fullness of the shade and the slowness of the creek made the place feel like a secret that had been kept from everyone but us. Up ahead, a white egret landed on a rock, its wings spread out in flight. In a matter of seconds, the bird went completely still.

I pointed at it. "You seeing this?" I said.

"Wow, look at him," Andrew said.

When I was alongside Andrew, the world looked so much more alive, like all of the blood had rushed to its surface. The whole purpose of sharing your life with another person might be for witnessing these moments together: The postman returning to his truck to grab a treat for a resident's dog. The long-legged old man jogging around the park listening to Mariah Carey sans headphones. The teenage couple lying together under a tree, their bodies pretzeled together so tightly it was hard to distinguish one from the other. This egret standing in the creek. That galloping, insistent heartbeat. All the small moments that are made strange or disquieting or beautiful when you see them with someone else.

A baby growing over the length of a pregnancy was like that. Maybe that's why this deployment felt so wrong. By the time Andrew left in five weeks, I wouldn't even be showing yet. But I'd be huge when he returned, nearly full term. I'd feel the baby's first kicks, hear its heartbeat on the monitor, see it move inside me on the screen.

"You seeing this?" I'd say, and he wouldn't be there to answer.

CHAPTER 19

—

DEPLOYMENT

In the following weeks, I became so crushed with exhaustion that I often fell asleep on the couch at 7 p.m. During the days, I edited manuscripts and graded papers and went to book club and the sand rushed through the hourglass, until suddenly, I was eleven weeks pregnant, and we had arrived at the day of Andrew's departure. We spent it packing him up, cleaning, eating sandwiches at the table, having sex, trying to savor the time together, to delay the inevitable, but wanting to just get on with it too, because the length of the day was a kind of quiet torture. Just putting away the dishes felt so heavy with dread that getting in the car at 5 p.m. to leave was a relief.

On the ride, Andrew held my hand, releasing it every so often to pull down the sun visor or grip the wheel. Watching the tattoo parlors and used car lots on Victory Drive pass by, I had the sensation that someone had put me on mute. I could just barely feel the sun through the window, the buzzing of my phone on my lap when Hailey texted: *Thinking of you. Lemme know if you need anything on this shitty day.*

Jack had left the day before. Rachel's husband wasn't leaving until later in the week. I was doing this drop-off on my own.

I'd never been inside the company operations facility on the day of deployment. I had assumed it wasn't an option. But after we arrived in the shadeless parking lot, Andrew guided me through the chain-link fence surrounding his unit's compound right to the door of the warehouse-like building.

"I can come in?" I asked, looking into the dark space, the smell of sweat already hitting me.

"It's fine," he said, and took my hand, leading me into the zoo. Now that he was a sergeant and team leader, Andrew was far more relaxed in his work environment. This was a brand-new COF and the team areas were now called "cages," because each one locked up like a giant cage in an animal shelter. When we walked into Andrew's, his guys paused, nodding at me in unison before returning to packing AA batteries and razors, opening and closing lockers, and strapping M4s to their carry-on packs. They were revved up and in sync, moving together in an unspoken choreography. High voltage coursed through every handshake and back slap. Outside the cage, other guys from the company whizzed by, yelling questions at each other:

"When are we transing down to the airfield?"

"Look at this new knife my wife got me."

"You got any extra 550 cord?"

Andrew kept his hand on me, gently but consistently, as though he was afraid I might disappear when he wasn't looking. He didn't need to; I was glued to his side, my whole body responding to some magnetic force at the center of the cage. For all of our conversations, I had never felt like I'd gotten a really good explanation from Andrew about why he wanted to go to war. But I thought I felt an answer to my question here, not in the room exactly, but from inside myself, the strangest, most senseless pull: *Take me with you*. Because who wanted to be a pregnant woman left behind to face a hot Georgia summer alone? Not me. I wanted more of this jittery aliveness, whatever it was. I wanted to yell and hear my voice bounce off the walls.

Once, not long after we'd moved to Georgia, I'd passingly called war "tribal," and Andrew had argued with the term. "What I'm part of, it's not just tribal," he'd said. "It's not just about hitting back when someone hits you, or about taking care of the person next to you. It's about those things, yeah, but it's a lot bigger, too. Wars are about ideas. You have to believe in your idea. You have to look at the way the Taliban has taken Islam to its extreme and warped it and know that it's wrong. Because, let's face it, the Taliban isn't really an existential threat to us. So you have to believe your idea—our idea, liberal democracy—is better than fundamentalist Islam."

"But is that even why we're there? To import our ideals?" I asked.

"Well, we were attacked and we responded. It took a long fucking time to kill bin Laden. At that point, we had a presence. We couldn't just leave. We have a responsibility to the populace. And the Taliban's ideology goes against everything in the Universal Declaration of Human Rights. Remember that presentation you gave in high school?"

I'd forgotten about the project I did for the "women's club" about the Taliban's crimes against women in Afghanistan. I certainly had not drawn the connection in the weeks after 9/11 when I'd passed building after building papered with the faces of the missing. I had been totally naïve, had known vaguely what the Taliban was but nothing about how it had provided safe haven to the perpetrators of the attack. But were the Taliban's violations of human rights what really swayed Andrew, or any of the guys in his unit, to put their lives on the line? I didn't think so. I thought whatever brought them to this echoing warehouse was something much harder to explain, something powerful enough to obscure, or maybe outweigh, any questions about a war's objective and worth, strong enough, even, to make leaving behind your pregnant wife not just possible, but inevitable. Easy, almost.

"You're the air I breathe," Andrew had said during our last counseling session. We had been to eight of them now, and, while we hadn't exactly solved the problem of Andrew's career or of my lonely pregnancy ahead, it had felt like we'd reconnected, at least.

"I'm your partner, not oxygen," I'd said. The phrase sounded romantic, sure, but it had pricked me right in my softest spot. Andrew's love for me, and mine for him, had long seemed an incontrovertible fact of life. I had agreed to the Army because I'd believed that such love could sustain an entire marriage. I'd known that even in the strongest relationships, fissures develop, and they either heal and mend or continue inevitably toward breaking. I knew that we had those. But I hadn't understood that we had a big old crack, right at the center of it all. That crack was his career, because every time Andrew left, for a training or a deployment or the mess of Ranger School, I felt, on some level, betrayed. I felt betrayed now—not just that he was leaving, but that he refused to fully take in my sorrow about it. It had taken couples therapy for me to understand that this was what I was feeling. I didn't feel like he was taking me for granted. I was pissed off that I didn't have the luxury to take *him* for granted. The wives were the ones I breathed like air. Andrew's presence in my life was far more precarious.

Andrew walked me through the parking lot to my car to say goodbye. I could barely feel the asphalt beneath my feet. When he leaned in to kiss me, the sun was so glaring, I couldn't make out his features.

"Kiss me again," I said, because I couldn't feel it, and he did. But I was numb to everything except that intense energy in the COF, which was still jangling around inside me.

I kissed him back, long and deep, until, finally, my body turned on like an engine, and suddenly, I was all want, all need, trying to take in the taste of coffee on his mouth, the warmth of his lips. But it wasn't enough. No amount of kissing would be enough. A kiss wasn't what I wanted. A goodbye wasn't what I wanted. I wanted for Andrew to stay here or take me with him. I wanted to swallow him whole.

"You have your St. Michael's medal?" I asked when he pulled away. I placed my hand on my own, running my index finger over the raised image of the archangel holding a sword and shield. For this deployment, I'd decided, we needed double the protective shields.

He pulled it out from behind his tan undershirt. "Yep, right here."

"I love you," I said.

"I love you too," he said, opening my door. "If I can, I'll find a way to get through to you when we stop over in Germany."

"Stay safe," I said. That's what we all said to our husbands, a comforting mantra that was more for us than for them.

Andrew gave me another kiss, a quick peck this time, and I got in the car, turning my key in the ignition. The motion felt slow and difficult, but the sound of it was tight and sharp, metal scraping against metal. When I looked through my back windshield, Andrew was already gone, back in the COF. How had he moved so fast? Inside that place was a crazed excitement that could light up or destroy the world, but all I could see was warm asphalt, dead air, a half-empty parking lot, and it felt wrong, like there was a hole in my vision, or maybe the world. I thought of the easy drive home, the quiet of my house, the nothing that awaited me, and I wanted to scream.

Without thinking, I yanked the key from the ignition and ran to the chain-link fence that separated the parking lot from headquarters.

A soldier came out of the building just as I approached the gate. It was one of Andrew's guys.

"Can you get my husband for me?" I called to him. He nodded easily and went back inside.

Andrew appeared a few moments later, squinting into the glare.

"What is it?" he asked from behind the fence. He looked as confused as I felt.

"I don't know," I said, lacing my fingers through the openings in the chain links. "I couldn't leave." Tears were running down my face now. Andrew opened the gate and came out.

"I just had to say 'stay safe' again," I said. "So, stay safe."

"Always," he said.

"I love you, stay safe," I repeated. I couldn't say it enough times. These words were the only thing that could begin to touch the hot panic inside me. They weren't what I wanted to say. I wanted to say, *Don't leave.* Don't leave me in any of the ways a person can leave, through deployment or death or disinterest or divorce.

"I'm sorry, I really have to go," he said, and then gave me one last kiss.

—

I was thirteen weeks along and sure that something was wrong with me or the baby. Every time I stood up, I got dizzy, and just taking a walk around the block was an athletic feat. I couldn't remember how long I'd felt this way. A day? Two days? More? It had been two weeks since Andrew had left, and time had taken on a strange quality. An hour felt like a lifetime, but a week dissolved, leaving behind not even a smudge of memory.

I was waiting in an exam room at the hospital on base to see an OB. I'd called that morning and gotten an emergency appointment with a doctor I'd never seen before. It seemed like they were running behind. I shifted on the tissue paper and took my treasurer binder out of my tote bag. Audrey had told me the treasurer work wasn't terribly time-consuming, and she'd been right—until this new FRG leader, hand-holding, overly zealous Bianca, had come along. Every day, she was texting and emailing me, asking me for updates on the account balance, requests to create fundraisers, even demands for the bank card itself, which I wasn't supposed to give anyone access to. Maybe this was her way of working out deployment anxiety. Whatever the case, I'd been spending so much time just fending her off that I had gotten behind in adding up receipts.

I was taking out March's spreadsheet when the OB came bursting into the room.

"What are you doing here?" I blurted out when I saw who it was. The receptionist had told me that my OB's schedule was full and had slotted me with a different doctor. A midwife, actually. But here was Dr. Fink.

"I saw you on the schedule," he said, a little out of breath, like he'd been running down the hall. Dr. Fink was somehow never in a hurry during appointments, but always in haste when going between them, near-running in the hallways and bursting through doors, as if he were perpetually on his way to deliver a baby, ready to take on whatever disaster or miracle was coming his way. I loved this about him. He made me feel like I was an urgent matter that needed tending to.

"What are *you* doing here?" Dr. Fink asked, sitting across from me on his doctor's stool. I liked the way he always sat rather than towering over me. I had met Dr. Fink when I was trying to get pregnant. In that first appointment, right after he'd shaken my hand, he'd paused over my chart for longer than I was used to doctors doing. When he was finished, he'd looked directly at me with boyish brown eyes and said, with utter sincerity, "I'm so sorry you have interstitial cystitis. It's such a painful condition." I was stunned. No doctor had ever apologized for my pain. From that visit on, we had an easy rapport.

"I know, I just saw you last week," I said.

He nodded patiently, as if he had all the time in the world. His mouth twitched. Was he trying not to smile?

"You're in fatigues," I said.

In our previous appointments, Dr. Fink had worn a white doctor's coat. But today he was in uniform, and, as he sat down across from me, I wanted, instinctively, to reach out and touch the starchy fabric. He had black hair and pale skin, just like Andrew. Did he have that rough-hewn Army smell too? I doubted it. There was something almost effeminate about Dr. Fink, in his nervous laugh, the delicate way he moved his hands, his quiet confidence. He was chubby and soft around the edges, and he looked impeccably clean, down to the foundations of his being, like he'd never been anywhere near a combat zone.

"I only wear the coat when I'm on call to deliver babies in L&D," Dr. Fink replied. There was just a foot between us. He was looking right at me, his head tilted to the side.

"I think I need my iron checked," I said. "I'm so exhausted. This can't be normal. And my blood pressure—"

"It's still a little high," he said. "But about the same as last time. We'll keep watching it." He was smiling fully now. "You're pregnant," he said. "Exhaustion is normal."

I nodded, as though reassured, but I was fairly certain Dr. Fink was wrong. Since Andrew had left, I hadn't had one decent night of sleep. Every night, I lay in bed, tossing and turning, sleep maddeningly just out of reach. The sleep deprivation might be a logical explanation for my crushing tiredness, my heightened blood pressure, the first-trimester nausea still going strong. But I was not currently in the business of looking for logical explanations. Insomnia made everything seem more complicated and worse than it was. Maybe I was having a stroke? Maybe I was about to miscarry? Maybe my body was racked with some other illness, a virus, and maybe that virus could hurt the baby?

"I wouldn't personally know, but being pregnant is hard," Dr. Fink said.

The crushing tiredness and nausea were the manageable parts, though. *My mind is the problem, Dr. Fink*, I wanted to say. In the past couple of weeks, it had been hijacked by worry—for Andrew, for the baby—and it would not rest for an instant. As a child, in times of stress, I'd retreated to nonsensical rituals: starting and ending every stairwell with my left foot; spitting out the last bit of water I'd drunk from a fountain; counting up to ten and back again, over and over. I told myself these practices kept me and my family safe. I hadn't engaged in them since adolescence, but in the days after Andrew left, it had begun to feel compulsory that I listen to a song on the radio to its very last beat, even if it meant spending four minutes in the parking lot of the grocery store, idling. I could not miss a phone call from Andrew and had to end every one with the words "stay safe." When I purchased something—anything, even a pack of gum at a gas station—I asked for the receipt and saved it, adding it to a growing pile on my desk. I had no accounting plans for these receipts. It just felt imperative that I keep them all.

A week after Andrew had left, I was running errands when I decided to drive an extra mile out of the way to cruise by my own house. I wasn't sure what I was doing at first, but as I reached my corner, I found myself craning my neck, scanning the street.

I was looking for notification officers.

My driveway and stoop were empty. This reassured me for a moment, but then, I caught sight of a black car parked two houses away from mine and all the oxygen went out of my lungs. No one had ever told me that a notification car was black. I conjured this from my imagination, because, of course, what other color could it be? I drove up to it and peered in. It was empty. I exhaled—just a little, not all the way, never all the way—and kept on driving.

Now, I was doing this nearly every time I was out. I didn't want to be caught unawares like that woman from the story Maggie had told me during Andrew's first deployment. Three years on, that terrible anecdote, the image of those plastic grocery bags cutting into her fingers, had stuck with me. I wanted to be prepared. At night, I stood at my living room window watching the road, my heart catching in my throat as a passing car's lights illuminated the dark slats in my half-open blinds.

But you're gonna have to serve somebody. That line had been running through my head ever since Andrew had left. My father had often quoted that Bob Dylan song when he talked about teaching. He took the lyrics to mean that we need to be useful in this world, that we need to be *needed.* I liked his interpretation, but I had always thought Dylan meant that someone owned every last one of us, from *the heavyweight champion of the world* to *a socialite with a long string of pearls.* We all served someone, or something. Andrew was serving our country, and I was serving my anxiety. Anywhere it told me to go, anything it asked me to do, I dutifully obeyed.

"Are you sure it's normal?" I asked Dr. Fink. His face was kind. I wanted so badly for someone I trusted, someone as comforting as Dr. Fink, to give me a certain answer to something right now.

He laughed. "I'm pretty sure that you're just anxious," he said. "And that's okay." He placed his hand on my shoulder. It was brief, but so unusual for a doctor that it disarmed me.

"It's not good for you or for the clinic when you come rushing in here at the last minute," he went on. I looked away, down at the linoleum floor, the heat moving from my cheeks to my chest. Was he admonishing me? Was I going to cry? What was *wrong* with me?

"But your blood pressure is still high," Dr. Fink said. "A little bit higher than last time, which is concerning."

"Concerning?"

"Well, it's not so high that I want to medicate you at this point. Just high enough that I want to keep watch. So, I'd like to see you every week. To . . ." He trailed off for a moment, searching for the right words. Whatever they were going to be, I could tell, didn't even matter. They were filler. He wanted to find a way to reassure me.

"Check your blood pressure," he finished. "How does that sound? I don't want you to do it if it feels like a burden."

How did that sound? It sounded like the clear, sweet chime of a bell.

—

Anxiety During Pregnancy, I typed into Google that night. Links to Healthline and Mayo Clinic articles filled the screen: *Tips to manage anxiety during pregnancy. 7 ways to calm anxiety. Risk factors for anxiety during pregnancy.* I clicked on that last one, glimpsed the word *preeclampsia*, and immediately returned to the search results, scrolling down to the bottom of the page to an article about something called "perinatal anxiety." The subheading: *Anxious negative thoughts about the future may include imagining the worst-case scenario, worrying, and doubting.*

Was perinatal anxiety why I couldn't sleep? Or was I this anxious because I didn't have to be all that creative to imagine the worst-case scenario? Worry was practically the vocation of the wives. "Even after ten deployments, my heart still jumps at every knock on the door," Maggie told me once. Some women relied on Xanax or Valium for deployments. No one told me this directly, but someone always had "a friend" who used them to get through. If I could now, I would in a heartbeat.

After skimming the article, I clicked on others, reading about peri-natal and postnatal anxiety until my eyes began to burn. I closed my laptop and picked up my phone from the armrest and looked at the time. It was almost 10 p.m.

My anxiety is so bad, I texted Rachel. *It's like I'm nine years old again, watching through the window for my mom.*

More than any of the other wives, Rachel knew about my lives that had come before this one. I had told her about the night I found my mom, and all the other nights I'd stayed up as a kid at our living room window, attempting with the power of thought to keep her driving straight, to get her home safe. Since Andrew's departure, I felt like that little girl all over again, trying to control fate. But this time, I was waiting for someone I hoped would never arrive. Because the only person who could show up at my door at nearly 10 p.m. and break this tension was a notification officer. I was watching a pot obsessively and pleading for it to never, ever boil. It was exhausting and impossible and made me feel insane. I had never been so tired in my life.

A minute later, Rachel texted back.

Come over now, in your pajamas.

CHAPTER 20

—

PERIOD OF DARKNESS

Rachel had been living a mile away for six months. It was a short distance, but it felt like more. I hadn't seen her quite as much as before. Perhaps this was due to my own busyness. In my mission to say yes to things, I'd had more on my plate recently. Or maybe the distance was due to her baby, who was no longer a baby, but a beautiful, fat thirteen-month-old toddler, with dimples for knuckles and chestnut ringlets like Rachel's. Since having Violet, Rachel spent afternoons at the public library's story hours and with her church group.

As I drove down her street, I began to feel nervous. Why had I texted her something so naked, so vulnerable? *I feel like I'm nine years old?* Jesus. What a ridiculous thing to text a person late at night, when her toddler was finally asleep. She was so gracious, of course she had responded. But she probably just wanted to go to bed.

When I reached her house, I paused on the sidewalk for a moment, watching her shadow through her front blinds as she moved across the living room, probably tidying up. Her porch light was on. She was painstakingly frugal, and always kept it off to save electricity. She must have left it on for me.

"I obeyed your command," I said when she opened her door, sweeping my hands over my hoodie and sweats. She was in a pair of faded polka-dot pants she'd owned since I'd met her and a ratty T-shirt and was as beautiful a sight as land coming into view after a long plane ride. I hugged her and she smelled earthy, like the essential oils she dabbed behind her ears.

Rachel took me into the little family room that sat at the center of the house between the kitchen and the hallway that led to the master bedroom. When Dan was here, she tended to keep this room relatively orderly. But he was with Andrew in Afghanistan—Dan had actually joined Andrew's company recently—and the den was a mess of toys. On the coffee table were plates from the night's dinner, a pack of wipes, and an antiquated baby monitor that had no screen, only audio. Her TV was on, a rerun of *Friends*. Even though I hadn't spent much time in the new house, the space felt familiar to me. There was her old checkered rug and the smell of her roasted chicken and sweet potatoes with rosemary hanging in the air.

I slumped onto Rachel's love seat and she sat down next to me, picking up a glass of wine from the coffee table. Wine had gotten me through trainings and deployments more often than I liked to admit. Three glasses could soothe the loneliness of evening and make me pass out, drooling onto my pillow. I wished for that kind of amnesia now. At the end of my appointment with Dr. Fink, I had even ventured to ask if I could, maybe, you know, drink a small amount of red wine with my dinner? He had given me a half-smile and said, "As your OB, I am never going to tell you it's okay to drink when you're pregnant."

"Pregnant deployments are the hardest," Rachel said.

"I bet deployment with a toddler isn't much better," I said. She looked even thinner than usual. "Please tell me you're eating."

"I am," she said. "It is hard. But she keeps me busy. Pregnancy is . . . something else."

"I had no idea," I said, watching Ross tear into the unrealistically vast Manhattan apartment on-screen. In reality, I did have *some* idea. I'd heard wives say before that being pregnant during deployments was the worst. I hadn't known exactly what they'd meant by it, had just assumed the hormones made that edge of madness a little sharper, that the physical trials of the experience exhausted you. I never asked, and they never elaborated. It was just a truth, universally acknowledged and accepted, that I'd never quite understood. Until now.

We spent the next hour watching TV, occasionally making jokes about our scuzzy houses and ancient pajamas. I didn't have the heart for small talk or deep talk. What I was going through felt like such an assault, such an upending of my entire world, that I wasn't sure I could explain it if I tried. Eating popcorn with Rachel and watching reruns of *Friends* seemed like the most appropriate antidote on offer. Andrew was the true fix, but not being alone right now would have to do.

"I cannot tell you how much I want to be sharing a glass of wine with you," I said.

"Oh gosh, I'm sorry—I wasn't thinking," Rachel said.

"Are you actually apologizing right now?" I said. "Please drink extra for me."

On-screen, Ross and Rachel were tumbling out of a Vegas wedding chapel, laughing and drunk.

"I never wanted to get married," I said.

"Really? *Never?*"

"Not really," I admitted, almost sheepish, my eyes still on the TV. "I mean, I wasn't totally against it. But I could just never . . . see it."

"Wow, I've been planning my wedding since I was, like, six."

"That's a shocker," I said dryly, and she swatted me on the shoulder. "I don't know, I think part of me wanted to. I used to talk about marrying my first boyfriend when I was seventeen. But I was a kid. It was fantasy. The real deal absolutely freaks me out."

"Freaks?" she asked.

I laughed weakly. "Freaked."

"Why?" Rachel said. I could feel her watching me intently now, so I met her gaze for just a moment before breaking away. She was always doing that, looking at me closely right when I least wanted her to.

"I used to think it was about my parents' marriage. And, it's true, they did absolutely nothing to sell me on the institution. But I'm beginning to think that I was just really scared to tie myself to someone I love. Scared that I'd end up devoting myself to waiting for them to come home every night, the way I did with my mom." *The way I'm doing now*, I thought but didn't say.

"Well, Andrew *is* in Afghanistan," she said, reading my mind, as usual.

"True," I said. "But I'm worried this feeling will never go away. Like, he'll get home and I won't be able to shut it off."

On-screen, the credits were rolling. Violet's cry broke through the monitor.

"Shit," Rachel hissed, and, with one swift, silent movement, she was gone, her faint, tender whispers coming through the speaker, Violet quieting in her arms. Rachel sang softly, wordlessly. She had such a sweet voice, and listening to it, I felt myself uncoil, just a little. I pictured her holding her child in the dark of the bedroom, and an Anne Sexton line I had always loved went through my mind . . . *when we touch/we touch entirely. No one's alone./Men kill for this, or for as much*. I wished, for a moment, that it was me singing, giving myself to someone who needed me so completely.

When Rachel got back, a new episode was beginning. She took the last sip of her wine and shut off the TV. "I should probably join Violet."

"And I should go home," I said, though I made no move to do so.

Rachel walked into the hallway that led to the guest room. "Come on," she said. I got up automatically, following her silently until she stopped at the end of the hall, just past the bathroom, and opened the door. This had been the baby's room, or Rachel had intended it to be. The last time I'd been in it, Rachel had been pregnant with Violet, and I had helped her hang Etsy-purchased animal prints. She had painted the walls a pastel green and covered the natural wooden crib with jungle-themed sheets. But Rachel had dismantled the crib once it became clear that Violet would sleep nowhere other than at her breast, and had transformed the space into a guest room, moving in a double bed and covering it with a cheap duvet from Marshall's. There were no photos on the wall, just a small lamp on the nightstand. A large antique brass mirror she'd picked up at an estate sale and hadn't gotten around to hanging sat against the wall.

Rachel walked over to the bedside table and turned on the lamp. "I had no idea you were experiencing this kind of anxiety," she said so gently I could feel her voice in my chest.

Usually, I'd dismiss such a statement. *Oh, it's not that bad.* But it was 11 p.m. and I was at her house because it was exactly that bad. "It's pretty terrible," I said. I didn't say more because I didn't know how, but also because I didn't have to. That was the bewitching power of spending time with the wives—the shorthand, the way we could say so much about our lives to one another without saying much at all. Rachel knew pregnancy, and she'd been through more deployments than I had at this point. She was well acquainted with uncertainty and terror kicking up childhood anxieties she'd thought she'd left behind. She knew, too, what it was to raise a child with her husband in a combat zone. Part of me wanted to ask her what it was like, to siphon out some of her wisdom in case we did end up in Washington and she wouldn't be a mile away when I had my own child. But she was tired, and I could offer her no comforting shorthand when it came to that particular hardship.

"Please stay the night," she said, resting her hand on my shoulder as she returned to the threshold. "And get some sleep. Violet is going to be waking us both up in the morning." She smiled faintly and padded away.

I walked into the room and closed the door. It was cooler in here than the rest of the house. A print of an elephant still hung above the nightstand, but otherwise, the space felt like a proper guest room for grown-ups, with just enough to make it comfortable, but nothing more. I pushed the dozen throw pillows off the side of the bed, pulled back the creaseless comforter, and crawled in. The pillowcase smelled of Rachel's all-natural lavender-scented detergent. Andrew's smell was nowhere. There were no half-read paperbacks or crumbs in the sheets. It was a perfectly sealed vacuum, like the exam room I'd been in that morning.

As I pulled the sheets over me, I suddenly remembered those emails that Bianca had sent the company spouses. *If you are going to travel, please make sure you let me and your key caller know where you're staying. We need to know about your plans in case we need to get in touch with you.*

Get in touch with you was a euphemistic way of saying, *knock at your door and inform you that your husband is dead.* This didn't exactly constitute travel, but I was away from home. It was too late to text my key caller or email the new FRG leader, though. And it was past notification hours, anyway. They'd start up again early—5:30 or 6 a.m., if I remembered correctly. But it was just one night. One night they couldn't track me down. One night I didn't have to wait and watch for someone I hoped would never come. I turned off the lamp and fell into a sleep so deep it was like sinking, hard and fast, underwater.

—

Two weeks later, I had spent so many nights at Rachel's that the Maps app on my phone had begun registering her address as home. My clothes were draped over the guest room dresser, a stack of my books sat on the nightstand, and the hall bathroom was filled with my toiletries. I had developed a ritual of getting naked in front of the bedroom mirror and I was doing this one evening when Andrew called. It was the end of his workday in Afghanistan and his voice was tight. I had learned what that meant: He'd just come back from a mission.

"I'm seventeen weeks today," I said, turning sideways in the mirror. The pregnancy was becoming more obvious. "The shrimp is the size of a pomegranate and the weight of a mozzarella ball." Shrimp was his name for the baby. I had started to feel movement in the last few days. Not kicks, but flutters. Tiny pulses. *I'm here. I'm here. I'm here.*

"Wow, that means I've already been gone for six weeks," he said.

I studied my profile. Never in my life had I looked at my naked body with any sort of awe or appreciation. It was mostly something I had put up with, but I was enjoying its visible changes—the tautness of my stomach where I'd always been soft, the fullness of my breasts.

"I'm starting to look pregnant," I said.

"Okay, I really wish I were there," Andrew said suggestively. Andrew had a thing for pregnant women. We were losing valuable time.

"Me too," I said. We'd been together long enough that he'd seen my body change, my weight fluctuate, the smallest of ripples appear on my thighs. Those changes had sometimes made me shy. But I was not shy about this one. I wanted him to see me, to touch me. Andrew required empirical evidence for every goddamn thing, but, for him, pregnancy and childbirth were miraculous and sublime. The baby hadn't changed him, though, not in the way it had already changed me. After four months of pregnancy, my whole world had somehow both expanded and shrunk. The things I had cared about before this baby, work and national politics and art, seemed utterly beside the point. *I* seemed beside the point. I couldn't even remember what the desire to write felt like. Only this life, growing inside of me, mattered. Only Andrew staying alive and returning home to be a father.

"You should send some new pictures," he said, and I could hear him smile. In every package, I included photos. But so far, they had been wholesome shots of me holding Violet, photocopied ultrasound images. He hung every single one with Scotch tape on the plywood wall next to his bed.

"I thought your mail was searched," I said. We were both more at ease on these monitored phone calls than we'd been on his first deployment because we better understood the rules now, but I thought it was probably best if I didn't mention the second part he'd told me: Anything X-rated was confiscated.

"It's okay if it's tasteful," he said.

"Whatever that means." I laughed, imagining the twenty-one-year-olds in the mailroom inspecting silhouetted pregnant photos of me under the fluorescent lights. "But all right, you may get some in your next care package. If you're lucky."

"I'm a lucky guy," he said, his voice suddenly expansive, like he wasn't rushing to get off the phone. He hadn't sounded like that in a while.

"I've started to feel quickening," I said.

"Quickening?"

"The baby moving, just a little."

"It's getting real," he said.

"Oh, it has been real."

"Well, I can't wait to feel the baby's kicks when I get back," he said.

I tried to think of some other bit of optimistic news to share. "I'm supposed to go to a spouse retreat tomorrow," I landed on, after a moment. "It's just a one-day thing downtown. I don't know, though. Rachel isn't coming. Violet would freak at the childcare. And Hailey's kids are sick. Or maybe that's an excuse."

"Maybe you'll meet some new wives," he said.

"Maybe. I am curious about the speaker. An Army psychologist. The FRG email said he was a cross between Robin Williams and Dr. Spock."

"Dr. Spock? Wasn't he a pediatrician?"

"Yep. Maybe he'll be talking to us about the care and feeding of our husbands."

"I can think of a few ways to care for and feed your husband," Andrew said, and I laughed. He paused, then, and the silence felt weighty.

"So," he said, his voice suddenly serious. "I'm going to sign the reenlistment papers soon. And we can still go to Washington, if you want."

I paused, watching my brow furrow in the mirror before I rearranged my face into a neutral expression. "Oh yeah?"

"Yeah, we can get it in the contract. But I just want to make sure it's what you want."

"Don't you want it?" I asked.

He exhaled heavily. "I have mixed feelings. I've gotten so tight with these guys this deployment. It's hard to imagine leaving them.

It's hard to imagine starting over. I'll be really sad to leave. What do *you* want?"

It had been so long since I'd asked myself what I wanted. And what did it even mean to want something? Was desire ever uncomplicated? I had wanted to marry Andrew, but I had not wanted to marry a soldier. I wanted this child, but I did not want to parent alone half the time. The things we wanted always came at a cost, and it was never entirely clear to me whether it was worth paying.

"I have mixed feelings too," I said.

"Well, I'm on board with whatever you want," Andrew said. "I want this to work for both of us. So, think about it." Short, clipped voices entered the background of the call.

"Everything okay?" I asked.

"Yes," he said, an edge creeping into his voice. "Everything is fine."

I looked back in the mirror at my body, put my hand to my stomach. What else could I say to keep him a moment longer? There was so little in my life that was noteworthy these days. All the action was in my dreams. *I think it's time to go our separate ways*, Andrew had said to me in last night's. When I'd woken to Violet's babbling down the hall, I had breathed a sigh of relief, remembered that Andrew hadn't left me, that he'd never leave me. And then I'd taken in the vastness of the bed, felt the flutter of the baby, and remembered that he already had.

"I gotta go," Andrew said. "I'm sorry, I'll call again soon. I love you."

"I love you. Stay safe," I said.

"Always," he said.

CHAPTER 21

—

PSYCH EVAL

When I didn't see a single recognizable face in the Marriott conference room, I considered, for a moment, turning back from the door and heading home. It was silly. I was no longer a private's wife. Half the women here were probably under the age of twenty-five. Some of them had probably only recently moved out of their parents' homes. But I never knew what to expect from a room of spouses. In civilian life, groups tended to become more homogenous after high school. You found your like-minded people in jobs, marriages, college. At Columbia, where students had come from all over the world, I'd made friends with Mormons, devout Muslims, staunch atheists. We shared in certain core life experiences, though, like college, and all lived in the same political neighborhood, generally. I had a sense of what I was getting into when I struck up a conversation with any of them. But who knew when you walked into a room like this? Some of the women had graduate degrees. Others hadn't made it through high school. A few had cheered when Obama became president, and others joked hopefully about his assassination. How many of them had voted for Trump in the primaries?

As I walked hesitantly toward the tables, I caught sight of a woman who appeared to be waving at me. I squinted. It was Mallory, Eddie's wife, the diminutive woman from the FRG volunteer lunch. I had been five weeks along then, the pregnancy a secret I was too excited to keep. A different life, almost.

"There's room here!" Mallory called when I got close. She looked tired as she got up to hug me, her under-eye concealer visibly cakey.

"I think you are going to love Doc Radley," she said, sitting back down. "He is just so funny and smart." According to the FRG email, this "doc" was a high-ranking military psychologist who had worked exclusively in Special Operations units in the Army. I wondered how Mallory knew what I would love. Then again, our reputations did often precede us. Or rather, our husbands' biographies did.

Andrew had told me a little about Eddie, which meant I knew a little about Mallory too: They had both grown up in the Cleveland area and gotten together at the end of high school. He enlisted at seventeen, deploying multiple times in the conventional Army at the height of the war. Mallory had been a stay-at-home mom ever since having her son eight years before. She also had a three-year-old girl. Eddie had scars on his back from those early years of enlistment, though he got them not in Iraq, but in a knife fight at a Cleveland bar a few days before he deployed. Andrew had told me that he and Eddie had once counted up all the time he'd spent in combat deployments to Afghanistan and Iraq. It was five years. One night, Mallory and Eddie were watching a TV documentary about Afghanistan only to realize halfway through that Eddie was *in* the documentary, helping to get a wounded soldier onto a medivac helicopter.

I looked around the conference room and saw that I wasn't the only one who'd be sitting out the whitewater-rafting "bonding activity" after the talk. There were bellies everywhere. "I guess I'm not alone here, am I?" I said, sitting down next to Mallory.

She laughed. It was a light, tinkling sound. "How far along are you now?" she asked.

"Second trimester finally," I said.

"How are you feeling?"

It was the question we all asked each other, whether we were pregnant or trying to get pregnant, or had just finished being pregnant and were waking every hour of the night with a newborn. Could I tell her just how dangerously sleep-deprived I was? That this morning, after a 1 a.m. Benadryl, I had woken up feeling like my brain had been scooped out and stuffed with cotton? Or that, returning home from Rachel's, I had tried, for a brief moment, to open my front door with my debit card?

"This whole pregnant deployment thing is hard," I decided on.

Mallory nodded absentmindedly, her leg jiggling up and down. There was something skittish about Mallory, her sentences trailing off, her gaze darting around the room. Her heavy makeup seemed designed to hide her face rather than accentuate her features, all foundation, no lipstick.

"Riley was a mess when I left her with the day-care providers," she said, her eyes on the doors that led to the lobby. She paused for what felt like a full minute before finally looking at me. "Sorry. Anyway, yeah, I think being pregnant during deployment is pretty unavoidable," she said.

Ouch. Mallory struck me as kind. I had hoped that she would look at me and confirm, "It's hell. You are going through hell." But maybe it didn't feel like hell for Mallory. For her, dropping her husband off for deployment probably felt about as dramatic as leaving her three-year-old at the day-care center in the next room. Sometimes, life with the wives, especially the most seasoned ones, could be incredibly lonely. It had been this way for so many of them for so long, there wasn't even a question about another life. To suggest that there might be was dangerous, even uncouth.

Maybe a fresh start in Washington would be for the best. I could make friends like those I'd had in New York, people who enjoyed dissecting things, pulling at the seams of their lives to see what held together and what fell apart. Even Hailey, one of the smartest people I'd ever met, wasn't interested in this kind of activity. Peel back your protective layers just for kicks? Life was hard enough.

I turned my attention to the broad-shouldered man adjusting the mic at a podium. He looked to be in his early forties, wore a suit and tie, and had a combination of a high forehead and receding hairline that gave him, under the gleaming lights, the appearance of an egg. He seemed nerdy and approachable, but there was something piercing in his gaze and authoritative in his stance that gave away his military training. I was pretty sure he was not here to talk about babies.

He introduced himself briefly, then took a step toward us, eschewing the podium. He was going for folksy, living up to his name. "After I finished my medical degree, the Army had me working in psychiatric units at hospitals. I absolutely hated it. Then, I got lucky. I got sent to your husbands' unit, to screen soldiers during their psych evals. What a revelation. Suddenly, I was working with healthy people."

"Healthy, huh?" a brazen woman called from the back.

"Healthy sociopaths?" he replied, raising his eyebrows in question, and the room erupted into laughter.

I'd heard that Andrew's unit looked for candidates with socio-pathic tendencies. This information wasn't part of any official mes-saging, but rather an unsubstantiated rumor that most of the guys accepted as fact. I hadn't believed it, but I wondered now if it was true. I didn't know a lot about the screening process, but I'd pieced together the basic gist: Candidates underwent personality assessments and spoke with psychologists like Doc Radley, who were trying to suss out if you were the right psychological fit for the job. "Low empathy," Andrew had told me, was one of the primary qualities the Unit looked for.

"I've deployed with your guys, gone to Ranger School with them," Doc Radley said, putting his hands into his pockets in a way that looked casual but was probably rehearsed. He'd been on missions? I knew chaplains sometimes tagged along, but psychologists? "Working with this community has been a humbling honor," he went on. "Over this time, I've gotten to know the Special Operations brain. I won't talk at you for too long, but I wanted to share a bit with you this morning about what I've learned because I know being married to these guys is not exactly a cakewalk."

The crowd laughed again. Mallory and I remained quiet.

"In a nutshell, these guys are way above average IQ, have a lot of emotions but don't use them to react to things very often, are able to stay calm under pressure, and are relatively low stress and anxiety. And when they do experience stress, they have fairly healthy ways of dealing with it, like the gym."

Always with the damn gym, I heard someone mutter one table over. Physical fitness was the mistress every wife was a little bit jealous of. It probably did keep most of the guys sane. Andrew absolutely needed it. But I wasn't sure about this "fairly healthy ways of dealing" business. That strange and unnerving night at Mira's right after Andrew's first deployment, she'd complained to me about how much time Tyler spent working out in the garage. Emmett could bench more than anyone else on Andrew's team, but, since his wife had called Andrew in tears the night she took him to the ER, the Unit had been on the edge of either sending him to rehab or kicking him out. Guys who hacked it, though, who made it through an entire career, had figured out a healthier way to deal with their stress, and I supposed those were the ones Doc Radley was talking about.

"They are obviously all individuals, and can differ in some real ways, but that's the basic psychological profile." Doc Radley paused and took a step back, leaning against the podium. "And it's one I've seen in action overseas. I've watched guys see their buddies get shot, get them to the medic, and then just keep on going, in a gunfight, with a kind of strength that seems superhuman. They've been trained to do that, but they're also that sort of person to begin with. Some people call it low empathy, but I think it's more about compartmentalization. They're able to take whatever emotion they're experiencing and set it aside. Not everyone can do that, no matter how much training they get."

I glanced over at Mallory. Her leg was jiggling again. Andrew had possessed that kind of strength for as long as I'd known him, and it made his very presence feel like a buffer against all that was most terrifying in the world. Pre-Army, his ability to shelve his emotions in a crisis had seemed superhuman to me. But now, when I watched half of him depart before he'd even left for deployment, or when I felt like I only had 10 percent of him on the phone, he seemed borderline *in*human. He could talk about killing, then go pick up tacos for dinner. Was that superhuman or sociopathic? Or was it just the inevitable result of the life he'd chosen? Lately, I could feel that he was learning how to better navigate this superpower of his, going back and forth between calls with me and life on deployment with more agility. I was happy that he was figuring this out, and yet, I was also lonely. I longed for the full chaotic mess of him, for his unbridled laughter after playing a practical joke on me, his surprising tenderness that always took me off guard, even his bad mood at the end of a pulverizing day.

"But, as you know, that particular skill set doesn't always translate so well to being a spouse," Doc Radley said, laughing wryly.

No one laughed with him this time. He had our attention, though. Even Mallory's leg had stopped jiggling. Across the room, I spotted one young woman actually taking notes. Our husbands were the maddening puzzles at the center of our lives, and this man understood them, to some extent, loved them in the way that only a scientist can love his subject. Many of the wives knew just the barest facts about their husbands' jobs. They loved their husbands. They knew their husbands, or the essence of their husbands, at least. They just didn't exactly understand their husbands. I thought I understood Andrew, but I was less sure of this now than ever. Maybe, with each passing year, I knew him a little more and understood him a little less. The Army was changing him, making the soft parts of him hard, the warm ones cool to the touch. Then again: *They're also that sort of person to begin with.* Was I just unwilling to fully take in who my husband really was?

"So, here's the thing," Doc Radley went on. "When they say they don't remember you asking them to pick up milk at the grocery store, that's because they didn't hear it. There's a crazy-high incidence of ADHD among these guys, and you have to pay attention to something to make it a memory." Someone in the back groaned. I looked at Mallory and she gave me a prim, closemouthed smile. A lot of these guys had struggled in school because of undiagnosed ADHD, he told us. As a result, many had high IQs but low verbal abilities.

"That's one way to put it," said one of the women in the audience. Once, Andrew and I were talking on the phone about a book we'd both recently read, and he used the word *protagonist.* He was on his way out of work with a group of the guys, and I heard one of them ask, *What the hell are you talking about?*

Talking was our main mode of connection. It always had been. This didn't seem to be the case for too many of the other couples I knew here. "Sometimes Dan will tell me about a beautiful sunrise from a helicopter," Rachel told me once. "But mostly, it's a lot of fart jokes." Fortunately, Rachel liked fart jokes, and I knew there was more than that. Every time he left, Dan hid Post-it notes with sweet nothings on them for her to find around the house. He'd written her stacks of letters during Boot Camp that, in her first year in Georgia, she had often returned to, trying to remind herself why on earth she'd upended her life for this guy who was never around. I sensed that she wished Dan liked to talk as much as she did, though, especially because, oftentimes, talking was all that was available to us.

"They are usually introverts by nature, too," Doc Radley said. "Though they're good at faking it. I call them 'socially skilled introverts.' I see it on deployments. They're all psyched to be together at first, but after two weeks, everyone's put up a blanket between their bunks as a curtain."

Andrew didn't have ADHD tendencies, but "socially skilled introvert" described him to a T. *There is no such thing as personal space in the Army*, he'd said to me once, a tinge of resentment in his voice. Andrew needed alone time, and he never got it these days. Of the two of us, I was the extrovert. Sometimes I thought if I were a little less isolated and he were a little more, the fights that had started between us here would disappear almost entirely.

"The good news is your husbands can do things to make the transition home a little smoother, to be more present spouses," Doc Radley said. Mallory's leg was moving again, but the other seasoned wives in the room looked relaxed, almost skeptical, leaning back in their chairs, arms folded over their chests. *Good talk, guy. When's lunch?* The younger ones were leaning forward, though. I was sitting up just a bit straighter.

"For starters, I bet all of your husbands need to fix their sleep. Because it's a mess, right?"

"Yes," a few women said empathetically, and I caught myself nodding. After Andrew had returned from Afghanistan, he'd toss and turn at night and then fall asleep at the table during lunch. When he was home, he had to get up at 4:45 a.m., but sometimes he wasn't drifting off until midnight. I'd heard stories from wives about first sergeant husbands who left for work at four in the morning and were still up at 1 tinkering with something.

"With all the night trainings and time zone shifts, their circadian rhythms get jacked up. So, they take Benadryl to sleep. But with Benadryl, you're never getting into deep, REM sleep," he said. I thought of the bottle that had been sitting on Andrew's nightstand for the past year. Now I had my own bottle of Benadryl on my own nightstand, and Doc Radley could pry it out of my cold, dead hands, because no one was going to give a pregnant lady sleeping pills. "I see it a lot; they start taking Benadryl to sleep overseas. Not getting any REM sleep is bad news for anyone. Bad, bad news. It affects some major stuff, like the ability to remember what your wife told you." He smiled knowingly, and this time, I laughed. "But it's especially bad news for these guys. They're more exhausted; it can exacerbate moodiness, can even make PTSD worse. They really need their REM sleep."

Across the room, the woman taking notes was scribbling furiously. What could she be writing? A proposed sleep regimen for her husband? I looked back to Doc Radley, who was going on about how we needed to keep a watch on our husbands' sleep when they got home, and I had the impulse to interrupt and ask: What about us, Doc? How do we fix ourselves at the end of this time? Better yet, how do we fix ourselves *now*? Because I could use some REM sleep myself, and this growing fetus could use a break from this round-the-clock bath in cortisol. Can you tell me, Doc, how to put my racing thoughts on a shelf, how to turn

off my dreams, to manage the clean, swift back-and-forth my husband
has mastered? Can you show me how to give in and do battle in the
very same instant like Jo? Can you tell me how a woman who was in
no way built for this life can bear it?

—

We were at the halfway mark of the deployment, a little over two months
in, and we had arrived at June, which meant that at 8 a.m., standing next
to Rachel in an empty Phenix City parking lot, I was already sweating.
I was nearly twenty weeks along. The baby was growing hair, a recent
BabyCenter email had told me.

"I know, we still need a sign," Rachel said, hitching Violet up on
her hip. This was Rachel's new church? An empty storefront next to
the Pizza Hut in a run-down strip mall? Violet, squinting into the sun,
looked about as confused as I felt.

The evening before, Rachel had asked if I'd come along and watch
Violet in the empty nursery while she practiced with the worship team for
an hour before the start of church. The worship team was the church's
music group that played Christian rock similar to the kind that was
always on in Abby's café. With its Celebrate Recovery meetings and
life groups for kids, today's Evangelical Church seemed to be striving
for a vibe that landed somewhere between twelve-step meeting and
summer camp fireside chat.

Rachel's "home church" was part of the Free Methodist Church,
an evangelical institution that believed the Bible was the inspired
word of God. I had gone to that church once for Violet's christening.
It wasn't a megachurch, Rachel had assured me, but it was the closest
to one I'd ever been inside of, on a sprawling campus, with a tub for
adult-sized baptisms on a huge stage lit in blue. The church had just

opened this offshoot in Phenix City, and Rachel had volunteered to help "grow" it, as she put it, inviting potential congregants, attending its weekly Bible study, and singing with its worship team during Sunday services.

"I don't think anyone is here yet," Rachel said, unlocking the glass door and switching on a light. I followed her though the lobby into the main space. I loved churches, loved their light and hush and shadows. Walking through their grand double doors always made me feel like I was entering a portal to another world. This place, though, had a damp mothball smell, fluorescent lights, and fifty foldout chairs. It felt a little like an Al-Anon meeting I'd once attended when I was a teen. When Rachel told me about this new venture, I'd understood that her motives were altruistic. But this was more than altruistic, I was realizing. This was devotional.

"This is where I'll be practicing, if you need me," Rachel said, pointing toward a low stage. She turned to me with a tight smile. It was obvious that she was nervous. Violet was rarely away from her.

"And we'll be right here if you need to check in," I said, gently touching her arm. The truth was, I didn't feel particularly relaxed either. I'd taken care of babies and toddlers in my early twenties, but I had been stupid and young then, blithely unaware of the dangers that lurked in electrical sockets and kitchen drawers. Now that I was pregnant and anxious and had researched every possible harm that could come a baby's way, I wondered how any of us made it out of infancy alive. That morning, as I'd watched Rachel pack the diaper bag full of snacks, I'd wondered, what if Violet chokes on a raisin? You couldn't just do the Heimlich on a fourteen-month-old, could you? Why on earth had responsible adults left me alone with their babies when I'd been hungover and clueless? I could not be this ignorant when my own baby arrived.

Rachel led me down a hallway to a small room, stopping at a short swinging door, similar to the closure of a barn stall. She opened it, placing the diaper bag on a plastic chair inside the entryway.

"This is the nursery." The room was tiny and windowless, the shape and size of a jail cell. Rachel placed Violet down on the play mat, which was covered in a smattering of old-looking toys, and crouched next to her. Watching them from the threshold, I felt the baby move. It was getting stronger, the sensation no longer just flutters.

"What does it feel like?" Andrew had asked me on the phone the night before, and I'd had to take a moment to think about it, lying on my side on Rachel's guest bed and feeling for the small taps, that miraculous Morse code sent from within. There had been nothing at first, so I'd poked my stomach a few times, hoping for a response. And, finally, after a minute, there it was.

Tap. A long pause. *Tap tap.*

"Like popcorn popping," I said. That wasn't exactly right, but it was close. It was indescribable, this feeling. "It makes me realize that the baby isn't just coming," I said. "The baby is already here."

"That makes sense," he'd said, but I wasn't sure he understood, or if he ever could.

"Look at the new toys they have," Rachel said to Violet in a singsong voice, picking up a pig and pressing a button on its nose. It let out an oink, and Violet giggled.

"Again, again," she said, and Rachel complied, pressing the button and letting rip her own high-pitched oink. One of Rachel's great strengths as a mother was her utter willingness to act a fool.

"We're gonna play, just me and you," I said to Violet, sitting down next to her. She smiled and kicked her feet, not understanding what was about to happen.

"Again, again," she said, and I took the pig from Rachel and pressed the button. Rachel stood up slowly, strategically, as though trying not to set off a bomb. When she reached the door, Violet's face shot up.

"Mama's going to be right back," Rachel said. Violet's bottom lip began to quiver as tears pooled in her eyes.

"I promise, sweet pea," Rachel said, and, as she slipped away, Violet broke into a full-on wail. "Mamaaaaa."

"Oh, look," I said, pointing to a sad, decrepit Barbie house.

"Mamaaaaa," she cried, the decibel so fierce it hurt my ears.

I crawled over to a wicker basket of dolls next to the house and fished out an old topless Barbie doll. "Who's this?" I asked Violet. It was a good question, actually. Who *was* this? She was blond and faceless, all of her features rubbed away by time and grubby little hands. Violet stopped crying suddenly, as if turning off a faucet, her face paused in an uncertain pout.

"Do you want to play with the dollhouse?" I asked, pointing again, and she nodded hesitantly, sniffing. Then she looked back at the door.

"Mama?" she said, her voice shaking as though she was about to burst into tears again.

"She's singing," I said. I racked my brain for ways to keep her calm. Then, I remembered the sweetness of Rachel's voice through the monitor that first night I'd stayed at her place.

"This little light of mine, I'm gonna let it shine," I began and she looked at me, frozen for a moment, before reaching her hand out for the doll.

As I sang, Violet stood up and waddled over to the dollhouse, the Barbie snug in her tiny hand. She'd only recently started walking and was not entirely sure of her footing. I looked around the room, taking in the peeling paint of the changing table, the stash of diapers sitting on its bottom shelf. There was little color, only a single image framed on the wall, which wasn't much of an image at all, just a psalm bordered by leaves: *Delight yourself in the Lord, and He shall give you the desires of your heart*.

I envied the way Rachel's faith seemed to carry her through deployments. In her daily life, there was so much she tried to control, making sure her and Violet's food was organic, that there were no parabens in their shampoos or artificial fragrances in their home.

"The world is dangerous," I'd said to her once. "Why try to manage any of it?"

"That's why I need to control what I can," she'd answered. But when it came to something like her husband's safety, she knew she had no hand in it. She didn't expect God to protect him, but certainly she prayed for it, and then she let "Jesus take the wheel" and went to sleep. This seemed far more restful—and rational—than my approach. I knew intellectually that I couldn't orchestrate Andrew's fate, but still, I tried. I was so tired, though, and part of me longed for a God who would do it for me, who would give me the desires of my heart so that I could stop collecting useless receipts or saying "stay safe" exactly twice at the end of each call with Andrew.

Violet and I had been in the room for about half an hour when a woman came by with a red-cheeked toddler on her hip. I was feeling pretty good about my caretaking skills. Violet was playing happily. She had eaten raisins and was still alive, and I'd successfully changed a dirty diaper. The mother opened the half-door to the nursery and plopped the boy down next to Violet. *Thank you*, she mouthed, flashing a dimpled smile at me. And then she was gone before I even had a chance to say hello.

Who was that woman? A member of the worship team, late for practice? But I was pretty sure they were only practicing for forty-five minutes, so she must be very late. I fished my phone out of the pocket of my skirt and looked at the time. It was fifteen minutes to nine. Service would be starting soon. Maybe she was a congregant. But why was she leaving her child with me?

A few minutes later, another mom appeared. This one looked less put together, more harried, her auburn curls still wet from the shower. *Thank you*, she mouthed, just like the first mother, before shoving a brother-and-sister duo into the room and scooting away. The girl was young, around two. She clutched a blanket in one hand and a sippy cup in the other. Her brother looked like he was a couple of years older. They both stared wordlessly at me, unimpressed.

Almost as soon as their mother disappeared, another showed up, this one young and slim and tired looking, with braids that reached the small of her back. And then there was another, and another. A whole stream of kids flooded the room, until it was bursting with boys crashing cars against the walls, Violet asking for snacks, the two-year-old girl crying for her mommy, a four-year-old throwing his snot across the wall in a Jackson Pollock–inspired motion. Where *was* Rachel? Maybe I had misunderstood. Maybe I was the caregiver for the entire nursery. I rifled through the diaper bag and found an applesauce pouch. *I can do this*, I told myself as I opened it and handed it to Violet. It was only, what, ten kids? Twelve? How long was a service? An hour, maybe an hour and a half? I could, at the very least, keep us all alive for that length of time.

Across the room, the boy of the brother-and-sister duo smacked his sister in the face with a truck so hard it left a red mark across her cheek, and she burst into hysterical tears.

Oh god, who was I kidding? None of us were going to survive the next hour.

I was in the middle of the room, pushing a wobbly chain of railroad cars around an old plastic track, a pile of toddlers climbing on me, when I looked up to see Rachel rushing through the door.

"Oh my gosh," she cried, but she was laughing. Violet sprang up from her seat on the floor next to me. "Mama, Mama!"

"I was wondering why you hadn't come over to the chapel yet," Rachel said, and now she began to really laugh, so hard her face turned red. It was full-throated and contagious laughter, and Violet began to laugh too. The boy who'd hit his sister in the face looked at both of them like they were insane.

"The nursery care worker never showed up?" Rachel asked between breaths.

"There was supposed to be a nursery care worker?" I asked. "I kinda thought *I* was the nursery caregiver."

Rachel started laughing all over again, her chest shaking as she gathered a delighted Violet in her arms. She wiped tears from her eyes and blew out a stream of air to calm herself. I was so relieved to see her I could have kissed her. "I know you don't go to church, Simone," she said. "But you're a better Christian than most people I know."

CHAPTER 22

—

RED MESSAGE

Two weeks later, in the quiet of morning, my phone buzzed on Rachel's coffee table. It was only 7:30. Who was calling this early? Rachel and Violet hadn't even gotten up yet. Hopefully they'd sleep a little longer.

In the last few days, a low-level friction had begun gnawing at my interactions with Rachel. "Can you please remember to turn the lights off?" she'd asked more than once, trying to hide the annoyance in her voice. "I can't find anything in this fridge anymore," she'd complained the other morning. I had started adding groceries to it and it was getting full.

"I'm sorry," I'd said. "I'll bring some stuff back to my place."

She'd closed the fridge, put her back against it, and sighed. "Don't do that. Life is not necessarily easier together, but it is better." Rachel had her own set of aphorisms, but, unlike Maggie's, they were unfailingly optimistic, church sayings that she actually meant. This one had been a kind of apology. She didn't need to apologize, though. She had shown me a kind of generosity I'd never seen, the way someone might show a child the ocean for the first time. I didn't know how I would ever thank her.

The phone buzzed again, and I felt the vise around my stomach tighten. I was twenty-two weeks pregnant, which was supposed to be the easiest time in pregnancy, but I had never felt worse. This tightness had started in the past week. It lasted for only moments at first, but now, it sometimes went on for hours, and there were times I genuinely felt like my stomach might actually split in two. Rachel thought they were contractions, and she urged me to tell Dr. Fink.

Another buzz. Finally, I leaned forward to look at the phone and my chest went still. *Vera.* My key caller for this deployment.

"Apologies for the early call," she said when I picked up. Her voice was low and flat, embellished slightly by the hint of accent she'd retained from her early childhood in Russia. The only wife I knew who'd been born in another country, she had moved to America when she was thirteen, and possessed both a can't-be-bothered attitude and a stubborn refusal to look on the bright side of things that felt distinctly un-American. She was, you might say, *over it* —"it" being just about anything.

"I have a red message."

Her words split a seam in the atmosphere. Someone was hurt or dead. That someone wasn't my husband. This was the second time I'd gotten a red message from Vera this deployment. Last time, it had been an injury, and thankfully not a KIA. We were never told who it was, or what had happened.

"Last night, while conducting combat operations in Kandahar Province, Afghanistan, a soldier from D-company was injured. Next of kin has already been notified."

I touched my hand to my stomach. It felt like steel.

"D-company? So, not our company," I said.

"Right," she said.

"Do we know what condition he's in?"

"We don't," she said. I wasn't going to get information, comfort, or even a change of inflection from Vera.

After a moment's pause, she spoke. "You're pregnant, aren't you?"

"Yes," I said.

"I'm sorry, pregnant deployments are fucking murder," she said. "Try not to worry."

Rachel stumbled into the den just as I was hanging up. Her cheek was creased with sleep. She did not look terribly happy to find me here, in the quiet of her den, in the sacred sliver of time before Violet was awake. I was heading to California next week for a baby shower my mother-in-law was throwing me. It would be good for both of us to have a little space.

"Hailey is the coldest key caller ever," Rachel said as she plopped down next to me on the love seat. "Sorry, but it's true."

I laughed. Hailey, of all people, had been assigned as Rachel's key caller for this deployment. The two of them did not click. Rachel was too earnest for Hailey's taste, and, either to survive her childhood or her current life circumstances or both, Hailey had mastered a biting sarcasm that Rachel found off-putting. Hailey wasn't actually cold. Her truest, most open self was loving. She excelled at bringing people together, and was definitely the entire reason the book club had survived. She was thoughtful and always remembered birthdays, bought all her friends who were new moms a Baby's First Christmas ornament, and, if she was in the right mood, she could brighten a room just by walking into it. But in the wrong one, she could turn it instantly drafty. In the past couple of weeks, she had been particularly irritable and distant, and I was starting to wonder if I'd done something wrong.

Rachel put her feet up on the coffee table, shoving aside a pack of baby wipes with one of them to make room. "I wonder what happened," she said.

I shook my head. The red message truly could mean anything. Maybe the guy was on life support in Germany; maybe he was limping around the forward operating base on a pair of crutches. Maybe a stray bullet had clipped off the tip of his thumb.

"Don't you think they should make injury, I don't know, yellow?" I asked, turning to face her. She looked confused. "Like, maybe orange for serious, beige for minor? Save red exclusively for KIAs. There should be some kind of clear, chromatic hierarchy, so we're not sitting there the first five seconds of the phone call, wondering if somebody died or got a fucking hangnail."

Rachel laughed. "That would make too much sense for the Army, Simone." Her smile suddenly died and she looked away. "I think Dan wants to get out after this contract."

"Really?" I asked. His first contract had been shorter than Andrew's, so he had already re-upped. He had another year and a half left on this one.

"I mean, we'll see," she said. "You know how they are, changing their minds every week. But he's been talking about it. I think this has been a hard deployment for him."

Maybe Dan and Rachel talked more deeply than I realized.

"What will he do?"

"I have no idea, but he's resourceful. He'll figure it out," she said. It amazed me that Rachel would shout obscenities over Dan being late for dinner, but having their family's entire future up in the air genuinely did not seem to faze her.

"Andrew is about to sign his papers," I said. I took a breath, focusing on the blank TV screen across from me. "We have an option to go to Washington." I felt the vise tighten. This was the first time I'd mentioned this to her.

I felt her look at me. "You do? Oh my god, you totally should!"

I turned to meet her eyes. "I should?"

"Yes, it's gorgeous. I actually dated this Marine who was stationed there. He was an asshole, but I loved it. He lived right on this beautiful lake surrounded by mountains."

"But what about how I'm not allowed to leave?" I asked.

"Oh, Simone," she said, and her eyes had a sudden shine. "It's hard to imagine you not being a mile away. But it's how it is, right? We won't be here forever either."

"No, you won't," I said hesitantly, unsure of what it was I felt right now. I should have been relieved, and I was, but somewhere in my chest was disappointment. Fear. An anticipatory grief filling me the way it had that day in the park before Andrew had deployed.

She paused, looking me up and down. "Hey, you look ready for the day."

"I woke up at five thirty. Couldn't get back to sleep."

"But the skirt, the makeup—you look nice," she said, gesturing toward my body, my face.

"Ah well, I'm getting to that point where maternity skirts are the only comfortable option," I said.

"Right," she said, sounding unconvinced. "Do I smell perfume?"

"Maybe," I said tentatively.

"Do you have an appointment with your boyfriend?" she asked.

Every week that I went in to see Dr. Fink, I did my hair, chose, with deliberation, what earrings I'd wear, prepared witty conversation while I waited in the exam room. When he came bursting in the door, I'd take in what was new about him. Was he in his uniform or doctor's coat, had he gotten his biweekly haircut at the PX barber shop yet, did he look a little trimmer? It wasn't that I had a crush on him. It was that, during our hour together every week, my life wasn't about Andrew. It wasn't even about the baby. It was about me.

"He is not my boyfriend," I said.

"Simone and Dr. Fink, sitting in a tree, K-I-S-S-I-N-G—"

"Shut *up*," I said, trying to sound forceful, but my voice cracked. We both buckled over in laughter, and then I felt the baby kick.

"The baby," I said, putting my hand to my stomach.

"Oh, let me feel it."

"I'm not sure you can yet."

"Dan could at this point," she said, inching closer to me before putting her hand to my stomach. After a moment, I felt it again, like an insistent knock: *Let me in.* Her eyes widened.

"It feels impossible," she said.

"The kick?"

"No. It feels impossible . . ." She trailed off, searching for the right words. "This baby is gonna grow up. And I won't be there for any of it. That can't be true, can it?"

"It can't be," I said.

—

Dr. Fink breezed into the exam room and sat down on his stool across from me, close enough that I had to curb the impulse to smooth down an unruly lock of his hair. He was wearing his white coat.

"I heard you're a little grumpy today," he said.

"Was it that obvious?" I asked sheepishly. These contractions in my uterus, if that's what they were, made me feel ill at ease in my skin, the sun coming through the windshield on the way over too bright, the air-conditioning in the waiting room too high. When the women at the front desk had been so enmeshed in gossip they'd failed to notice me waiting, I'd felt annoyed and impatient—and, apparently, I hadn't hidden it well.

Dr. Fink laughed. "It's okay. I'm having one of those Mondays too."

It was hard for me to imagine Dr. Fink grumpy.

"You're starting to look pregnant," he said, nodding at my belly, which was, it was true, really beginning to show itself. "And your blood pressure is still higher than I'd like, but it's holding steady, at least."

"So I can fly back to California for my family baby shower?" I asked.

"Yes, I think it's safe for you to fly," he said.

"What about these contractions I've been having?"

He looked at me with a raised brow. "Contractions?"

"I think that's what they are," I said.

"Are you sure they are contractions? At twenty-two weeks?"

"My stomach has been hard," I said.

"How hard?"

"Rock hard," I said.

"Have you been feeling the baby kick?" he asked. "When you're resting, lying on your side?"

"Yes," I said. I loved the baby's kicks. They were so reassuring, I sometimes drank apple juice or prodded my stomach just to wake the baby up so I could experience them. Feeling the tap back was as joyous a relief as receiving a call from Andrew, and I waited for the sensation with the same stilled breath.

"Well, I can't hear you mention what sounds like contractions and then just send you on your way. You're my last appointment. I'm heading to L&D for the night. How about you come with me and we have a look?"

Rachel had been right, it turned out. I was having contractions, but they were fortunately disorganized. "Irritable uterus," it was called, frequent contractions that don't produce any change in the cervix. A pissed-off uterus, essentially. That's what I got for living in a constant state of anxiety. After an hour of monitoring me, Dr. Fink released me to go home.

"Just keep watch on the timing," he told me, unaware that he was adding one more obsessive ritual to my already exhaustive list.

"I don't know what is considered strong at this point," I said. "I don't want to cry wolf."

"Consider this your new baseline," he said. "If it gets worse, then come back. It's our job to take care of you. You do not need to worry about crying wolf."

By the time I got home from L&D, it was evening. I was tired but antsy and shut-in feeling, so I walked down to the park. The creek that had been full when Andrew left was just a trickle now in early summer. The sun had begun to set, which meant I was waiting, counting time not just in hours but in minutes until Andrew hopefully called. There was a kids' baseball game going on, so I sat down on some cement steps behind the bleachers to watch. The stands partially blocked my vision, but I was able to catch glimpses of boys rounding second base under the bright lights, could hear the sound of parents cheering, the clink of the bat hitting the ball.

I took out my phone, opened Google News, and typed *Afghanistan* into the search bar. I knew I wouldn't find much that was relevant. "You won't see our unit on the six o'clock news," the officer on rear detachment had told us during the pre-deployment brief. The Unit did everything in its power not to publicize its work overseas. It was also true that American news outlets didn't care all that much anymore. It was the summer of 2016. Trump dominated the headlines and US news had stopped tracking much of the violence in Afghanistan. But I was a sleuth, and I'd discovered in my internet digging that Pakistani, Indian, and some UK media were still very much interested in the ongoing violence. I was checking them every day, sometimes multiple times a day. This ritual felt wrong, taboo somehow, so I hid it, even from Rachel, and definitely from Andrew.

Pakistan focused primarily on the loss of Afghan National soldiers, and some outlets reported on the deaths of terrorists in groups like ISIS, which had a stronghold in Afghanistan. American-led missions were almost always responsible for these deaths, at least according to these articles. I had no idea if any of this information was all that accurate, but I pored over it like it was a holy text that would reveal an essential truth. It never did. It only made me hungrier for more. It also made me feel sick. Because what did it say about me that the death of thirty-five civilians in Kabul did not keep me up at night the way the death of one, or two, US soldiers could? *Two soldiers killed in an ambush. One soldier killed overseas, a roadside IED. Leaves behind a wife and a baby boy, born during the deployment. Two children. Three children. One pregnant wife.*

I scrolled through an article about a suicide bomb in an open-air market in Kabul that had killed ten Afghan civilians. The Taliban had taken responsibility for the attack. After the 2013 MASCAL, the battalion commander's letter to the spouses about it had said the mission Andrew's unit had been conducting had prevented a high-profile attack from taking place in Kandahar City, "saving countless innocent lives." What did *countless* even mean, though? A journalism professor had taught me to never use the word because it meant nothing. Andrew told me his unit went to great pains to avoid casualties. Rules of engagement were the strictest they'd been since the start of the war. And yet, according to a UN report I'd found online, civilian casualties had reached a record high in Afghanistan the previous year, at 3,545 deaths and 7,457 injured. The Taliban were responsible for the majority of these casualties, but terrorist groups, the Afghan National Army, and the US military were certainly at fault, too.

How many civilians had died in the last month of US combat operations? How many had been saved? Was the price of forty lives worth paying for one hundred others? How could anyone make such hypothetical calculations? There was so much gray in war, even for the ones fighting it. Maybe especially for the ones fighting it. It was easier to sit on the sidelines and look at these numbers and come away with a black-and-white opinion. And insurgencies were the foggiest of wars. It wasn't always clear who was a civilian and who was a combatant, whether an Afghan soldier was on the side of the Americans or the Taliban. It was really only clear, Andrew had told me, that you were being shot at, and that the Americans you'd trained with were the people you trusted.

"Not all lives are equal," Andrew had said during that discussion we'd had about tribalism and the war of ideas. "We were raised to believe in that ideal, but, when the chips are down, it's not really true. Alliances matter. If you had a Sophie's Choice kind of situation where you had to choose between your mother or a stranger dying, you'd choose the stranger, wouldn't you? We're protected from having to think about those kinds of things, but a lot of people in the world aren't." We hadn't been in Georgia all that long when he'd said this. I'd gotten angry. It went against everything I believed, or thought I believed. All lives mattered equally, didn't they? But maybe he was right. And maybe I had spent my life lying to myself because I'd had the luxury to do so. Because the chips, for me, had never been down. But they were down now, in some sense, and sitting here, pregnant, I saw what he meant with a ruthless kind of clarity: If it had to be their man or my man, it was theirs. Every single time. When I read these articles, I thought almost exclusively about the Americans, about our unit, about my husband. I had almost stopped worrying about what it meant that he could kill. I just wanted him to make it out whole and alive. I wanted him to meet his child.

My phone buzzed in my hand. It was Rachel.

Just heard from Dan. All is well.

A phone call from anyone's husband usually meant all was quiet on the western front, at least for this moment. Rachel tried to let me know when she heard from Dan because she knew it reassured me. It was always possible Andrew was still out on a mission while Dan wasn't, but I tried to believe that a text like this was equivalent to a call from Andrew. It kept me—sort of, kind of—sane.

One of the many times I'd asked Andrew why he wanted to join, he'd told me, "I want to see what's behind the curtain." He meant that he didn't want to read about the things our country did on Google News. He'd also meant this in a more existential way. In American society, you could read about war in books, watch movies like *We Were Soldiers*. But that got you about as close to it as I was right now, safe on these park steps, listening to a kid hit a pitch. Curiosity, not patriotism, killed the volunteer soldier, I was pretty sure. Andrew wanted to see and, to some extent, understand a reality, a story as long as life, that most people tried to avoid knowing about, if they could afford to. War had never been a place I wanted to go, but it was disquieting, and oddly heartbreaking, not to be able to go with him. He'd left me behind. Checking the news felt like the only way I could follow him.

The parents yelled and the stands shook with enthusiasm as the sound of the kids' excitement filled the air. Maybe the batter had gotten a home run. I wondered what it would be like to have such an ordinary, beautiful life, to sit on the cool metal of the bleachers, released, finally, from the heat of the relentless Georgia sun, your children playing under the bright lights and your spouse sitting beside you in a ball cap. Your head full only of what base your child just slid into, what you'd make for dinner when you got home. This safe, reliable family ritual seemed to me the most extraordinary thing in the world.

—

A few days later, my contractions had gotten so strong I couldn't focus on work, or even muster a decent appetite. And they had begun to hurt. For much of the deployment, I'd been distracting myself with slow walks around the park or downtown, but it was late June now, and too hot for that. So, I decided to stop by Hailey's instead, where I found Chloe skipping around, chanting, "We're going on a ghost tour!" Chloe was deep in a ghost obsession, and Hailey had promised her all the ghost tours she could handle on a weeklong trip to Savannah during post-deployment leave.

Leaning against Hailey's bar, I watched her aggressively scrub her dishes and wished I hadn't come. I had the distinct feeling she was angry with me. I even asked her, point blank, if she was.

"Boiling," she said. It was her trademark sarcasm, but her voice had genuine bite. There were just a few weeks left of the deployment. The wives were frustrated and wrung out, and the air had become charged with these emotions. The guys were exhausted too. Andrew and I mostly spoke on the phone because the connection on Skype was often terrible, but wives who did use the app said their husbands were looking particularly haggard. I could hear it in Andrew's voice. He was feeling ready to get out of there. He'd been talking more and more about the pleasures of home, sex and a rare steak and a bed with soft, freshly laundered sheets.

But Hailey was annoyed with me, I could tell. Maybe she thought I was, indeed, crying wolf with this irritable uterus stuff, because, in the circle of the wives, I was feeling very much like the weak link. *Are you bleeding out? Nah, you're good? Then chill the fuck out*, I could practically hear her thinking.

When I left Hailey's, I decided to go home to my own bed. If I'd gone to Rachel's she would have taken me to L&D immediately. The contractions were still irregular, so I was trying to ride this out with the maximum dose of Tylenol I was allowed. But when I woke to deep, painful cramps in my pelvis, I decided to drive myself to the hospital.

The OB on call looked to be in his sixties, with a bald head surrounded by a ring of feather-like tufts and a beakish nose. With spindly, gloved fingers, he slid the ultrasound wand across my stomach. I followed his gaze to the screen.

My breath caught at the sight. My baby. No longer a bean sprout but a person, with arms and legs and a spine and tiny ribs. I could even make out the tip of a nose. I could swear it was sloped like mine.

"The sac looks to be intact, and the baby's heart rate is 150, which is normal," the OB said, nudging up his glasses and leaning a little closer to the screen. "Looks like it's a girl," he said. My mouth twitched into an involuntary smile—a girl! My girl! With my nose!—and then I felt myself turn cold. I glared at the doctor. He was in profile, the light through the expansive windows illuminating the pores on his nose and gray hairs crawling out from his ears.

"I didn't know the sex," I said icily. Andrew was supposed to call into my scan next week.

"Now you do," he said, and finally met my eye, but all I could see was the light reflecting off his glasses. The nurse began to wipe off the ultrasound goo from my stomach in frantic, quick motions.

"My husband is deployed," I continued. "I wanted to find out with him over Skype."

"I'm going to sit you upright now, then get you hooked up to the monitor," the nurse said, her voice tight.

I was facing the doctor now. "What about this pain?" I asked him. "I can't keep popping this much Tylenol, can I?"

"We'll see what the toco says." He nodded toward the contraction-reading machine that was sitting on a wheeled cart to my right. "You've been in here before with disorganized contractions and pain. This is probably what that is again. We still need to keep watch for preterm labor, though. And your blood pressure is high."

"But, I mean, in terms of my life. This pain, it's not livable," I said.

The doctor blinked once, then twice, as the nurse wound the toco belt around my waist.

"Well, you're alive, so this is livable," the doctor said.

"Drink the ice water." It was the nurse, rushing in with a soothing tone, and I took her in for the first time since I'd arrived. She was pretty in a tidy, dish detergent–commercial kind of way, with a straight blond ponytail and a sprinkle of freckles across her nose. And she was pregnant. Quite pregnant.

"You're so light on your feet," I said.

"Am I? I feel like a block of cement. I'm running after two at home," she said. "My husband's deployed too."

"That sounds . . . impossible," I said.

She shrugged. "It's easier, in some ways. You know how husbands are."

"Right," I said hesitantly. I'd heard that one before. When the men were gone, life was more streamlined, lower maintenance—less laundry to do, a lower level of stress permeating the household, fewer demands to meet. Dinner could be microwaved chicken nuggets. There were no boxer briefs to pick up off the floor, no one requesting sex when all you wanted, after an achingly long day, was to sleep.

"We need to get enough contractions going to read a pattern, so drink up to get her moving," the nurse said as the belt tightened around me. "I'll be back in a few minutes to check on you."

Next to me, the toco churned out its page of seismic waves, charting the little earthquakes inside me. Seeing them gave me a feeling of calm, and the sensation of the belt, the faint ticking of the clock, and the occasional beep of the vitals monitor registering my blood pressure were all reassuring too.

You exist, the sounds said. *You're alive, so this is livable.*

A knock came at the door. I looked up, expecting to see the nurse.

"Dr. Fink!" I said. He rushed across the room in his tan Army boots, his steps even more urgent than usual. When he reached my side, he stuck out his bottom lip in a childish, empathetic pout and then leaned down, laying his hands on both of my shoulders in an awkward way that said, "I would hug you if I could." After he stood back up, I could still feel the warmth his palms left behind.

His hair was rumpled. So were his fatigues. Why was he wearing those? The Labor and Delivery uniform was a white coat.

"You're on call right now?" I asked.

"No, I'm in the clinic. I've got a day full of appointments."

"Why are you here, then?" I asked, suddenly aware that my hair was a mess and I didn't have any makeup on. Sweat from the hot morning had dried on me in the cool, air-conditioned room, and I probably smelled.

"I heard you were here," he said.

"You came all the way over to L&D just to see me?" I asked.

"I have to make sure you're okay," he said in a mock-stern tone.

"I'm okay," I said. "But that OB is a jerk."

Dr. Fink let out a laugh, exposing his well-ordered white teeth. I could tell that it was bigger than he'd intended, and I watched as he tucked himself back in, straightening his posture and trying to draw a serious face. "The thing about surgeons is, they're not altruistic people," he said.

"But you are."

"I'll tell you a secret, something I don't tell my patients," he said. "I don't like surgery."

I raised my eyebrows.

"I mean, I am very competent at it, don't worry. But I do this because I love being in the clinic, with patients. That's not true of all OBs."

"He was so cruel," I said.

Dr. Fink took a measured breath. "You did the right thing coming in," he said.

"I did?" I asked.

He leaned down and tore out the page from the toco printer, studying it for a moment.

"Your contractions are thankfully not organized, but they're real all right." He looked at me, then, closely, studying me the way he'd just studied the earthquakes on the page. "How can we get you to relax?"

I sighed. "I'm relaxed right now."

He gave me a skeptical look.

"I know I've been anxious," I said. "But I don't actually *feel* that anxious anymore." I meant this, though it would have been more honest to say that I had become so accustomed to anxiety it was no longer something I felt; it was something I did. I'd been managing it so diligently that I believed I had, on some level, mastered it, my rituals becoming so ingrained in my daily routine that I barely noticed myself driving past my house like a stalker, scanning the street for notification officers, listening to the end of "Landslide" in the grocery store parking lot because something horrific would happen to Andrew if I failed to hear its very last beat. I could have found a logical reason to avoid hairline cracks in the sidewalk. My anxiety had become the guiding compass of my life.

"You can feel fine and . . ." Dr. Fink started, looking away for a moment before returning his gaze to mine. "Not be. Anxiety can take a real, physical toll." He was talking about me, I was pretty sure, but I couldn't stop thinking about the baby. Because what kind of toll could it be taking on her?

Not long after I'd arrived in Georgia, when Andrew first deployed, I'd asked my very first key caller if this life ever got any easier. "It doesn't get easier, but you get used to it," she'd said. This hadn't made sense to me then. Doesn't getting used to something make it easier? But I understood now. You got used to being unable to sleep at night. You got used to feeling exhausted even when you *could* sleep. You got used to seeing your friends melt down over a missed phone call. You got used to your life being defined by uncertainty. You got used to it never getting easier. I had gotten used to this. And now my baby, who was just beginning to perceive light and dark, was being forced to get used to it too.

PART IV

"Don't think I don't know you love me. You think we going to make it?"

—James Baldwin, *If Beale Street Could Talk*

CHAPTER 23

—

RULES OF ENGAGEMENT

July 2016

It was 95 degrees in Atlanta, our pilot told us from the cockpit. "San Francisco summer was nice while it lasted," my flight neighbor said gloomily, looking out at the hot tarmac.

I had missed the wives while I was in California for my baby shower, but it had been a welcome break from both the humidity and the gossip that must've been going around about the most recent red message. At the shower, I'd inhaled the scent of my ninety-three-year-old grandmother's perfume, unwrapped soft baby blankets, seen an old friend who gushed about a guy she'd recently met at a poetry reading, and remembered that my world hadn't always been so small, or its stakes so high. Life in Georgia, I realized, had become a lot like life with family: claustrophobic, necessary, and never quite enough. I wanted more.

At my anatomy scan, Andrew and I had seen the baby floating on a huge screen in a dark room, kicking her feet and punching the air. He had Skyped in through my cell phone, and even though, thanks to Dr. Birdman, we already knew the baby's sex, it had been electrifying to see her with Andrew. Our entire marriage these days was made up of quick emails, one-sided care packages, and monitored phone calls that were always too short, so this forty-five-minute span of time had felt luxurious. At one point, I saw Julia's husband, Anthony, pass behind Andrew on the screen. "Ah man, congrats," he said, and Andrew had smiled in response. So had I. It hadn't felt like an invasion. It was, instead, an expansion, our daily lives converging to create what felt like a 3D moment. Real life, almost.

I took out my phone and turned it back on, watching as the screen lit up. Already, my world was shrinking back down to size.

"How much longer until your husband gets home?" my flight neighbor asked. We had chatted on the flight. She and her daughter, a nineteen-year-old college student, had been on a trip to Napa together. They were both petite, with long, wavy brown hair, and between them, they shared a kind of unspoken intimacy, as if they breathed an air that belonged only to them. I hoped that my daughter and I would someday have that kind of bond.

During the deployment briefing, the officer on rear detachment had reminded us of what to say to this question: "I'm not sure—I usually don't receive notification until just before he returns." People didn't want that answer, though. They wanted something hopeful sounding. They wanted something at least vaguely concrete. I understood. So did I.

"Maybe just a few weeks," I said, which was true. Now that we were nearing the end of the deployment, I was finally allowing myself to relax, just a little. In California, the conversations I'd had with Andrew had been charged with future-looking excitement rather than tension. When he'd mentioned Washington again, I felt clear.

"I don't want to pressure you, but we gotta decide soon," he'd said.

"Let's do it," I said.

Andrew laughed. "You sound pretty sure about that."

"I feel pretty sure about it, at least right now. So go sign the thing before I change my mind."

A few days later, I was still feeling pretty sure about it, thankfully. I looked down at my phone as it came to life. Immediately, a new Facebook message appeared and I clicked on it. Vera. That was strange. I'd never had a key caller contact me through there.

CALL ME ASAP.

I dropped the phone. "Shit," I said, and both the woman and her daughter looked at me as I leaned over to retrieve it. My stomach was just big enough now, at twenty-four weeks, that contorting my body like this was becoming a challenge.

"Honey, get that phone for her, will you?" the woman said to her daughter, and, like a dancer, the girl extended her body out from the window to the aisle seat, down to the floor and back up again, in such a quick, seamless movement, it was as though the limitations of space and time did not entirely apply to her.

"Here you go," she said, handing me my phone in that blithe, slightly spacy way of the young.

"Thank you," I said. My voice came out shaky, but inside, I had gone still. I scrolled through my contacts list three times before I found Vera's name. The dulcet bell dinged, letting us know we could take off our seat belts, and people shot up, jostling around me while I stayed glued to my seat.

Vera picked up after a single ring.

"There you are." Her voice was high-pitched, which was so radically out of character I wondered for a moment if I'd picked the wrong name from the list.

"I was on a flight," I said.

"Sorry to do this to you when you're pregnant."

"Is my husband okay?" I asked her, and immediately felt the heat of concern radiating from my neighbor.

"He is *fine*," she said, sounding again like the sangfroid Vera I knew. "You're never going to get a phone call from me if something happened to your husband." I knew this by now, of course, but how was I supposed to react to a text like that, in all caps? My fingers were starting to ache, I was clutching the phone so hard.

"I have a red message," Vera said. "The nature of the mission has changed, and so has their timeline."

I let out an exhale. I had been holding my breath, I realized. For thirty seconds, two minutes, who knew. I stood up and walked out to the aisle. Everyone was alive. No one was injured. But *the nature of the mission has changed*? Even for the Army, this was vague.

I cradled my phone between my neck and shoulder and struggled to free my bag from the overhead bin. A hairy arm came into view and grabbed my suitcase, and I turned to see a tall man bringing it to the floor. I released its handle and gave him a stiff smile.

"What the hell does that mean?" I asked Vera.

"I don't know."

"You don't *know*?" The plane was suddenly stuffy. There were people on every side of me. I glanced back at my seatmate, who was now standing behind me. There was visible concern on her face, so I gave her a weak thumbs-up with my free hand.

"They're not coming home in two weeks," Vera said.

"The flights are delayed?" The line of people ahead had finally begun to move, and I felt some of the tension in my body ease as I began to walk down the aisle.

"No, they're extending the mission. Changing the mission. I don't know. Could be weeks, could be months."

"*Months?*"

"Honestly, I'm freaking out. I've never seen a message like this."

The moment I was inside the airport, I called Hailey. Since Maggie had left, she had become my new font of information. As a key caller, Hailey knew a tiny bit more about what was going on than I did—or rather, she knew the tiny bit we knew, just earlier.

"Well, I appreciate that you're calm," Hailey said after we talked for a minute. I was resting against a wall next to a restroom, watching the quiet airport chaos, passengers streaming by and dashing to gates, mothers picking up tired preschoolers. Once, people had called me *Zen, unflappable*. I couldn't remember the last time I'd actually felt like either of those things. But I was still pretty good at faking them.

"Because the wives I called today were losing it," Hailey went on. "I seriously do not know why I signed up to do this."

"Because you're a glutton for punishment?" I suggested.

"I always think I want to be a joiner, but every time I join something, I remember that I am not," she said. I thought of Rachel sitting in the dark of her bedroom, nursing Violet, gritting her teeth at Hailey's aloof delivery. Had she been one of the ones to lose it?

"Do you think it will be long?" I asked.

"Jack didn't give me a lot to go on, obviously, but he made it sound like it would just be a couple of weeks."

"That's nothing," I said, straightening my posture and stepping away from the wall. "I can do a couple weeks." I sounded jaunty and sure of myself. Hailey, who did not have a lot of patience for whining, always brought out this attitude in me. As I stepped onto an automatic walkway, my suitcase trailing behind me, I thought about how, during birthing courses, women stuck their hands into buckets of ice, trying to leave them for the length of time that a labor contraction lasted. The last few months had been one long contraction. I had been submerged not just in a bucket, but an entire tub. What was a couple more weeks?

"But it could be much longer," Hailey said, in her most resigned voice. Hailey had a curated collection of resigned voices, some of them sighing, others rippling with a current of resentment. This one was the full expression of surrender.

"Who knows," she said, and, as I stepped off the walkway, the ground stopped beneath me. There it was. There it always was.

Who knows.

—

That night, our husbands called to reassure us. *Shouldn't be too much longer. Don't worry, everything's fine.* "Probably just a few more weeks," Andrew said to me. He was calm, even bright, but his voice sounded stiff. I knew what he was doing. He was managing me. We wives may have been the men's primary source of support, but we were also their greatest liability. A few weeks I could handle. Even a month. But any longer? He'd miss the baby's birth. He could not miss the baby's birth.

"But what is this 'nature of the mission' stuff?" I asked. "Why are you staying longer?"

"I can't talk about it, you know that," he said. "But I'm not worried, so you don't need to worry."

And with that, the door that had briefly opened between us in California closed again.

That night, I tossed and turned. Around 3 a.m., I picked up my phone, but instead of watching cat videos or scrolling Facebook, I looked up the news in Afghanistan, hungry for any scraps of information I could gather about the "change in mission." It was hopeless, I knew, but I did find two *New York Times* articles from the summer about Obama's decision to re-expand the overall mission in Afghanistan.

The one from June said that Obama had recently decided to loosen the US Army's ROE, or rules of engagement, in Afghanistan, and began with this comforting opening line: "As the United States braces for an especially bloody summer fighting season in Afghanistan . . ." According to the article, Obama was once again granting American soldiers the ability to fight the Taliban directly, wage ground combat, and conduct airstrikes with "greater flexibility," whatever that meant. The US Army didn't need as much substantial intel in order to make a call on whether or not to conduct an airstrike? Or the US was allowed a greater number of civilian casualties without penalty? Those explanations were so abstract they were almost meaningless. I was beginning to see why Andrew and other guys in the Unit clung to words like *kill* and made such dark jokes. No one else was going to tell the truth of what they did.

The other article, from the beginning of July, mostly covered Obama's decision to keep more troops in Afghanistan than he'd originally planned. The Afghan National Army troops were still nowhere near strong enough to fight the Taliban on their own, and had been unsuccessful in quelling a spate of recent attacks and suicide bombings. This was no surprise. The guys did not trust or have faith in the Afghan soldiers, and tried to stay far away from them on missions so they didn't accidentally get shot. All of this felt like a policy shift only on paper to me, and the *Times* seemed to agree: "The guidelines reflect what has been apparent for months: American troops, primarily Special Operations forces, have continued to actively fight the Taliban since the declared end of the American combat mission in 2014."

At 5 a.m., I was still awake and wanting to talk to Andrew so badly it felt like thirst, like a physical need. I'd never let on to him that I was unraveling because I thought that protecting him from my reality was the best way of loving him. He didn't need to worry about me. He needed to stay safe. But all I'd done was lay down more and more bricks on the wall we'd slowly been building between us since he'd joined the Army. What if the wall grew so high we lost sight of each other completely? What if we lost each other over time, almost by accident, so slowly and quietly we didn't even notice it happening? Such an outcome would have felt utterly impossible even a year before, but I could see, now, how it happened to couples. My mother had left my father because she couldn't bear to be alone inside a marriage any longer. At thirteen, I had blamed her. But I didn't now. I understood.

Maybe Andrew and I had both fucked up. I'd hidden too much and not asked him enough, and he had hewn to the rules of OPSEC too strictly, failed to understand that I didn't just need a phone call; I needed *him* on that phone call. I needed to hear what he'd written in his very first boot camp letter: *I'm really starting to see what a sacrifice this is for you, because it is for me too.*

I sat up against the headboard of Rachel's guest bed and started an email to Andrew on my phone. *I can tell it's harder for you, as time goes on, to talk*, I typed. *You seem less able to ease into it, which I suppose makes sense. You are OK, though? Could you maybe write me and tell me why it's hard for you? Is that too much to ask? . . . I just really want to know your internal world, what goes on inside of you.*

I paused, considered how to end it. *Maybe they could send you home because I'm in my third trimester now and have high blood pressure? A girl can try.* I knew this was crossing a line. You did not ask for an exception, ever. But I could see the sky beginning to lighten through the blinds and the screen was blurring in my vision and none of this even felt like real life anymore. I titled the message *Can't Sleep*, and then, after a moment's hesitation, I sent it and finally passed out.

When I woke, sun was filling the room. My head felt a little clearer. I turned over onto my side toward the windows that faced the street and remembered an email Andrew had sent earlier in the deployment. What was it he had written? I searched for the note, bringing it up on my phone: *For whatever it's worth, I feel more fulfilled than perhaps ever before in my life (though I certainly feel a part of me is missing, being separated from you). I really love my job, and I believe the work I am doing is important and meaningful.* I hadn't replied. I hadn't replied? That was him, letting me in, and I'd said nothing. I thought of my email I'd written in the middle of the night and felt sick. I hadn't shared myself with him the way he had with me. I'd asked him to wave a magic wand and make all of this go away. I grabbed my phone sitting on the pillow next to me. It was a little after 7 a.m.

Maybe Don't Read My 'Can't Sleep' Email, I wrote in the subject line, leaving the body blank. I sent it, then, feeling restless and unsettled, got dressed quickly, and drove down to the café, not even pausing to brush my hair. "A Case of You" was on when I got to the parking lot, and I sat in my car idling, because it was one of my favorites and because I still, more than four months into this deployment, was maintaining my ironclad routine of listening to a song to the very end. Before I got out of the car, I took out my phone and typed a third email: *Actually, Don't Read the 'Can't Sleep' Email.* In this one, I wrote a message: *What you need is for me to be strong and OK, which I can do.*

I was keeping it together *great* on the home front.

"Decaf?" Abby said when I got to the register.

"Full caff," I said.

Abby placed my coffee on the counter in front of me. When she met my eyes, the smile on her face disappeared instantly.

"What's wrong?" she asked, looking at me with the same concerned expression Dr. Fink had when he saw my blood pressure.

"What do you mean?" I tried to bring a faint smile to my eyes and felt the sudden, involuntary prickling of tears.

"Is it your husband?" she asked, and in a rush, she came out and wrapped her skinny arms around my stomach. Abby was so small, and I was now so big, that she could barely get them around me. As she released her arms, I realized that a line was beginning to form behind us. Abby didn't appear to notice, or care.

"He's fine," I said, wiping at my eyes with the heel of my hand. Abby returned to her place behind the register. She had to see the line now, but she remained focused on me. "It's just that they've been extended. I don't know when they'll be back."

"Oh gosh. Will he make it for the birth?" she asked. Her voice was so kind it hurt.

"I think so," I said. "But I really don't know."

—

CHAPTER 24

OPERATIONAL SECURITY

Deployment informational update brief, the leadership was calling it. This antiseptic title did not fool us, though. We knew this was not just any old deployment meeting. Our FRG typically held these in fluorescent-lit classrooms full of those tiny desks attached to chairs that couldn't possibly accommodate pregnant wives. Five-dollar Little Caesars Ready-to-Go pizza was usually on offer, and at most, two dozen women showed up. But the FRG had known to prepare for a packed house this time and had called us all to the vast and stately Marshall Auditorium. Easily one hundred women were here, possibly more. Many of them I had never seen before. There was no pizza in sight.

Hailey and I sat next to each other in the center of the audience, with Jo and Julia behind us. Rachel had come in late and was standing toward the back, Violet strapped into a carrier against her like a shield. Onstage a young officer with a heavy brow was standing behind a projector, looking through a folder of documents. His pomaded hair glistened under the lights. Every so often, he looked out at us in a disinterested way. A blank screen hung behind him.

"I went over to Sadie's and had a drink when I got the news," Hailey said, picking at her cuticles.

"A drink?" Hailey didn't drink. She had never developed the taste for it, she said. Plus, she liked to have her wits about her.

She looked up and made a face. "A strawberry Mike's Hard Lemonade."

"Gross," I said. "That's not a drink. That's a punishment."

"Never again," she said, shaking her head. She looked sad suddenly. "Chloe was so excited for the ghosts." Hailey wasn't up for wrangling a four- and eight-year-old alone. She was hopeful they could reschedule the trip, but she wasn't sure. School was starting soon, and she had signed up to be a substitute teacher at her kids' school. A college degree wasn't required for the position in Alabama, and she wanted to get a sense of what teaching was like. She had recently hatched plans to start taking some general eds at the local community college, get an AA and become a paraeducator. I was excited for her.

"Did you know Steve was shot four times?" she asked.

The auditorium blurred in my vision for a moment. Steve. It took me a moment to remember who he was. I'd never met him. He had been Jack's boss but had moved over to a different company before Andrew had arrived. Andrew worked with him at training events, had described him once as a mentor.

"Wait, was this the last red message?" I asked. "The one where the calls went out early in the morning?"

She nodded, her eyes on the stage. "He's lucky to be alive."

I put my hand to my stomach instinctively. I didn't want to hear this right now. I didn't want to hear this ever, maybe.

"Jack told you that?" I asked.

"Yep," Hailey said.

The officer cleared his throat in an aggressive manner and the room stilled instantly.

"As you know, our unit has received a change of mission," he said, beginning to pace. Was he nervous? I would be if I were him. Even though the room had quieted, the energy in here felt unpredictable, like someone could go off the rails at any moment. And there were so many of us, and only one of him. "Our country has asked us to extend this deployment," he went on. "It has also asked us to increase our force, so we are sending over another company in the next few days."

The entire room seemed to contract. Another company? That was over a hundred guys. What on earth did they need all of them for? And why so suddenly? I looked over at Hailey. This time, she met my eyes and shrugged, but I could feel that her body had gone rigid like a cornered animal's.

"We know this is a deviation from the norm that will cause additional stress on the families," the officer said, finally stopping, mid-pace, and turning toward us. His gaze panned across the crowd, his dark eyes gleaming in a strange, hard way. Slowly and deliberately, almost angrily, he said, "But I'll remind you that this unit has a no-notice deployment capability."

"Oh gee, I forgot," Hailey whispered in a Valley Girl voice.

In quick succession, PowerPoint slides appeared behind the officer as he clicked through them. One gave the contact information for the Unit's family counselor. Another reminded us that "seeking or giving any additional information" beyond this briefing was a violation of OPSEC. The crowd was getting restless. Toddlers were squirming. A baby began to cry so hard that the mother had to take him out of the auditorium. Women were getting out their phones, uncrossing and recrossing their legs. None of us cared about any of this. We were here only for the answer to the question that had been clanging inside our heads the last three days:

When are our husbands coming home?

Finally, the officer landed on the final slide. QUESTIONS? The letters were big, but the blankness of the screen surrounding them was even bigger. This was the last slide of every briefing. Usually, it invited silence. But this time, hands shot up all over the room.

Rachel didn't even wait to be called on. "How much longer will they be gone?" she asked, pitching her voice from the back. It was high and a little panicked, the way it sounded when she couldn't find Violet in the house momentarily.

"We don't know for sure, but command is projecting thirty to sixty days," the officer said.

Fuck. The whispers went through the room in a wave.

The officer called on a woman a couple of rows in front of me.

"What about if our husband is in the company that deployed to Iraq?" she asked.

"They're on track to come home at the usual time," the officer said, and there were a few audible sighs across the room. A handful of women got up and left, content that they had gotten what they'd come for—the clear and official confirmation that none of this applied to them. I wanted to be happy for them. But hearing the door close softly behind them made me feel achingly alone.

The officer called on someone in the back of the room. It was Rachel again, raising her hand this time.

"Why is the mission changing so suddenly?" she asked.

The room went silent. This was a serious faux pas. You didn't ask why. I looked back at Rachel and smiled encouragingly, but I couldn't catch her eye.

"I can't tell you that," the officer said, smiling tightly. "But I can tell you that your husbands are the best trained fighting force on the face of the planet. We are ready and able to conduct the mission we are being asked to execute."

"But why can't the next battalion just do it?" Rachel insisted. "Aren't they scheduled to arrive in a week or two?"

The officer looked at her and blinked his eyes, like he was just now adjusting to the harsh stage lights. "That's. OP. SEC," he said, coming down hard on each syllable, and the air in the room went instantly taut. OPSEC came up frequently in deployment briefs and mass FRG emails, the letters highlighted in red type, reminding us to protect the tiny shred of sensitive information we were privy to: the windows of time during which our husbands were leaving and returning home. This was the first time I'd ever seen a higher-up use the phrase with a spouse as a conversation stopper, though.

The officer returned his gaze to the room. "This briefing is over. I know many of you have to get back to work or kids," he said. "If anyone has any more questions, I'll be here, by the stage, and you can come ask me." He said the word *questions* like it brought a bad taste to his mouth. "The FRG is here to assist you. I and the other NCOs on rear detachment are here to assist you. But remember, your primary support team is to your left and right. Just stay away from the rumor mill."

"Good luck with that," Julia said from behind me.

Gossip was already making the rounds. There was talk of a very big mission, a "historical" mission, whatever the hell that meant. The guys were gearing up for something major. How could we lean on each other and keep that noise out of our heads? You had to be as compartmentalized as a soldier. Only the most seasoned wives came close to achieving this. Maggie had been like that. She didn't spread information or ask for it. She knew just enough about the war and her husband's role in it so that she could carry on a conversation with him about his work, but not so much that it crowded her mind. She had focused on the things she could control, keeping herself busy with the other wives, but never getting too close for comfort. It seemed lonely but also wise. Because what happened when a whole network was enduring the same stresses? Who carried the weak when most of us were only playing at strong?

Afterward, out in the lobby, Jo, Julia, and I gathered around Hailey, who was leaning against a pillar. McGinnis-Wickham Hall was full of pillars. With its unit flags and memorial plaques and wall of windows that faced an outdoor courtyard of fountains, it was the only building I'd been in on base that lived up to the Fort Benning of my imagination. I glanced around, looking for Rachel, but couldn't find her anywhere.

"I've got a little intel," Hailey said, her voice low.

"You do?" I asked, and she looked suddenly hesitant. The squeaking of boots approached, then two soldiers passed.

"It's not much," she said once they were out of earshot.

"Spill," Jo said.

Hailey sighed. "One of the guys on Rear D, I know him. He said it's a matter of acclimation."

"Acclimation?" Julia asked.

"Like, the Unit doesn't think the battalion that was supposed to be taking over for them in two weeks will be ready to do this kind of mission. Our guys are used to the elevation and have been doing missions for months."

"Huh," I said.

"Huh," said Jo.

Hailey shrugged.

This sounded reasonable and unsensational enough that it was probably true. And even if it was false, there was some relief in having new details to cling to, even though they changed nothing about our circumstances.

—

A few days after the briefing, I was in my bathroom getting ready for a book club meeting when my phone began to vibrate on the sink. My shoulders jumped. The thing was beginning to feel like a loaded gun.

Julia, the screen read. That was a surprise. Had she ever called me? I couldn't remember a time.

"Julia?"

"Simone, I'm fine, but I got in an accident on the way to Hailey's."

"Are you okay?"

"It was not my fault," she said, sounding pissed off and righteous, which was not a tone I'd ever heard her take. "This car just blew right through a stop sign and hit the front of my car."

"But you're okay?"

"I'm okay. But the cops, they're saying my car is undrivable."

I was touched. Of all the wives heading to Hailey's, Julia had called me. We were friends, but not the kind of friends who called each other in emergencies. We'd never even had a coffee or gone out to lunch together. Then again, she was still a relatively new wife. This was her first deployment with the Unit, her first deployment ever. I wasn't sure how many of those friends Julia had.

When I got to her on the side of the quiet wooded road where she'd crashed, her blond hair was slick with sweat. The sun outside was merciless.

"Thank you for getting me," she said almost breathlessly. Her cheeks were beet red. Two cops stood by the stop sign where she'd been hit, looking bored.

"I brought water," I said, thrusting a big plastic bottle toward her that I'd picked up at a gas station.

"You're my hero," she said.

"When do you think the tow truck is going to get here?" I asked. "Because I seriously need to pee."

She glanced at the bored cops, and then at a field of tall grass across the street.

"No idea," she said. "But I'll shield you from those cops if you want to pop a squat."

I laughed. "Pop a squat" was the last phrase I expected to come out of Julia's mouth.

We waited for a white truck to pass and then ran across to the other side, finding a spot well away from the road line. Covered by Julia, her back to me, I pulled down my maternity skirt. The dry grass scratched at the back of my calves.

"What did you think of the book?" Julia asked. Hailey had picked this one, *The Curious Incident of the Dog in the Night-Time*, a short novel about a boy on the autism spectrum trying to solve the murder of a neighbor's dog.

I stood up in a half-crouch and pulled up my skirt. The hem suctioned to my skin. "Shit, I'm pretty sure I just peed on my leg."

Julia laughed.

"Honestly, I only read, like, thirty pages," I said. "I can barely make it through an email right now."

"Me too," she said, sounding relieved.

"I have a feeling we're not even going to talk about the book," I said.

"Thank god," she said. And I actually agreed. I had fully given up at this point in the deployment on reading anything other than work I was editing.

"I don't know if I can do this for sixty more days," Julia said, once we were back at the road together, waiting for the cars to pass. She was staring dazedly at her totaled black Jetta across from us, her dark eyes stunned and deer-like. She wasn't the youngest of the wives. She was twenty-six, if I remembered correctly. But she was still new here, still in the first year of her marriage, still likely reeling, I imagined, from leaving her career at the ballet company. She didn't have kids or a job. Her husband was an officer, so they'd be moving on to somewhere else soon enough, and living with that knowledge, that you'd always be in motion, suddenly struck me as unbearably lonely. Julia looked so small and lost standing on this country road in her cutoffs and tank top, I had the urge to put my arm around her. To keep the world at bay. But I wasn't sure I knew her well enough for that.

"Thirty to sixty," I corrected, trying for a mix of authoritative and comforting.

"I have to ask, are there usually this many red messages?" she asked. A car rushed past us, kicking up dust.

"Well," I said. "No one has been killed." I could see, from the pained look that came over her face, that this had not been the right thing to say. I rushed to rephrase. "What I mean is, there have been worse deployments. But this does feel like a lot of red messages."

He's lucky to be alive. That's what Hailey had said about Steve, who'd been shot four times a few weeks back. What did that mean? Had he been close to whoever shot him? And with what kind of gun? I didn't have enough details to conjure a clear scene. This was the problem with getting only bread crumbs of information. I traced their trail, but it only led me in circles. I did this out of desperation, and I could hear that desperation in Julia's voice now. She had gathered each red message like a clue, thinking that together they might mean something.

Did they? Was there a unique chaos to this particular deployment? It was beginning to feel like it.

Considering what to say, I remembered how I'd felt when Hailey had told me about Steve. The sudden chill in the warm auditorium. The impulse to cover my ears. We needed to protect each other from the full truth, and so, as we began to cross the road together, I said something to Julia that I hoped was true but wasn't sure I believed.

"They'll be home soon. I don't think we'll see any more red messages from here on out."

—

Babies were the one true constant in our lives: It seemed like everyone was always pregnant or having babies or had just had babies. When Julia and I got to Hailey's, we found the wives gathered under a white tent, all of the babies cradled in arms and car seats looking peaceful and relaxed. But the women were tense, their nervous energy filling the air with a kind of static. Hailey was messing with her hair, Jo was rocking her new baby in her car seat, and Alex, the young wife I'd met the first time I'd gone to Hailey's, the one who'd wanted the recipe for the buffalo dip, was jostling her leg up and down, up and down. She wasn't part of the book club, but she was here because her husband was in the company that had been sent over with three days' notice. She'd just started the second trimester of her second pregnancy and was struggling to keep it together. Sadie was the only one who looked at ease. I was beginning to think she was just very good at pretending, though. Rachel wasn't here. She had gotten so busy with church commitments that she'd stopped coming to book club.

Julia and I sat down on two empty lawn chairs facing the street, her next to Hailey and me next to Jo. Not a book was in sight, so I left mine in my purse.

"I've seen extensions before, but we always knew when they'd be getting back," said Jo, looking across the way at the neighbor's two pit bulls tussling behind a chain-link fence.

"Tommy says it's just work," said Sadie. A drop of condensation fell from her Corona Light onto her tanned thigh. It looked ice cold and delicious. In my prepregnancy days, Corona Light would have been my last beverage of choice, but Sadie had a way of making any drink look like an elixir of the gods.

"Doesn't sound like 'just work' from what Nate told me," said Alex.

The women glanced at each other: *Alex's husband needs to shut his mouth.* It definitely sounded like he was telling Alex details none of us were supposed to know, the kind of information that, in theory, could put the whole Unit at risk if it got out. I wasn't worried about Alex's husband, though. I just wished that Alex would shut *her* mouth.

"Thank god this baby is such a dream," Jo said, clearly trying to change the subject. "I'd be in deep shit otherwise." Two months before, Jo's husband had appeared for the planned birth, and then gotten back on a plane again ten days later. The baby, Zoey, was fat and serene. The other day on Facebook, Jo had posted a meme that read: *A woman is like a tea bag. You can't tell how strong she is until you put her in hot water.*

Jo unearthed a mesh sack from her diaper bag. It was full of sunscreen and snacks and toys, as though she'd prepared for a day at the beach. She grabbed the sunscreen and offered it to me. I took it from her and inspected the label.

"What are you looking for?" she asked, peering at me quizzically.

"Is this okay to put on while pregnant?" I asked hesitantly. I knew I sounded ridiculous.

"Without question," she said, giving me a skeptical look. "In fact, you need it."

Hailey rose abruptly. "I'm gonna get some snacks for the kids," she said. "Anyone want to come with?"

Julia and Sadie scooped up their babies and followed as I began to apply the sunscreen to my arms, struggling to think of what to say. I had never been alone with Jo, had only spoken to her in the kind of group conversations that moved in and out of lulls, shifting seamlessly from disciplining children and feeding babies to sales at Target, birth stories, and complaints about husbands. This kind of talk had an easy intimacy, but you could easily walk away without knowing the most basic details of someone's life.

Finally, after a long, awkward silence, I landed on something that felt safe and well-trodden. "How did you and Blake meet?"

"Oh, that's a long story," she said, smiling wistfully.

"Let's hear it," I said.

"It's also a sad story," she said.

"I like sad stories," I said.

She raised her eyebrows at me.

"It can't be too sad, can it? It's a love story."

—

When Jo was fifteen, Patrick landed in the seat next to her in sophomore World History at their Michigan high school. He was funny, sweet, and skinny, the kind of guy who walked the girl home from school, talked to her on the phone on the weekends, and helped her with her homework, all while silently pining for her. That girl, of course, was Jo, and she adored him, but she wasn't romantically interested in him. She was an athlete, and she liked jocks.

Their senior year, Patrick bloomed into, if not a jock, a stronger, less puny version of his previous self. He had been preparing himself to try out for the Unit, and maybe, in some sense, readying himself for Jo. He got rid of his glasses. He grew a few inches. But Jo couldn't see him any other way than she always had. During spring break her freshman year of college, she flew down to Georgia, where Patrick had been stationed. She had nothing going on and she longed for the warmth of the deep South. She'd stay in Patrick's barracks. This was not technically allowed, but the Unit was on leave before deployment, and the barracks were practically empty, a ghost town.

When she got to Patrick's door, two guys answered it. They were wearing the Unit's black workout uniforms, which were made of thin, moisture-wicking material that clung to every edge of their bodies. One of them was the best-looking guy she'd ever seen.

"I was gaga for him the minute he answered that door," she said.

This was Blake: tall and sinewy, quick-witted and sharp, with a tousle of dirty-blond hair that softened him, just slightly. I'd met him a couple of times. The centerpiece of his face, of his whole presence, really, was his wide grin, which projected a quality that was a near requirement for membership in the Unit: a confidence that verged on arrogance.

Like so many relationships that begin in the military, there was the quick lighting of the flame between Jo and Blake, and then, waiting. Learning to live both with and without someone from the beginning. After a week with Blake, Jo returned to Michigan to finish college, and, once she graduated, moved down to Georgia to be with him. They married several months later. Patrick eventually married a hairstylist named Linda, and over the next few years, the four of them became a tight band of friends. Then, before a deployment, Linda got pregnant. She and Patrick were overjoyed.

Jo was a storyteller who relished the smallest details, and she was doling out this narrative so slowly that I was starting to get a little bored. She'd gotten to how she met Blake, but she was blowing right past that now. Where was this going? Where were the other wives? I was sweating profusely in the heat and I could feel that my thighs had adhered to the lawn chair like Band-Aids. I was dreading the moment I'd have to peel them away.

"The guys had been gone for a month when Linda called me," Jo said. "She was ten weeks along and bleeding."

"Oh wow," I said, stiffening. "She was miscarrying?"

Jo nodded.

"You weren't kidding when you said this was a sad story."

"This is just the beginning," she said. I wasn't sure I wanted the rest, but Jo was full speed ahead.

Linda and Jo went to Applebee's for lunch after leaving the hospital, because these were the wives, and they did stubbornly hardy and possibly inadvisable things like eat burgers and fries after a D&C. A couple of the sergeants who'd stayed back on rear deployment joined them for the meal. When one of the guys received a call, his joking demeanor turned suddenly serious.

"Something might have happened overseas," the soldier said after he got off the phone.

Jo and Linda looked at each other. "It couldn't be either one of us," Jo said.

"Just give me a call, let me know everything is all right," she told the guys before they left.

The moment she got home, the sergeant from lunch was calling. "You need to get to Linda's house *now*," he told Jo.

"I ran every single stoplight there, trying to beat the notification officers," Jo said, looking right through me. It was as though she wasn't even on Hailey's lawn anymore. She was in her car, rushing down Victory Drive, the heat of panic spreading through her body and into the atmosphere, into me.

Why had she told me this story right now? Why had we signed up for this life? How had she lived through multiple deployments after that one without breaking? I had spent these last months terrified that I'd lose either the baby or Andrew. But both? On *the same day*? This was a fate too cruel to fathom, a fear too outlandish to even allow myself to have.

"Blake watched it happen from the helicopter he was on," Jo said suddenly, as though she'd just remembered this. "There was a sandstorm during a night mission, a helicopter crash."

I didn't know what to say. When I finally did speak, the words came out quiet and weak.

"I'm so sorry," I said.

"It was a long time ago," Jo said. "But we were all devastated."

The afternoon had gotten unbearably hot, and Hailey was calling us to come inside and talk about the book. Jo rose, her baby swinging in the car seat from her hand, and I followed, Hailey's front lawn coming slowly back into focus as I walked with her to the doorstep. Hailey's house was gray and vinyl-sided, the exact same as all the others along the road, but it looked suddenly menacing from the outside. I glanced back at the dogs across the street. It didn't feel much better out here either. I couldn't think of a single place on earth that felt safe—not my house, not Rachel's den, definitely not my own mind.

It took a moment to adjust to the dimness as I crossed Hailey's threshold. The shades were drawn, the lights low, the cartoons playing so quietly the sound was almost imperceptible. A scented candle was burning on the mantel. It was always like this at Hailey's. Quiet. Mild, like a tepid bath. But right now, the hush of the house was unsettling. Shadows played against the wall behind the candle's flame. The dog would not stop barking at the sliding glass door. Hailey was at the sink. Sadie stood at the kitchen bar and opened a fresh Corona. Across the room, her baby was fussing on a blanket on the floor.

Finally, Hailey broke the silence. "All I've gotta say is, thank god Hill and Adler are gone." Hill had been the company's last commander, and Adler had been the first sergeant who worked alongside him. The guys referred to the duo as Bert and Ernie, or, when they were feeling less charitable, "complete morons." Hill, especially, had "zero tactical sense," they said. During the last pre-deployment validation, he'd even arranged an exercise in a way that had accidentally created a Polish Ambush, a setup that involved two friendly elements shooting directly at each other. They were sure that unforgivably stupid calls like this were the reason their company had been skipped over for the last deployment.

Hailey turned off the kitchen sink and dried her hands with a kitchen towel. "Because if they were leading our guys over there, it would be time to break out the black dresses, ladies," she said, and for a moment, we all forgot ourselves, and our laughter filled the room.

CHAPTER 25

—

THE FIRST SHOT

A week later, I was returning from a birthday dinner in North Columbus when I noticed that the outskirts of my neighborhood seemed abnormally dark. Weren't the headstones in the historic graveyard usually lit at night? And the light at the intersection looked like it was out. In fact, all the streetlights were out, I realized, and the traffic light wasn't just dark, it was dangling precariously, swinging like a pendulum in the wind. I'd seen lightning in the far distance through the windows of the restaurant, but the streets on my ride home had been quiet and dry. There must have been a storm, but when? Where?

A quiet tension had been brewing since the book club meeting at Hailey's. A few days before, Rachel had told me she'd be visiting her college friend in Florida "sometime in the next week," and I knew what that meant because I recognized magical thinking when I saw it: Dan had told her the big mission was coming up, and nothing could reach her a state away, the way nothing could reach me at her house. Hailey had gone silent, dropping off text and social media. She did that sometimes, hibernated to wait out a squall. I hoped she wasn't avoiding me specifically. She knew that Washington was on the table for us. I hadn't told her it was definite, but Jack would've relayed the news. That's how it was. Everyone just knew things, and sometimes we talked about them, and sometimes we didn't.

The commander had tried to cheer us up with a sleepaway camp–style newsletter: "Deployment Cycle Edition 2016." *We are so grateful to have you on the team!* was its opening line. The PDF was full of photos of the guys: eating, practicing shooting, gathered in prayer before a mission. Andrew found those prayers odd. "*May this .300 Win-Mag fly straight and true* does not exactly jibe with Christ's actual message," he'd said to me. Toward the end of the newsletter, there had been this upbeat, off-color note from the chaplain:

Hello from the beautiful beaches of Club Med! Ah, I wish . . . Though the scenery is unique, ultimate vacation destination this is not. But that's OK, because we're here to uphold freedom and sovereign truth. And we're definitely not doing that in our board shorts.

I'd reached the corner of my block. People were out in huddles. It looked like the whole neighborhood had lost power. This was not good. I took a breath, then inched toward my house. I'd go to Rachel's. She would be prepared. She always was. She'd have flashlights and candles. I loved the thrill of a nighttime storm—a glitch in the order of things, forced togetherness. It was fun if you weren't alone.

I spotted Pure Race Guy across the street, taller than the rest of the neighbors around him, the flashlight he was holding lighting his face. I sped up a little and passed my house, turning right to make my way to the street parallel to mine, but immediately, my headlights revealed a tree barricading the way. There had to be a route to Rachel's. I backed up, then swung around and drove toward the main road that circled my neighborhood. As I passed my corner, a ream of yellow caution tape emerged out of the dark and a policeman appeared, a flashlight in his hand.

I rolled down my window. "How do I get out of here?" I asked.

"You don't," he said, looking down at me. His face was difficult to make out with the glare of the flashlight in my eyes. "Not until we clean up these trees."

"Will that be tonight?"

He let out a quick laugh, so short it was more of a bark. "Not a chance."

I turned back and parked in my carport, keeping my eyes averted from the group across the street. Inside, the house was thick with stagnant, hot air. Using my phone as a light, I rustled around in the kitchen cupboards for candles or a flashlight. I was not prepared, though I should have been; there were tornado warnings here with some regularity.

I gave up, returned to the living room, and sat down on the couch in the dark, looking at my phone to check the battery. Thirty percent. Hopefully, that would get me through the night. I did not like being here at this hour. I did not like being here at all these days. Walking around in this house, which had slowly been falling apart over the last three and a half years, felt like walking around in the wrong body. I was thirty-one weeks pregnant. Most women in the position to do so were nesting at this stage in their first pregnancy, folding baby blankets and lining up tiny socks in drawers. I hadn't done any of this. We were likely going to be leaving for Washington only two or three months after our daughter was born. Why would I want to begin the process of nesting? I fantasized about taking a match to all of it.

Dr. Fink had told me earlier in the day that he was leaving. An emergency assignment at West Point. The birthday dinner I'd gone to after our appointment had been a pleasant diversion, but, now that I was alone in the dark, it was sinking in that one of my primary life rafts was gone. Before he'd told me, Dr. Fink had inched his stool back, sitting up unusually straight, and I'd known something was coming. I was well versed now in what the delivery of this kind of news looked like. Little eye contact. Some physical distance. Andrew sometimes tried to couch such announcements by saying, "I've got good news and bad news," before proceeding to give me two pieces of shitty news, the first just slightly less shitty than the next. But Dr. Fink had no slightly-less-shitty news to give me. He was leaving in a week, my blood pressure was ticking upward, and he and the OB who was taking over my care had decided together that I should get twice-a-week monitoring from here on out.

There was a loud, clear knock at the door.

When had I last talked to Andrew? It had been a couple of days. But he had sent a quick email the previous night. If he'd gone out on a mission, it was over by the time he wrote. Maybe. I wasn't sure, though. I hadn't seen a car roll into the driveway, hadn't seen headlights come through the blinds. So, there couldn't be a car. There couldn't be a notification officer at the door. But maybe notification officers hid, waiting to let themselves be known. Maybe I should hide.

There was another knock, more insistent this time. I tiptoed to the door and peered through the peephole. But of course, there was no stoop light.

Another knock.

Finally, as if working against some gravitational force, I opened the door with painstaking slowness.

"Simone?" A rough voice came out of the darkness. A flashlight beam lit up the ground. In the shadows, I could make out the pitted skin of his face, the hollows under his eyes.

I couldn't remember his name, but I did remember the feeling of his presence—big and quiet, a little menacing. Pure Race. I would have preferred to see almost anyone other than him right now, but at least he was not going to tell me my husband was dead.

He was in a faded T-shirt and jeans. He tried for a smile. It came out as a smirk.

"I thought you might need this," he said, taking another flashlight from his pocket and handing it to me. I could hear voices from across the street. "You lost some shingles." He nodded toward my side yard. "We did too."

"Thank you," I said, clutching the flashlight in my hand.

"Do you know what happened?" I asked, trying to keep the conversation going. I didn't want him to stay. But I didn't want to be alone, either.

He shook his head in a kind of disbelief. "Something I haven't seen before. The news is calling it a microburst. Quick and fast. It's over now, but it's bad. Houses with their roofs caved in, blown clean off."

The group of people was still in front of Pure Race's house, and I could feel that he was about to invite me out. Part of me wanted to say yes. The night was alive with voices, and my own home was utterly silent. He'd been thoughtful to bring me the flashlight, too. Maybe he wasn't so bad. Maybe I could set aside my reservations about him. I'd already surrendered quite a lot in the last several months, in the last three and a half years, to avoid loneliness, rearranging my priorities so that I cared about not whether I enjoyed a person's company, but whether they picked up the phone when I called. I had allowed a gun in my home. I'd pushed the boundaries of my own beliefs and ethics to make an extremely conflicted peace with my husband's work. I'd set aside my writing entirely during this deployment because my mind had become too dangerous a place to fully enter.

He cleared his throat as if he was going to speak again, and finally, I remembered his name.

"Thanks, Joe," I said, and closed the door.

—

A few days later, I was sitting on Rachel's guest bed, my laptop warm against my thighs, when Rachel appeared in the doorway holding a glass of red wine. Beyond her, the house was silent. It was 8:30 p.m., early for Violet to be asleep. She must have gone down easily.

"Writing?" she asked.

"Just editing," I said, scooting myself farther up the headboard. Editing was one word for it. Scrolling was another. I was anxiously waiting for Andrew to call and I couldn't get myself to concentrate. I always felt edgy and distracted at this hour, but after seeing Rachel on Skype with Dan earlier, I was feeling especially nervous. There had been a preciousness about their conversation. She'd been secretive, speaking in hushed tones, sequestering herself away in a corner of the formal living room while Violet played on the rug in the den. Dan must have been telling her something she didn't want me to hear. Rachel was trying to protect me the same way I had tried to protect Julia. But I knew. The big mission that had been hanging over all of our days for a month now was finally about to go down.

"Has Andrew called you tonight?" Rachel asked.

I met her gaze, and the air between us was suddenly tense.

"No, why?" I asked.

"No reason," Rachel said. She was trying to sound breezy, I could tell, but her hand was so tight around her wineglass that I was beginning to worry she might break it.

"By the way," Rachel started again, her voice oddly frail, "I'm leaving for Florida tomorrow. Probably just a couple nights. You're welcome to stay here. You'll be coming by to feed the cat and water the plants anyhow." She smiled in a way that was clearly supposed to be reassuring. But staying in Rachel's house alone? Sometimes, when she was making a stew, or Violet was playing in my lap, I crawled into the illusion of safety as though it were a cocoon, believing for a few minutes that nothing could touch me here. It was their presence, not the house, that did that for me, though.

Rachel's phone rang from the next room.

"Shit, I left the ringer on," she said, sprinting down the hall to get it before the singsong tone woke Violet. I could feel my heart thumping in my chest. The baby was big enough that she had begun to roll, and she was doing it now, landing on my right side and wedging her butt up against my hip with an aching firmness. I remembered how, before Andrew had left, I'd nipped nearly every argument in the bud. "The stress is not good for the baby," I'd said, so definitive and self-assured in the way that only uncertain and inexperienced first-time mothers could be. As if a marital spat would do the baby in. I would laugh now at who I'd been just a few short months earlier if I weren't thrumming with anxiety.

I shifted on the bed and my phone vibrated next to me. An unknown number. Andrew.

"Hi," I said, trying to make my voice both bright and nonchalant.

"Hi, how are you?" Andrew sounded preoccupied. It was close to 9 p.m. here, so almost 7:30 in the morning in Afghanistan, which was often when he was going to bed. I wanted to believe that he was just tired, but I knew it was more than that. I tried to tell him about the baby's tidal-wave rolls, but voices in the background kept cutting in. Often in our phone calls, I could hear the faint hum of conversation, a chuckle, a guy saying hello to Andrew. But this was different. This was real commotion in the background. The voices sounded urgent, and even when they grew quiet and muted, I could sense the seriousness of their conversation. I could feel how Andrew had one ear on it, half-focused on what I was saying. I couldn't blame him. *I* could barely focus on what I was saying. I wanted to know what they were saying.

"Anyway, it doesn't matter," I said. "This baby is just huge. I am huge. How are you?"

"I'm fine. You probably won't hear from me for a couple of days."

One of the voices emerged from the commotion, then, so close to the phone it could have been Andrew talking.

"Shut it down NOW."

"I have to go," Andrew said. "I love you."

"Already?"

"I have to," he said, and though his voice wasn't loud, it felt rougher than the one I'd just heard say *shut it down now*. Almost cruel. It felt like he was throwing me out. Like he might never let me in again.

"Stay safe, I love you," I managed to say, and then the line went dead.

—

Rachel and Violet were already gone when I woke the next morning and got into Rachel's hall shower. It had been a bad night, the baby insistently kicking as I tried to find a comfortable spot on my side, and I felt woozy and sick to my stomach as the hot water bore down on me. I felt a little like I was dying. Maybe I *was* dying. At least then I wouldn't have to get through this fucking mission.

Alas, I survived the shower. One four-minute chunk down. That was how I was going to get through the next couple of days: in bite-sized chunks. I survived another as I got dressed. Another as I choked down a yogurt cup. Another as I backed out of Rachel's driveway. The whole day moved this way: an eleven-minute drive to Marshall's to buy a tiny pink dress I didn't need for the baby; an unbearably long eight-minute walk along the sidewalk of the outdoor mall, heading to the movie theater to buy a ticket for a matinee. An impressive twenty-two-minute chunk spent eating half a bagel at Panera, waiting for *Ghostbusters* to start.

During the trailer, the couple in front of me spoke in a hush. *We need to remember to pick up milk. Did you let the dog out before we left?* That easy intimacy felt so tantalizingly close yet out of reach that I could hardly bear it. The movie theater was too cold, too dark. It was the weekend, I suddenly remembered, and nearly everyone here was on a date. I left, tossing the full bag of rubbery popcorn in the trash.

I spent the rest of the afternoon at home, looking compulsively at my phone and my email inbox, both of which were maddeningly silent. I didn't want to bother Rachel in Florida, though. And I didn't want a phone call or text. I wanted to accompany her to Target on an evening errand like I had the week before, when she'd persuaded me to ride around on one of those motorized carts. "When are you going to have the excuse to do this again?" she'd said. I'd put Violet in my lap, and she'd laughed as we whizzed down the aisles.

I scrolled through the contacts on my phone. My mother and I had been in pretty intermittent touch lately, and she didn't know about the mission. I called her anyway but got voicemail. It was early morning in Indonesia. My father was probably awake. He had been sending me emails and Facebook messages lately, short and sweet, but also a little stern, containing practical fatherly wisdom like "guard your health." But I needed a woman. And despite my father's anti-military leanings, he loved Andrew, worried about him, and always grilled me for every last detail I had of his whereabouts and work. I couldn't handle that right now.

There was Hailey. When we'd first gotten the news of the extension, she had been extroverted, getting us together for the book club and sending group texts inviting everyone over for the cinnamon rolls she'd been stress-baking. But then she'd gone into hibernation mode. I knew her. She wasn't going to resurface until this was all over. She was trying to keep her mask on for her kids, take them back-to-school shopping, make them Taco Tuesday, get through the motions without fraying her nerves to shreds. But she was spooked.

"Something bad is gonna happen, I just feel it," she'd said to me when we'd last spoken.

Julia? Somehow, texting any of the wives at this moment felt against the rules, like I'd be breaking a spell we were all trying to cast. Every one of us knew the mission was happening, but we weren't supposed to know, and so we acted like we didn't. Maybe Reina. I'd written her an email about how rough a time I'd been having and hadn't heard back. She'd been busy with work in New York. She was styling catalog sets these days, and the shifts were long and often grueling. But it hurt. Something about the pregnancy, or maybe it was the Army, had weakened the seams of our friendship.

I found her name in the Contacts list and called, but her phone just rang and rang. The voicemail beeped and I hung up. What could I possibly say in a voicemail right now? *Hi, I miss you, I think I might be losing my mind, are you still my friend?*

Some part of me longed to hear Reina say what she'd said when Andrew had first enlisted.

I'm scared too.

That's all I really wanted. Someone who could share my fear with me so I didn't have to bear it alone. It seemed like that should have been the wives, but this was the strange fact of our unorthodox arrangement. We had each other, but sometimes, we hid the way animals did to protect themselves when they're sick or hurt, choosing to endure the hardest things alone.

—

When I reached the park for a walk the next evening, the lights along the gravel path had come on. It was Sunday, always a quiet day in Columbus, and there were only a couple other people out walking and running. I felt weak. I'd barely allowed myself a moment of rest all day. So long as I kept moving, I reasoned, the specter of this mission couldn't catch up with me.

The sky had darkened completely by the time I heard the sound of approaching feet on the path, and I felt my pulse quicken. After a moment, a young woman in hot-pink running shorts ran past me, kicking up gravel in her wake, and I exhaled, half-wishing she had been something real to escape, or vanquish, like the dangers of combat. But that was silly. I had no idea what combat was really like. I only knew it held surprises. There was always a plan, but, as the Army truism went, *no plan survives the first shot*. Still, Andrew had told me once that even though being in the Unit was hard and stressful, nearly every moment was, in its way, a letdown—never quite as he'd imagined. It was real life, a known quantity.

Even with the sun gone, it was still very hot. I decided to stop at an oak tree and rest for a moment, leaning against its trunk. I should be at home. I was nauseous with exhaustion. Everything hurt. But I couldn't stand to be in my silent house right now. I felt a twinge in my pelvis. And then another, this one so sharp, it took the air out of me.

You're alive, so this is livable. You're alive. You're alive. I stood up and walked slowly away from the path toward the creek, saying this in my head over and over like a mantra, stopping only when I reached the bank.

What would my life look like if Andrew didn't come home? For months, I had stowed this question under Rachel's guest bed like the bogeyman, trying, always, to keep it just out of sight. I had never summoned the courage to let myself envision what it would be like to deliver and raise my daughter alone, to remake my world just as I became a mother. Pregnancy was high risk, Dr. Fink had told me. Combat was high risk. Loving someone was high risk. I knew all of that intellectually, but to fully let in those stark realities? Maybe you had to hide them all away to stay sane.

I'd gone too far, though, narrowing my vision so completely I had spent these past months seeing my world through the eye of a needle. It wasn't just Andrew who had missed so much. *I* had. Like this creek bed. There was a staleness to the park in midsummer, but a renewed trickle moved through it now, probably since the storm, and I hadn't even noticed it until this moment. Looking at it, I thought of the egret, and I could almost feel the warmth of Andrew's hand in mine, the leather of his calluses, the soft hairs over his knuckles, and all of these tiny details of him felt so good to remember that it broke my heart.

You're alive, so this is livable.

This was no way to live, though.

I stood up shakily, using the tree for balance, and began to walk, slowly at first, then picking up speed. When I was halfway up the hill, sweating and short of breath, my phone buzzed in my pocket, and my heart started beating fast, banging against my chest. It had been more than forty-eight hours since Andrew had called, since that voice had cut through the background, SHUT IT DOWN NOW.

It was a number I didn't recognize.

"Andrew?"

CHAPTER 26

—

REDEPLOYMENT

The sun coming through the window of Abby's café the next morning soothed me as I worked. I was editing the manuscript I'd been trying and failing to focus on at Rachel's. Finally, now that my mind felt open and relaxed, I was making progress. After hearing from Andrew, I had slept ten whole glorious hours. We had spoken for no more than sixty seconds, and he'd sounded exhausted, his voice ragged, but that was all I needed to tumble into bed with relief. He said that he hadn't slept, or even stopped, for two days.

Rachel had texted from Florida not long after I woke up. *I've loved having you, but, with the guys coming home soon, I think it's time to have the house back, get it ready for Dan's return.* I'd known this was coming. The Unit hadn't yet told us when the guys were getting back, but this last big mission was supposed to be the end of the deployment. It was time to go. I needed to return to my own house, and the baby needed me to get it ready for her. Still, I felt a tug in my chest when I read the message. I was ready for this deployment to be over. I was ready, even, for Washington, which we were supposed to relocate to in four months, at the start of 2017. But I wasn't ready to leave Rachel.

As I took a sip of my coffee, I felt the table vibrate. My phone was buzzing, but I couldn't make out the name in the sun. I curled my hand around the screen. *Vera.*

Vera? That was weird. Very weird.

"Hey, Vera," I said hesitantly.

"I have a red message," she said.

"You *do?*" There were always communication blackouts when someone was hurt or injured. Hearing from your husband meant everything was okay.

"On Sunday, in the early morning hours, five soldiers sustained injuries while conducting a combat operation in Afghanistan," Vera said, reading from the script in a robotic voice. "All notifications of soldiers' families have been made. If you have not been contacted telephonically by the battalion commander then your spouse is not injured. Please remain considerate of the families' privacy and be mindful of our operational security. Do not post information regarding this incident or our deployment on social media."

"*Five?*" I asked, and a few heads in the café turned in my direction.

"I know," she said.

"But I heard from my husband," I said, lowering my voice.

"Me too," she said. "It doesn't make sense."

"Wait, which company is it?"

"Usually they tell us, but they didn't this time," she said.

A few minutes later, my phone started buzzing with texts. *Just checking in on you*, Hailey said. Mallory, Eddie's wife, called, sounding as nervous as ever. I hadn't seen her since Dr. Radley's talk. "I've tried everyone," she said. "Who could it be?" Rachel was silent, so I decided not to bother her. She was probably happy to be a state away from all of us right now.

After I hung up with Mallory, I called Hailey. "You okay?" I asked.

"I'm okay. I guess. I mean, I'll be okay. When I hear from Jack."

"You haven't heard from Jack?"

"No, I am apparently the only person on earth who hasn't heard from her husband," she said.

"I'm sorry," I said. I was never sure how to comfort Hailey. Rachel was so much easier. Earnest affection, a listening ear. Zero criticism. But Hailey didn't trust people easily, even after years of friendship. Sometimes, she leaned into a hug. More often, though, she raised her porcupine quills at the first sign of tenderness.

"Thanks," she said, and I could hear the knot in her throat.

"We know he's okay, at least," I continued. "He's not one of the injured."

"I know. I just need to hear his voice."

"I'm sure he'll call soon," I said. I was sure of nothing, but how many times had she told me the same? *Soon, soon, soon.* You'll hear soon, you'll know soon, this will all be over soon. It was the only word left in our arsenal when there was nothing else to say.

"Five guys is a lot, though," I said.

"It was a big mission, I guess," she said. "At least everyone's alive." Her voice was measured again, and the very absence of emotion in it was calming. Hailey had told me once that she was not a particularly comforting person. She rarely knew the right thing to say, got visibly uncomfortable when other people cried, and didn't like to dig too deeply into difficult subjects. But she had a talent for making the terrible seem not so bad. That was how she took care of you. You saw that she was surviving, which assured you that you could survive too.

A crashing sound came through the phone. "Oh fuck, Asher is probably breaking something in his room. I gotta go."

"I'll let you know if I hear anything more from Andrew," I said.

"Just tell him to tell Jack to call his goddamn wife," she said before hanging up.

—

Two days later, we were all back in the same stately auditorium, the same unsmiling officer pacing the stage. I was several rows from the front, with Hailey next to me, Julia and Sadie behind us. Sadie held her smiley five-month-old in her lap. The auditorium was crowded with women, though slightly less so than last time. The deployment was coming to an end, and finally, the Unit was giving us our "re-deployment brief." Like the emergency one five weeks before it, this briefing had a serious, down-to-the-brass-tacks feel, with the bright stage lights and humorless officer and the huge screen behind him. As with so much Army lingo, "redeployment" didn't make a whole lot of sense.

"Like deploying again, but back home instead of away?" I'd asked Andrew once.

"Don't question it. It's the Army," he'd said.

Rachel had once again come in late and was standing in the back, Violet strapped to her in a carrier. Violet was whining and Rachel was jostling her up and down, trying to calm her. I knew her so well that, even from where I was sitting, I could see that she was a woman on her absolute last nerve.

Onstage, the officer was going over PowerPoint slides about things like *flight notification procedures*, which was not what any of us were here for. Those "procedures" were pretty much the same for every deployment: Sergeants on Rear Detachment called us when our husbands left "theatre," which served as a twenty-four-hour notification, and then again, eight hours out from their arrival. Sometimes, they called with a thirty-six-hour notification, or a fourteen-hour one. Always, some spouses fell through the cracks and didn't receive any calls. But we had our own grapevine. We all found our way.

The officer clicked to the next slide. *Spouses CANNOT go to the airfield to meet their husbands* was right at the top. The FRG and Rear Detachment sure loved typing in all caps. We knew this. Most of us did, anyway. Showing up in our cars would distract the guys from busing back to the COF to turn in their equipment. Many of these women had experienced every iteration of a homecoming and didn't need an officer who'd spent the deployment going home to his wife and kids every night to tell them what to expect. The one thing we were all here to find out was when the hell the redeployment window was going to start. We were patient women. But we were starting to crack. I, in particular, was done with vague assurances. I wanted to know that their work was finished. No more missions. I needed to exhale more than I'd ever needed anything in my entire life.

The officer took his time, flipping slowly through the slides. One was the exact same "5-day recovery model" list we'd received after the first deployment, about how the guys would come back smelling and gratuitously cussing, their training as good soldiers undoing all their training as good spouses. This time, though, the regimental psychiatrist had added a list of warning signs to look out for: sleep problems, signs of depression, anger, "marital discord" lasting beyond four to six weeks. What these symptoms warned of, exactly, wasn't clear.

The room was starting to get antsy. "When is he going to tell us the redeployment window?" I whispered to Hailey, and she just shook her head.

The officer stepped out from behind the projector to the front of the stage. "The mission they executed during this extension, it was a big one," he said, and began to pace. He'd been speaking slowly and deliberately for the last few minutes, but his speech was quickening, gathering heat. He was warmed up now, starting to enjoy himself. Everyone in the Unit hated missing something big. They still took pride in it, though. This officer hadn't been on the mission, but he had classified information on it, and I could tell that knowledge was with him in a real way right now. The mission belonged to his unit, so it belonged to him too, in some sense. It was almost as if he had been there.

"They've seen some stuff they haven't in a while. That they'd maybe never seen before," he said, pacing one more time across the stage before stopping and turning toward us. "Don't ask anything of them for a couple weeks," he said. "*Anything.*"

"Anything?" I asked Hailey under my breath.

"Anything, Simone," she said in a faux-somber tone.

Command always advised us that there would be a transitional period after deployments and long trainings or schools like Ranger School. We'd never been commanded to let our husbands completely off the hook for two weeks, though, had never been told so clearly and forcefully how to conduct our marriages and run our households, and I could feel a cold nervousness beginning to pool in my chest.

I looked back at Rachel. She was swaying, her head down toward Violet's. When Dan had gone on that deployment right on the tail of Ranger School, he'd been away for a solid eight months. By the time he returned, he was "broke off," as the guys would say. Pregnant Rachel was tired of doing everything alone, so the day after he got back, she gave him a honey-do list. This dynamic usually worked for them. Rachel was a woman who liked to project-manage, and Dan was a guy who liked to keep busy, who was always on his feet, mowing the lawn or repainting a room. He got to the first item on the list, scrubbing the tub, right away. When Rachel walked into the bathroom to tell him something, though, she'd found him crying.

"I'm sorry," she said, her hand on his back. "I didn't realize."

Would I find Andrew crying as he took out the trash?

Would I find myself crying while scrubbing the tub?

The latter seemed more likely, but anything was possible.

And if the husbands got two weeks, what did we get? When did Jo get to put down her brand-new baby and sleep more than three hours straight, just once? Some of the wives were fortunate enough to have family nearby, or parents who could afford the time and expense to come visit and help. But that was the exception. Some, like Hailey, basically had no parents to speak of. Most wives did it on their own, with a little help from the informal network of support we found in each other. The men had the architecture of the Army to hold them up wherever they were, and the women were the home they returned to. The wives, on the other hand, were left to erect their own scaffoldings.

A few hands rose from the seats.

"I'll take questions at the end—" the officer started.

"I've gotta go pick up my kid," someone called. I recognized that voice—flat but unyielding. I turned around to confirm that it was her. Vera. She was near the back, standing up from her chair, her black curls cut short at her ears. That was new. I liked it. "Can you just tell us when the redeployment window is?"

"God bless Vera," Jo murmured behind me.

"Sure," the officer said stiffly. "I was just about to get to that." He clicked the remote in his hand and a new slide populated the screen.

REDEPLOYMENT WINDOW: Aug8–Aug22, it read, in big, black letters. It was July 27. The end of that window was nearly a month away.

"Thank you," Vera called, her shoes clicking across the floor as she left.

—

The sky above headquarters was the kind of cloudless blue it hurt to look at, but I could not take my eyes off it today, and nor could Hailey, Julia, or Jo. We were standing in a circle by the locked fence of the battalion compound, all of us watching for the plane our husbands were on. Six weeks after they were originally due back, they were finally coming home. And surprisingly, they were doing it in the light of day.

It was an unusually temperate morning for August in central Georgia, but I could feel the afternoon sun as though it were under my skin. I'd seen the faraway look of women days away from giving birth and had always assumed they felt distant from their surroundings. But I realized now that maybe they were trying mightily to go inward. The world felt too close, like there was no clear boundary between the environment and myself.

Every one of us waiting at the gate was wearing a sundress except for Hailey, who was in her usual jeans. I had on a black-and-white striped cotton one I'd bought at Motherhood, new black sandals a size up to accommodate my swollen feet, and a delicate gold necklace with a butterfly charm a friend from my Maryland days had sent me as a "new mother" gift. In order to put it on, I'd had to take off the St. Michael's medal I'd been wearing throughout the deployment. I'd hesitated to do so, pausing in front of my bathroom mirror, grasping the medal in my hand.

The deployment is over, I told myself. *You can breathe now.*

But I wouldn't trust it was truly over until Andrew's feet hit Fort Benning. Because the planes out of Afghanistan kept getting delayed. Once they finally reached Germany, there were mechanical failures (there were always mechanical failures), then fog so thick they couldn't take off. We kept getting calls from Rear D with new times: It'll be twenty-four hours; no, thirty-six; no, two days. The guys making the calls sounded tired, like they'd been absorbing the frustration of too many wives and higher-ups. An outrageous rumor had begun circulating that a commander had taken one of the planes for himself and his staff, stranding the rest of the guys to sleep yet another night in the barracks at the airbase. At this point, this seemed both too insane to believe and totally plausible.

"Hurry up and wait, huh?" Hailey said, her arms folded over her chest protectively. "If I don't see their bus roll up in the next hour, I'm torching the place."

"Easy, Hailey," I said.

Hailey had finally heard from Jack a couple of days after the last red message. He had been one of many to get heatstroke on the big mission and it had taken him a couple days to gain back his strength. Around the same time, we got an email from the commander about the injured—the five soldiers were in another company, and none of them, thankfully, were critically wounded. Hailey had rescheduled their family trip to Savannah for next week. She was exhausted. A stomach virus had hit her house a few days before and their air-conditioning had broken in the 90-degree heat.

All of this waiting—waiting to hear from our husbands, waiting to find out who'd been injured, waiting to get one more phone call from Rear D with a new landing date and time—had pushed all of us to the brink. Violet was getting her molars, which meant she was cranky and not sleeping, and Rachel had called me in tears the previous morning. "I just lost it," she said. She'd called the sergeant on Rear Detachment and chewed him out, demanding answers about when exactly her husband would be home. She knew she had broken the Army wife's unspoken cardinal rule: *Thou shalt keep thyself in check.* She had also broken a spoken rule, one the FRG and Rear Detachment had told us on multiple occasions: *We're not here to be your whipping post.* She was too tired to care, though, too pissed off to give a shit about any of the rules. She had ranted to me over the phone for a solid ten minutes about the motherfucking dickhead sergeants on Rear D.

"I'm sorry," she said to me when she'd calmed down. "We're all going through this."

"I don't have a teething toddler," I told her. "You've been flying solo for too long." I knew some wives would harshly judge what Rachel had done. But I admired her fierceness. She said what the rest of us were too afraid to say, and it made me feel less alone.

Finally, the previous night, we got the call: They were up in the air. Dan was supposed to be on this flight too, but, as I looked around the parking lot, I didn't see Rachel's car anywhere. She was probably behind. When I returned my gaze to the group, Julia was looking at me.

"Did you get Andrew a homecoming gift?"

"A what now?" I asked.

"Julia got her husband a watch because her heart is not yet cold and dead like ours," Hailey said.

"Speak for yourself," Jo said, giving us her toothy smile. "I did not get Blake a homecoming gift."

And then, there it was, in our ears, in our chests, in the tips of our toes: the big, magnificent sound of a C-17. Enormous and gunpowder gray, the military used them primarily to transport troops and cargo to and from combat zones and tactical exercises. I saw them flying sometimes and always thought they were elegant and serene in the way they glided slowly through the sky. But none had ever looked as beautiful as this one as it came into view. We all turned our faces upward and Jo raised the baby like an offering. "I'm handing Blake his baby! That's his homecoming gift!" Her expression was a wild mix—giddy, righteous, indignant, every last recognizable emotion right there on her face.

—

The men had always looked similar, especially in uniform, with their heavy brows and pronounced jaws and clean-shaven faces. But this long and ambitious deployment had cemented the mold, and they were nearly indistinguishable from one another as they rushed, en masse, off the white buses. The guys often said the number-one rule was always look good, and they especially prized a head of hair that had "nice flow." Some had tried Andrew's American Crew pomade and began asking their wives to send it over in care packages, and now their heads positively shone in the sun with my husband's influence.

One guy stood out, though. He was skinny and sallow. He was also on crutches.

"Is that *Jack*?" Hailey asked, pointing. He was a markedly reduced version of his usually robust self, but it was Jack all right, moving impressively quickly toward us on crutches, a white cast covering one of his legs from the knee down.

"Pretty sure that's your husband," I said.

"My husband isn't injured, though," she said. It sounded like she was gritting her teeth. She walked briskly ahead of me, and I followed her in a waddle. "Hey dude, you think you would've mentioned this to me!" she yelled, moving with a kind of clear purpose that fell somewhere between charging an enemy and attending a child in need. She embodied both of those energies at once, the same way Jo's face had held warring emotions. We were overjoyed. We were relieved. We were angry. When I caught up to Hailey, she was bringing Jack into a hug. Her eyes welled with tears.

I hugged Jack too, feeling his thinness. He pulled back and gave me such a sweet, gentle smile, I felt the impulse to ruffle his hair like a kid's.

"Welcome home," I said, and stepped away from him.

And then there were two strong arms wrapped around my stomach, Andrew kneeling on the hot pavement before me, kissing my belly, his dark hair shining in the sun.

"You're so big and so tiny at the same time," he said, looking up at me.

Public displays of affection generally made Andrew uncomfortable, but here he was, on the ground, so elated that he'd forgotten himself. He was safe. The baby was safe. I was safe. We were all, finally, safe.

—

The Army called it *reintegration*: the transition from being gone to being home again. The men had grown accustomed to living in a certain way, among other men. Now, they were weighing what to tell their wives, and what not to. The wives were weighing the same. We had each kept so much from the other over the past six months—classified information, an inappropriate attachment to a nerdy OB, overwhelming worry, nightmares about divorce. In some cases, we shared secrets we'd never discussed—the extent of Steve's injuries; the night the last big mission began; the fact that there had been a big mission at all.

To many of the women, especially women who'd been through this several times, the men seemed like invaders. To the men, home felt recognizable but somehow different, as though all the furniture had been rearranged. And sometimes, it had been. Many couldn't relax into being with their families again. Two days home, Andrew started getting texts. *What are you up to? Wanna get some beers?* The slides at the redeployment brief had told us this would happen. They'd also counseled us not to take a trip for three to six weeks, but, because this deployment had been extended, leave started for the guys pretty much the moment they got back. So, many couples, like us, put off true reintegration and entered a dream for a few days.

The resort we'd picked was on St. Simon's, a coastal island off Georgia. It had looked fancy online. In person, though, it had a pleasantly run-down beachside air, and the rooms were small, not the luxury suites they'd looked like on the website. But we could see the gray Atlantic from our French doors, and it was pure bliss just to lie next to Andrew in bed, his hand soft and steady on my stomach.

"Wow," he said, his eyes wide, the first time he felt the baby's powerful kick. *The first time.* All these months in.

In the mornings, we'd amble downtown and eat waffles. My pelvic pain had eased a bit, but I was so heavy now that just walking a small way felt like a marathon. So we took it slow. We walked on the beach and swam in the pool. Andrew took shots of me in a blue-and-white plaid maternity bathing suit and a big, floppy hat I'd found at JCPenney's shopping with Rachel. Under his gaze, I felt beautiful again, even glamorous. In the evenings, I was too tired to go out, and we watched movies and ordered in bad pizza. Afternoons, we napped with the breeze coming through the open doors. I did not worry about everything being just-so. Things were easy, and that was perfect.

In the afternoons, we had physically awkward sex that was funny and tender and sensational in the most literal sense—I was seven weeks out from my due date and struggled to maneuver my body, but I could feel him in a way I'd never felt him before, and climax sent tingles up my spine, through my arms, and down to my fingertips. Afterward, I finally slept. God, I finally, *finally* slept. Our last afternoon, it was dreary outside, and after a short walk along the beach, we retreated to bed, turning on our sides to face each other.

"I was thinking we should go back and see Gary when we get home,"

Andrew said. "Work on our lines of communication. They're a little rusty." I hadn't seen the Andrew who talked about couples counselors and lines of communication in what felt like a long time. Glimpsing him again made me feel almost wistful, like I had come across an old, lost photo of him.

"Sure, that sounds good," I said easily.

"Maybe we need to keep you pregnant all the time. You are the most relaxed I've ever seen you."

I laughed. "Trust me, this is not how I've been most of the pregnancy." Part of me wanted to say more, to tell him that this was not relaxation so much as exhausted relief, to say that I didn't know how I was going to do this again, and again, and again, but with a child. His face was so soft in the gray afternoon light, though. He had felt the baby kick. He had gotten on his knees in front of all those guys.

"How did Jack shatter his ankle, exactly?" I decided to ask instead. Chloe wasn't getting her ghost tours after all. "Maybe next year," Hailey had said over the phone, sounding resigned. Jack was having two surgeries. He had tried to tell Hailey about the injury before he got on the plane to Germany, but she'd been in the throes of Chloe's stomach virus when he'd called, rubbing her back on the side of the road as she puked into the brush, and hadn't had time to talk. The break had happened at the end of deployment, on a mission, and X-rays he'd gotten in Germany had shown that he had a compound fracture. That's all I knew.

Andrew rolled away from me onto his back. "Oh, it was this terrible mission. We were on irrigated farmland with a lot of sheer drop-offs. He fell into a huge hole in the dark. And the gear we wear weighs like fifty pounds, so he went down pretty hard."

"Wait, the big mission?" I asked, feeling the vise around my stomach as though it had never left.

Andrew's jaw tensed. I wasn't supposed to mention the "big mission" at all. "No, the one after that. The last one. It was shitty."

"There was another one?" I asked, feeling my heart rate go up suddenly. It was over now. Why did it even matter?

"Nothing happened. That was kind of the problem, actually. It just was stupid. Boring. We walked ten kilometers in the dark for no good reason."

"He hurt his ankle at the end?"

"No, right at the start."

"He walked ten kilometers on a broken ankle?" I asked.

Andrew cracked a smile and I felt myself calm. "That's the thing about these guys. They're the real deal," he said.

I rolled onto my back. I couldn't stay like this for long without getting dizzy, but my hips relished these brief moments. As we listened wordlessly to the waves, Andrew's hand found mine. He loved to finger my wedding ring, but my hands were so swollen it no longer fit. Along with the St. Michael's medal I'd taken off, it was in a small gauzy bag sitting on my dresser, a little pile of worry and longing and love.

"The best and worst people you know, right?" I asked, repeating what he sometimes said of the guys he worked with.

I couldn't see his smile, but my ear was so close to his face, I could hear it.

"Yep," he said.

That was all he said of the deployment on the trip, and all I asked. I had so many questions, and so much to tell him, but all of that, I decided, could wait.

CHAPTER 27

—

REINTEGRATION

The evening we returned from St. Simon's, it hit me: I was thirty-four weeks pregnant. And I had done nothing to prepare for this baby.

We were supposed to be leaving for Washington when the baby would be around two months old, so I wasn't going to set up a nursery, but I needed to put the bassinet together, to wash all the newborn onesies I'd picked up from thrift shops, to fold and find storage for the soft blankets I'd received at my shower. I also needed to figure out what the hell these blankets were even for, because I'd read a lot of articles about "safe sleep," and they all agreed no one should ever be putting their baby down with a real, loose blanket, lest it wrap around their tiny neck or suffocate them.

I went into a nesting frenzy, talking to the baby as I worked. She didn't have a name yet, so I called her baby girl, telling her how excited I was to meet her, how soon we'd be living among snowcapped mountains and evergreens. "Your first president is going to be a woman," I told her. "Can you believe that?"

As for nursing, I was arrogant. "How hard can it be? Babies come out looking for the breast, right?" I said to Andrew after an infancy-care class at the base hospital, in which the nurse had given breastfeeding an inordinate amount of airtime. Rachel had made so much milk her freezer was full of the stuff, and still used her breast to soothe Violet's every cry. It was a superpower I couldn't wait to possess. I fantasized about placing the baby in the soft woven sling an old friend had gifted me, her eyes opening and closing as she drank, Andrew bringing me glasses of water as I sang to her.

"Piece of cake," Andrew said. "And I'll be here to help." *For ten days*, I didn't say, as we walked into the hospital elevator and Andrew pressed the button for the underground parking. Then he'd be back at work. He was already slated for a training in Kansas when the baby would be around five weeks old.

One afternoon, about a week after Andrew had returned to work, he had a night jump. Since his unit was airborne, jumping every three months was a requirement to keep the qualification up to date. By the time a deployment was over, they were behind schedule. Night jumps made Andrew nervous. They were usually jumping from just one thousand feet. Inevitably, somebody got hurt. There were broken ankles, legs, once someone even broke his back. The year we'd moved here, a soldier in one of the Unit's other battalions died on a jump.

Andrew had done so many jumps now, he managed the anxiety well. But he seemed nervous as he opened the door and grabbed his keys from the bowl sitting on the bookshelf.

"When will you be back?" I asked.

"I don't know," he said. "Late. After midnight." He wouldn't look me in the eye. Or maybe he was just in a rush. Whatever the case, as he backed out of the driveway, I felt like I was saying goodbye to my husband all over again.

You spend enough time waiting for someone you love to be killed, you begin to obsess over life's fundamental fragility. Not long before Andrew got back, a healthy twenty-five-year-old woman had bled out giving birth at the hospital on base. On the Fort Benning Facebook page, a post asking for diaper donations had included a photo of the young father sitting there in the hospital with his newborn, like he and that baby were the last people on earth. I didn't worry about what could happen to me, though. I worried about the baby. I worried about Andrew getting shot in the next training; jumping from a plane on a Wednesday night; driving to the store to pick up a gallon of milk.

After a dinner alone of canned lentil soup and toast, I sat down on the rocking chair and went through the baby bottles that I'd washed by hand. It was so quiet in the house I could hear the hum of the refriger-ator. I could not figure out how to get the lid on the 14-dollar Italian bottle that was supposed to mimic the feeling of the breast. I tried again and again until I was so frustrated that I threw the lid against the wall, burst into tears, and screamed, "I can't do this anymore!"

I cried, letting some animal part of myself take over the way I had when Andrew had recycled the first phase of Ranger School. Every-thing was fine. The deployment was over. But Andrew had become my new watched pot. Ever since we'd gotten back from the trip, he seemed, even in the most mundane moments, ready to spring into action. A car backfired when we were on a walk and his whole body went rigid. We walked through a drugstore parking lot one evening, two cars heading for the exit from different directions, and he froze, suddenly, in a defensive stance as though we were being cornered. The moment was so brief, almost imperceptible, I wasn't sure a passerby would notice. I wasn't sure Andrew had even noticed. But I had. I was watching that closely.

I wanted to understand what had happened to him. I wanted to understand what had happened to me. I wanted to understand what was still happening to both of us. I wanted all of this to be over.

—

"Thanks for doing the dishes," Andrew said from behind me as I pushed the start button on the dishwasher. It was around ten o'clock the next morning. He'd just gotten out of the shower. I could smell the mint of his shampoo.

Andrew had been giving me a lot of thanks-yous recently. Thanks for supporting me. Thanks for managing while I was gone. "Thanks for being my strong little bird," he'd said the day after we returned from St. Simon's, and I'd shrunk when he'd reached to touch my shoulder. Somewhere along the way, Andrew had learned that a thank-you was a form of recognition. In fact, I'd probably told him that it was, and now I was regretting this. I was not a strong little bird. I was a woman about to give birth.

"You all right?" he asked, sidling up to me. He was wearing only a towel around his waist. The air around him felt warm and moist.

"You don't need to thank me," I said.

"Are you in a bad mood or something?"

I turned to Andrew. He looked tired, his eyes half-swollen with sleep. I was tired too. I had slept maybe five hours, and it had felt less like sleep and more like "time travel," which was how the guys described the Ambien-induced hours of unconsciousness on the plane to and from Afghanistan.

"I didn't sleep much," I said.

"How come?" he asked.

"Anxiety, I guess."

"What about?" The question sounded casual, but I sensed that he was investigating, trying to figure out why so much heat was coming off me this early in the day.

I didn't want to have to explain. I wanted him to be a mind reader. But of course, he was not. "You," I said tiredly. "The night jump."

"It was fine," he said, pouring himself a cup of coffee. "Though Mallory's husband broke his leg."

"Jesus," I said.

"I don't know what happened. It was his hundredth jump. I guess something's bound to happen eventually, right?"

"Fabulous," I said.

"Fabulous?"

"Fabulous that this is how we live. Just waiting for something bad to happen."

"Simone, what is the *deal*?"

The kitchen felt suddenly crowded. I walked to the dining room and looked out into the street. It was as dead and empty as it had been those weeks after Andrew had left on his first deployment, but now it felt supercharged from every time I'd stood here, waiting and watching and longing and worrying and feeling like I might howl just to confirm that I existed.

"The deal?" I said, turning back toward Andrew. He was in the doorway between the kitchen and dining room now, his coffee mug in his hand. The St. Michael's medal on his chest shone in the light. "I don't know. Maybe the *deal* is that I'm a billion weeks pregnant. Or that I haven't slept in six months. Or maybe it could be that I've done this whole fucking pregnancy alone. Or that you have ten days of paternity leave and will be off training a month later."

Andrew ran his hand over his face. "That's . . . a lot," he said. He looked so worn out, suddenly, the lines around his eyes deep. When had he aged like that?

"Yeah, tell me about it," I said.

"I am here now."

"You left me."

"On the night jump?"

"No. Yes. On the deployment, I mean."

"It's my job, Simone. I had to."

"You wanted to."

"Why is this all about you?" he asked.

"It's not," I said, shaking my head. "It's—"

"I'm the one who deployed," he said.

"You wanted to," I repeated with emphasis.

"I'm here for the birth. I'm here for the baby."

"You don't get it," I said. "The baby is already here. You've already missed so much. You're going to miss so much more." My voice cracked at this. I willed it to stay in one piece.

"I wanted to be there, but that doesn't mean I didn't miss you," he said. "People can want to be two places at once."

"It didn't feel like you missed me," I said.

"I called whenever I could."

"You didn't want to."

He paused, took a breath. "No, not always," he admitted.

"I'm an obligation," I said sadly, feeling as though he'd just yanked out my plug.

"No," he said insistently. "But I called and emailed because it was important to you."

"But not to you," I said.

"It's not that simple," he said. "Going back and forth, it's hard. It's really hard."

"You have no idea what I went through," I said.

"You don't know what *I* went through," he said.

"Then tell me," I said. "All I've ever wanted is for you to tell me." That wasn't strictly true. But right now, it was all I wanted.

"You know I can't talk about this stuff," he said.

"You can't tell me facts. But you can tell me how it felt, can't you?"

"How it felt? I don't really talk about that kind of thing."

"You used to," I said.

He paused for so long, I thought maybe we were done. Then, finally, he spoke. "I don't know, Simone. It felt . . . like being at the beating heart of the world, sometimes. Other times, it was just family movie night, eating our food from the chow hall on Styrofoam plates."

"Family movie night?"

"We watched movies in the evenings when there was time. I always chose serious stuff like *Charlie Wilson's War* and made Finley, our private, write reports on them. Well, before he quit."

"He quit?" I asked gently, trying not to scare him off.

"After Steve was shot, we took turns sitting with him at the base hospital across the street from the barracks so that he was never alone. Steve would do laps around the place multiple times a day, already trying to get back in shape, and we'd carry the bags of all his draining body fluids behind him. Finley was a senior private and had been a perpetual problem child for a solid year, still didn't have a good grasp on basic tactical stuff he should've known a month in. We'd have Finley carry Steve's draining fluids, and then later, we'd pressure him, ask, 'What are you gonna do out there when I get shot and you don't know how to do your job?' We could've fired him, but it was our responsibility to train him. We tried. He decided it wasn't for him. And it definitely is not for everyone."

I sat down at the dining table.

"We all lived together in the same room," he went on. "The ceilings were twenty-feet tall, and each bed was separated into its own nook by plywood that reached only six feet up. Anthony would leave before everyone and forget to turn off his light. It drove us nuts, so we decided to break the light bulb right at the base in a way that Anthony couldn't see, reattach it, and screw it back into the lamp. He spent a solid week getting new bulbs from supply before he realized what the hell was going on. He was so fucking pissed." Andrew smiled, remembering.

"One time, I lost it on him, I don't even know why. I was so tired and trying to take a nap, and he kept fucking with me, and I tackled him. I was so fucking angry, I tried to send him through the wall. And then, suddenly, we looked at each other and just stopped. Then walked away, like, *that was fucking weird.*"

"What about the missions?"

He paused again for a long time. "You see dead bodies, and it's strange, they don't look like real people anymore. They look like they're made of rubber. And then, you know, senseless shit happens. The first mission we did, we were waiting to get into the helicopter on the airfield. An incoming mortar round explodes and a piece of fragmentation slits one of the Afghan Army guys' throats and kills him, instantly."

"Jesus Christ," I said.

"And then we just went and did the mission. Like, no big deal. And for some guys who've been doing this forever, it really does seem like it's no big deal. It's just a particularly exciting day at the office. It's not like that for me. Every time I go out, I am hyperaware that everything is at stake."

"You are?"

"Of course. I think about you."

"You do?" I was tearing up now, and Andrew, half-naked in the door frame, was blurring in my vision.

"Every time. And every time, I think about our baby. You see kids out there, you know? You see a lot of shit, and it changes you. How could it not?"

—

Rachel was in her bathrobe when I arrived at her place for my baby shower, and her hair was twirled up in a towel. Violet, who was sitting on the floor stacking a pile of blocks, got up and squealed when she saw me, scampering in my direction. "Me, me," she said, putting her arms out, asking to be held.

"Just let me put this down," I said to Violet before placing the asparagus-and-cheddar casserole I'd made on the dining table, which Rachel had covered with a delicate floral tablecloth and little mason jars we'd glued ribbons around the week before. She had filled them with yellow and white daisies.

"I'm sorry, I'm so behind," Rachel said before disappearing to her bedroom in the back. Rachel had insisted on throwing me a shower, even though I'd already had one in California. Hailey had offered too, but Rachel had beat her to the punch. I'd asked Hailey if she wanted to throw it jointly. "No, thank you," she'd said.

I sat down on the couch and took Violet in my arms. "I've missed you!" I said, kissing the curls on top of her head. She smiled at me, revealing a newly toothy grin.

"Miss," she said. She was eighteen months old and starting to parrot us. Even though she was on the move now, she was still deliciously chubby, with dents at her knuckles and wrists. I put her down on the floor and walked back into the hallway. The door to the guest room was closed. I inched toward it, and then opened it, feeling strangely nervous as I did.

It looked just as I'd left it. I walked to the bed and swept my hand across the soft comforter, then turned to the mirror. My stomach was huge under the black maxi dress, extending so far out it now served as a ledge for my breasts. Something had happened to me in this room that not even Rachel knew, something unspeakable I shared only with the baby. I had been so anxious to leave that time behind, but now that I was here again, all those nights rushing back in, I wanted to stay put, wanted to remember the baby's first kicks and rolls and even the 5 a.m. emails and middle-of-the-night prayers. I could feel the accumulation of all those moments in here, and it was almost like another presence, a witness reminding me: *This happened. Don't forget that this happened.*

When I turned back to the hallway, Rachel was standing there in a long, flowing dress, her wet hair tied up in a knot.

"I saw the casserole. Don't tell me you cooked for your own baby shower."

"You're doing so much," I said. "And hey, I'm pretty proud of it. This is the first casserole I've ever made."

"You did not need to do that," she said, walking into the living room, where Violet was calling for her. I followed and we sat down on the couch, Violet climbing on her lap.

"I got you something," I said, fishing the gift certificate out of my purse, which was still hanging over my shoulder. "It's for a massage at that place you've been wanting to try forever."

She looked embarrassed. "Simone, you don't need to get me gifts to be your friend," she said.

"You did not need to let me essentially live in your house rent-free for the last few months, either," I said. "I wanted to."

I thought the gift certificate was a small gesture, but Rachel looked flustered, even annoyed, as she placed it on the end table beside her, almost as though she were upset with me. Had I done something wrong?

"I'll miss you," I said, and, to my surprise, she looked away. Rachel was usually so good at these kinds of heartfelt conversations, but maybe goodbyes were her Achilles' heel. Maybe she was mad at me for leaving. Or perhaps just sad. Rachel could be happy for me and also a little bit brokenhearted. I could want to leave and stay. Andrew could wish he were here but want to deploy. Somehow, we all managed to hold these fragile paradoxes without breaking them.

It seemed like Rachel was about to speak, but then the doorbell rang, and she looked immensely relieved as she ran to get it. The wives streamed in quickly over the next few minutes, one by one, with presents in their arms. Hailey, Sadie, Julia, and Jo. With the exception of Hailey, who was in white capris, they all wore summer dresses and strappy sandals.

When it came time to open gifts, we sat in a wide circle in the living room. Hailey was next to me. Her hair fell around her face in loose, perfect waves, just as it had the first time I saw her, standing at her kitchen sink. She didn't look like a kid anymore, but she didn't look burdened either, in the way she had then. She looked at home in her skin.

"I feel like I haven't seen you in forever," I said.

"It's been a long two weeks," she said. I could tell she didn't want to say more. "Jack stuck some things in there too," she said in an almost apologetic tone as she handed me her gift bag. "He's happy for y'all with the move. Me too."

"How's subbing?"

"I love it, actually," she said, and her face lit up in that beautiful way of hers, the door swinging wide open. "The school's a mess, though. If I get serious about this teaching stuff, maybe we'll follow you to Washington. The schools there are way better."

"Yes, do it," I said.

"We're talking about it," she said.

"Really?"

"Yeah, you and Andrew are bigger influences on us than I think you realize. And I think I'm gonna get a teaching degree. I want to teach middle school English. The teachers at the kids' school say I'm really good at this."

"No surprise here," I said.

In the bag of baby pajamas and books that Hailey had given me, there was a bottle of Merlot. And wedged against the side was a wooden sign with white lettering, the kind someone might buy from HomeGoods and hang in their office. I took it out and held it up to read it.

This isn't retirement. It's just a new beginning.

I looked at her with a questioning smirk. "Is this a sports metaphor? Like I'm retiring from the boxing ring or the soccer pitch because I'm having a baby?"

Hailey shook her head. "I apologize for my husband."

"You know, that's the very first thing you ever said to me."

"I say it a lot."

"I don't understand it, but I'm truly touched he got me something," I said, laughing.

From her perch on the rocking chair, Rachel took photos while I opened the rest of the gifts: a book from Sadie welcoming my daughter to the world; a blue-and-white quilt with whales on it and nipple cream from Rachel; a soft pink baby blanket from Julia; baby wipes, pacifiers, and diapers from Jo.

"I guessed you were probably drowning in onesies at this point," she said. "Welcome to the club."

"She was already part of the club," Hailey said.

"I mean, the motherhood club," Jo said.

These women were all so different from one another. But they shared something significant: a core philosophy of survival. They got through the days with their children by force of will, by relying not on family or husbands but on friends—and often, just themselves. They welcomed people's help with open arms but recoiled from anyone's pity. They snuggled their kids through every sickness. And on the overwhelming days, they let their kids cry, walked into the summer heat of the backyard, and chugged a beer. They were the toughest people I'd ever known.

"What am I going to do without you guys?" I said, feeling a terrifying sorrow approaching fast like a wave.

"We could all end up at Fort Lewis," Jo said. "Watch it happen."

I laughed, feeling grateful to her, and then, there it was, a hot prickling at the corner of my eyes.

"Simone, I don't think I've ever seen you cry," Hailey said.

"I have," Rachel said, one-upping her.

"The first time we ever hung out," I said, remembering that day we'd dropped off our husbands together, two strangers thrown into a strange land. "It's usually something I try to do in private."

"There's no private with us," Hailey said.

CHAPTER 28

—

THANK YOU FOR YOUR SERVICE

G ary the therapist's hair was as immaculate as I remembered. Better, even. I wanted to get up out of my leather chair and touch it, the way strangers had started touching my stomach in grocery stores and at the post office. Was the silver in his hair somehow brighter? Maybe it was the effect of the sunlight coming through the blinds. This was the first time we had been here during the day. Andrew had managed to get off early for an afternoon appointment.

Andrew and I had been avoiding making the follow-up with Gary, but, after our fight, we knew it was time. So, here we were, back in these leather armchairs. I was thirty pounds heavier, Andrew was trimmer, and each of us had lost a certain kind of innocence.

"Welcome home," Gary said to Andrew, then nodded toward me, smiling.

"Thanks," Andrew said, smiling hesitantly back at him. He was waiting for what usually came next: *Thank you for your service*. The well-meaning line made him uncomfortable. There were a few layers to the discomfort. He never knew what to say in response. *You're welcome?* That seemed arrogant as hell. He had signed up for this, it wasn't compulsory, he was being paid, he didn't need a thank-you. The job was messy and ugly and complicated, full of some of the worst things a person could experience. And were people really thinking about what he did, what he'd done, when they said it? He doubted it. He felt like it was knee-jerk and thoughtless. "Like Siri is wired into their brain and that is the response she gives them when they ask, 'How do I greet a service member after deployment?'" he said. He felt like if anyone needed to be thanked, it was the people who'd really sacrificed something—the soldiers who'd been killed or lost a leg. Not him.

But Gary did not say it. Gary knew better. Gary was a man of few missteps. He crossed his legs, revealing socks that were a surprisingly bold red.

"When you were last here, you were preparing for deployment. Now that it's over, how is the transition going?" he asked.

Andrew and I looked at each other. He gave me a half-smile. "It was going pretty well, actually. Until it wasn't."

Gary looked at me and nodded, encouraging me to respond.

"It was such a relief to have him home, I was kind of basking in that for a while. But then we got into a fight."

"I don't know why exactly," Andrew said.

I looked over at him. His gaze was on Gary. "You said it yourself. Our lines of communication are rusty."

"Sure," he said, shrugging.

"You did. Why are you being so dismissive?"

He looked at me now. "I'm not being dismissive," he said. "'Sure' means 'yes.' I'm agreeing with you."

"Really? You just shrugged. I think you don't realize when you're being an asshole because you're surrounded by assholes all the time."

Andrew laughed gently. "Yeah, they're assholes. They're also the best people I know."

"And the worst," I reminded him. "The best and the worst, that's what you say. I don't want to be married to any of them. I want to be married to you. And I want you to own up to the effects of your job on us. I think sometimes you don't because you feel guilty and you're trying to avoid feeling it." I looked back at Gary as if for confirmation, though I knew telling my husband how he felt about something was about as effective as him telling me to relax.

"Guilty for what?" Andrew asked.

"For the fact that your whole career choice is, like, a foundational betrayal in our marriage." I hadn't been intending to say this. The words had just pushed their way out, and I felt, suddenly, the kind of vertigo Andrew must have experienced when he was about to jump out of a plane into the dark.

"What?" Andrew asked. He sounded like he couldn't believe his ears.

"I'm sorry, I didn't mean to say that," I said. I looked at Gary. "Let me back up. When Andrew decided he wanted to join, we went to couples counseling in New York to hash out the conversation. At one point, he told me that if it was a choice between me and the Army, it was the Army."

"And how did that make you feel?" Gary asked.

"I mean, in a way, I admired it. His willingness to give me up. I'm not sure I've ever wanted something that badly." *Except maybe him*, I didn't say.

Gary nodded.

"It's part of what I love about Andrew. How he knows what he wants and goes after it. His passions and desires are so important to him. The whole way he lives—it reminds me that we only get to do this once. But I also kept having these dreams. Not that he was hurt or killed, though I had those too." I paused, swallowing. "But dreams that he was splitting up with me. I felt abandoned, and Andrew was supposed to be this person who was never going to abandon me."

"I would never leave you, Simone," Andrew said.

"You say that, and I believe you, but I feel like you're always going to be leaving me," I said, still looking in Gary's direction. There would always be one more training with live rounds, one more deployment, one more jump. The wars would end, maybe, eventually. But not really. I finally saw what Andrew had seen before he joined: Mankind was in a constant state of war. Our country was in a constant state of war, mostly in ways the public couldn't see. And that meant that as long as he was in the Unit, he was always going to be walking out that door. And I was going to have to learn to live with that fact, somehow. I was going to have to say goodbye to him with a baby in my arms. I was going to really, truly join the tribe of wives.

"I reenlisted," Andrew said, frustrated. "I can't just keep apologizing for it. I'm going to keep deploying. What can I give you to make it better? To make this work?"

Finally, I looked at Andrew. There was something almost unbearable about making eye contact with him in this room. "I don't want an apology. I don't want a thank-you. I want you to close the distance between us. Your whole fucking life is designed to keep me from actually knowing you, and the way the Unit expects me to be, all quiet and capable and resilient, is designed to keep you from knowing me. Do you know how that makes me feel?"

"I don't expect that of you," he said.

"You don't, and you do," I said. "When you were over there, you never really asked what the last six months were like for me."

"So tell me," he said, like he was daring me. "I told you."

How could I fashion the last six months, the last four years, into a story for him, with a beginning, middle, and end? It was too big and also, too small, what had happened to me. It wasn't war. It wasn't what people wrote songs and books and made movies about. It was so much quieter. We wanted a partner so we'd have someone with whom to share the unsayable secret of being alive. I had shared that, these last months and so much of these last four years, with the wives. And he had shared it with his guys.

"I'm trying to figure out how," I said. *And I'm trying to figure out how to forgive you for missing it all*, I didn't say.

Gary cleared his throat and we both looked to him. "We are about out of time, but I like the question you just asked, Andrew. You could ask it more gently, though. Your homework is to go home and do that."

I nodded, looking in Gary's eyes, and then over at Andrew. He was looking at me—not sternly, or softly. But steadily.

"Okay," he said, nodding, his eyes meeting mine. "I can do that."

Afterward, we paused on the steps outside. It was the start of October, and the air felt heavy, like it might rain soon. Andrew was wearing a red flannel that I had always loved on him.

"I reread an essay of yours yesterday," he said.

"You did? Which one?"

"It's called 'The Writer and the Army Wife'?" he said uncertainly.

"Oh wow. That was published forever ago. Why did you read that?"

"I felt like reading your writing. It had been a while. I missed it. I guess I wanted to . . . close that distance, like you said. I always get what you're saying best when you write it down."

"The concerns in that essay seem so silly now," I said.

"No," Andrew said, shaking his head.

"What do you mean, no?"

"I mean, your concerns aren't silly. Reading it reminded me of what you've given up. Not just your job and friends, but your old sense of self."

I understood that this was his offering, just like the desk had been his offering before he left on his first deployment. I took his hand in mine and fingered his wedding band.

"I did give up a lot," I said, my eyes on his cracked, dry knuckles. His beautiful hands. "But I never would have written that piece if we hadn't come here. You gave me a room of my own, remember?"

—

The morning I hit thirty-nine weeks and six days, I woke feeling like a starting shot had been fired inside of me. I felt great. I felt strong. I felt like I could pick up a car if I wanted to.

At my routine monitoring appointment, the nurse told me I was in early labor. When she brought in the on-call OB, I knew immediately that something was wrong. I'd never seen this OB before. She was probably not much older than I was, with straight blond hair and the kind of icy blue eyes that made a person look villainous, no matter how goodhearted she was. Standing side by side, the two women looked like they were about to escort me into my own trial. Maybe not for anything so transgressive as murder, but definitely something criminal. Auto theft, maybe.

"Your baby is having late decels," the doctor said.

"Late decels? What does that mean?"

"Late decelerations. Her heart rate is falling right after the peak of your contractions."

"Which means?"

"It means she's not tolerating your contractions very well, and these are just early labor contractions."

"Why wouldn't she be tolerating them?"

"She's not getting enough oxygen, likely."

"Why not?" My hand was on my stomach suddenly. It had become, at this point, a steadying landmark. My girl. She had tolerated so much. Too much.

"Well, we don't always know. The placenta isn't doing its job."

"Why not?"

"Why not what?" she asked.

"Why isn't the placenta doing its job?"

She took a deep breath and shrugged. "Hampered blood flow. Could be your blood pressure." I could see that her patience was wearing thin. Medical staff tired of me quickly. I asked too many questions. I always had. I missed Dr. Fink, the doctor of endless patience. "We don't really know. But I do know that we're admitting you right now."

"To monitor the early labor?"

"No. To have this baby. She's coming out," she said, and the nurse checked me into a labor and delivery room. I called Andrew, but his phone went straight to voicemail, which was no surprise. When I tried his office, it just rang and rang. A deep cramping had started.

IN LABOR. CAN'T GET THROUGH TO ANDREW. CAN YOU CALL JACK, I texted Hailey.

A few minutes later, my phone buzzed in my lap.

"I heard you're in labor!" Andrew sounded breathless and boyish, like a kid skipping down the autumn street. He sounded like I'd felt when I'd woken up. Invincible. I did not feel invincible now, but hearing it in his voice brought me back to the memory of this morning, the thrill in my bones, and I felt a flutter of excitement. Our baby was coming.

"Kind of. It's complicated."

"I'm there in five minutes," he said.

—

"She is feisty," the nurse said, placing my screaming child on my chest and then backing away as though she were on fire.

"She's so blond," I said to Andrew.

"And blue-eyed," Andrew said. We both watched her intently as she rooted around for my breast. A dusting of fine blond hair covered her, each one visible under the fluorescent lights of the operating room. Her skin was milky white and her eyes shimmered. Throughout my pregnancy, I had pictured her as a tiny female Andrew, with dark hair and green eyes, but she was nothing like either of us.

I looked up at Andrew and met his eyes.

"You're incredible. So tough," he said. "I could never do what you just did."

I'd been feeling more like something had been done to me. After drawing up a birthing plan, I hadn't had much of a chance to labor at all. The doctors had started me on Pitocin only to realize I had an infection that was dangerous to the baby. She had to come out immediately, which meant a C-section. I had been heartbroken, so desperate I even made the icy doctor call Dr. Fink at West Point, who assured me that he would do nothing different. Now that my baby was on my chest, though, I was mostly just grateful that she was here. Andrew was here. I was here. We'd all traveled a long way, and we'd made it.

We named our daughter Fiona. Andrew's ease with her was immediate. He wasn't experienced with babies, and yet he instantly knew exactly how to hold her. "Do you want my job? Because that is the best swaddle I've ever seen," one of the nurses said to him after he wrapped her up in a few swift movements in one of the striped hospital blankets. "That thing is Alcatraz. She's not getting out."

He was an expert diaper changer, a pro rocker-to-sleeper. She looked so at home against his furry chest, buttoned up asleep beneath his shirt. He was made for this. And despite having been the one who had conjured Fiona, I was not. Fiona broke out of all of my swaddles. My guts had been taken out and put back in, and I could not even go to the bathroom without help. I wasn't making much in the way of colostrum, that "liquid gold" the teacher in the birthing class had mentioned that comes in right before your milk. And that instantaneous transcendent love new mothers talked about? I was waiting for it to flood me the same way I was waiting for my milk to come in.

Fiona began to lose weight precipitously. There were crystals in her urine. I was discharged as a patient, but she was admitted and I stayed in the hospital with her. My mother and mother-in-law both flew in. Sensation finally began to flood me, but this was not some moony-eyed love. This was a fierce protectiveness, the overwhelming pressure of guardianship.

Fiona couldn't properly latch, even with the help of Andrew, my mother, and a lactation consultant Rachel had found, all of them huddled around me like a car racer's pit crew. I wished I had paid much closer attention in the infant-care class. By day five, Fiona had lost 11 percent of her body weight. The hospital would not let us go home with her dropping weight like this, and I didn't feel safe to do so, anyway. She was ravenous all the time. Trying to feed her was a round-the-clock, full-team effort. A doctor with wire-rimmed glasses who looked like a grown Harry Potter began to barge into my room at 5 a.m. carrying legal notepads full of complex mathematical calculations involving pumped milk and formula delivered to Fiona's mouth through a tiny tube. All of this had to be absurdly precise, as if feeding my baby were high-stakes medical research. Not too much formula, and not too long between pumping sessions, or I'd lose what supply I had. Keep bringing the baby to the breast, again and again and again, no matter whether she drank. I pumped around the clock, through the night, the alarm clock on my phone waking me every two hours.

I had never been hungrier for sleep in my life.

Around dawn on day seven, Fiona was finally sleeping peacefully in her little translucent box next to my hospital bed when someone walked in. It was either a doctor or a very large owl.

"It's time to pump again," the owl said. It was pitch dark outside.

"No," I said.

"No?"

"I can't keep doing this," I growled.

"You're telling me you want to give up?" the owl said. It wasn't a question. It was an accusation.

I sat up and looked at the owl doctor standing in the light streaming in from the hallway, and it was clear, suddenly, that he was very much a man. The small Harry Potterish doctor. I looked at my daughter, her lashes soft against her face, and then back at him, his beady eyes staring at me in the dark.

"Leave," I said. "Just leave. Now."

And, to his credit, he did.

Two hours later, I woke feeling better than I had in days, sun coming through the blinds in a gentle, pleasant way.

"Got you coffee from the Starbucks downstairs," Andrew said, holding out the steaming cup. It smelled delicious as I brought it to my lips. In the bassinet next to me, Fiona was beginning to squirm.

"Wait," I said, remembering. "I didn't pump."

"Bring her to the breast and then do it," he said, picking her up out of the bassinet. "It's okay."

Our nurse this morning was one I hadn't met before, compactly built, with short hair gelled to her head in a tight helmet. She looked to be in her late forties. After two minutes in the room, restocking the bin of diapers and pulling new baby blankets out of a drawer, she said, "I notice Dad's handling the baby a lot." She said this to no one in particular, but then she stopped, a stack of sheets wedged under her arm, and looked at me. I was sitting in the armchair next to my bed, Fiona asleep on my chest. "I know you just had surgery. But you gotta get in there. You cannot be afraid of your own baby."

Was I afraid of my own baby? She was the most beautiful creature I had ever seen. Her tiny fingernails. Her curled upper lip. Her warm, heavenly little sack of a body. But I couldn't quite relax into motherhood. What if I dropped her, smothered her? The sound of her shrill cry made my blood pressure shoot up.

"And this baby needs more food. Look at her. She's lethargic," the nurse went on, pointing down at Fiona. "That's not normal." I'd tried to offer her my breast, but she wouldn't wake for it, not even after I'd unswaddled her, tickled the bottoms of her tiny feet, wet her face with cold cloths.

The nurse put the sheets down on the bed and drew a small bottle of formula out of her pocket. She handed it to me, and I looked at it, hesitating.

"But what about nipple confusion—?" I started.

"Feed the baby," she said. "I worked in a NICU in Oakland for twenty years. I know babies. And that baby needs to eat."

I brought the small nipple of the bottle to her mouth. Her lips parted, and she began, still asleep, to suck it down. I watched, in awe and horror, tears falling involuntarily down my cheeks.

"She was so hungry," I said. "Why can't I make enough for her?"

"Stop beating yourself up," the nurse said, tucking in the corners of my hospital bed with military precision. "Maybe you'll get there. Maybe you won't. But this baby needs you right now.".

When she left, Andrew crouched down next to me. The gold flecks in his eyes caught the sun coming through the big windows. "I love this nurse," he said.

"She's a little abrasive," I said.

"She's old school. But I think she's right. Let's keep trying with the nursing. I will support you as much as I can. But you need some sleep. Fuck that doctor and his insane calculations. Our daughter needs you."

I looked down at her pillowy face, the little blue veins that traveled the length of her tiny, translucent eyelids, the dribble of formula clinging to her lower lip. "I'm not afraid of her," I said, feeling like I needed to defend myself. "Just . . . *for* her."

"She's going to be fine," Andrew said. "Look how peaceful she is now. You fed her. You're holding her in your arms, and she's totally blissed out. It's you I'm more worried about."

—

One week out of the hospital, I brushed my hair for the first time since I'd given birth, nestled Fiona into her carrier, and brought her to vote for the first woman president of the United States. The precinct was just two blocks from our house. It was November, the heat of the summer long gone, but it was lunchtime and the day's sun was high enough that all I needed was a long-sleeved nursing shirt as I walked. Patting Fiona's little body under the carrier, I felt both lighter and freer than I had in months, hopeful for the future.

Andrew had just returned to work. Fiona was two weeks old. "I don't want to leave you two yet," he'd said when he left, then took a photo in the dim light of me holding Fiona's little hand in her side-car bassinet so that he could look at it throughout the day. He was wearing a black wool beanie, and I was so exhausted, it struck me that his sweet face was just like our baby's, not the other way around.

Fiona's birth had shifted something between me and Andrew, closing that distance between us while creating a bulwark around us against the rest of the world. We had talked, finally, about how hard this deployment had been for me, and we were also getting excited for Washington, for the next chapter of our lives. We were ready for cool weather and evergreens, ready to elect the first woman president.

For the last year, I'd been driving behind *Make America Great Again* bumper stickers. The Black vote had pushed Muscogee County into the blue the last few elections, though, and, even if we did go red, I was pretty sure those bumper stickers were an aberration from much of the country. Andrew knew lots of guys at work who wanted Trump to win, but they'd never actually voted in their lives. I was hopeful they wouldn't start now. Andrew was voting for Clinton. Rachel was too. Hailey and Jack were still undyingly devoted to Bernie, but they were grudgingly voting for her. All the other states I'd lived in before this were absolutely, no question, voting for Clinton.

I was still pumping every two hours during the day and a couple of times during the night, supplementing with formula and coaching Fiona on her latch, using a nipple shield every time we nursed, which was a little bit like a flimsy bottle nipple that suctioned to the breast. Her pediatrician required that I take her in twice a week to get weighed, and she wasn't gaining at the rate she should be, but she was no longer losing, at least. Now that she was getting more nourishment, her feistiness had returned full force. Even the blueness of her eyes had intensified. She was happy during the day, but in the evenings, she cried and wouldn't stop, sometimes wailing until two in the morning while I bounced with her on the exercise ball.

I was consistently covered in a film of dried milk, exhausted, and still healing from surgery, but I found that I was surprisingly happy to be totally immersed in Fiona on my own. Finally, I was relaxing into being with her, relishing the sensation of her delicate fingers exploring my face as though it were Braille. I could do this, I realized. I *was* doing this.

When I reached my stoop after voting, I stuck the "I Voted" sticker to Fiona's carrier and took a selfie, posting it to Facebook.

This is the happiest post I've seen all day, a friend from college commented.

I sat down in the rocking chair and looked out at the street through the half-open blinds, remembering the terrible loneliness of those first weeks after we arrived. *I feel bad for you because you're all alone.* Isn't that what Hailey had said? I did not believe this baby was going to solve the incalculable problems of this life. She was going to present new ones, actually. But I could not imagine ever being that lonely again. I looked down at Fiona's downy head and inhaled her scent. The last several months had been like one long held breath. My whole life had felt this way, to some extent. Like I was always waiting for something big and bad to happen. Something big had happened all right, but I could finally exhale because it was the very best thing of all.

I will always be here for you, I whispered into her fine hair. *I will never leave you.* I rocked, repeating the words enough times that I began to feel like I was saying them not just to Fiona, but to myself.

CHAPTER 29

—

PERMANENT CHANGE OF STATION

Midtown Coffee was pleasantly busy when I walked in the next morning. One of Abby's daughters was roller-skating two bowls of granola to a pair of middle-aged women in button-down shirts and slacks. In the back corner, a college-aged boy sat quietly at his laptop. The same Christian pop was playing; the same chalkboard psalms were hanging from the wall. The same rich coffee smell was wafting through the air to greet me.

There was nothing new, nothing out of place. But it felt different to me.

I hadn't been here since before Fiona was born. That had only been a little over two weeks, but it felt much longer. Fiona's body was warm and buttery in the carrier against me. I put my hand on her back and thought about the night before, Fiona colicky in my arms as the results rolled in and the impossible began to look possible, then probable. Andrew and I had grown silent as Fiona cried, both of us so frozen that we let her go on for a little too long. Finally, I'd stood up and bounced her, looking into her little red face. I had thought we

389

were bringing her into a US that would elect its first woman president. Instead, her father's most powerful boss, the one who could send him into wars, could extend deployments and change troop counts, was an irrational, terrifying man.

"This is a nightmare," I'd said, looking down at Andrew, who was sitting up in bed, his back against the wall. "We are in a nightmare."

"It'll be okay," Andrew said, not quite looking me in the eye. "Presidents have less impact than we think." He wasn't convincing me, even for a second.

I walked up to the counter and waited for the barista to finish grinding beans. I wondered if maybe Abby was at home. Had she and her husband voted for Trump? They were obviously a deeply religious family. He was a veteran. In the past, I would have assumed they were conservative, but I no longer made such assumptions. And Trump wasn't exactly conservative. He was chaos. He was new, uncharted territory.

That morning on Facebook I'd found a mix of mourning and celebration. Clinton voters were incredulous and despairing. Trump supporters were well-rested and triumphant. One was thrilled to tell her children that the train had "indeed come in overnight." She was a wife and a pediatric nurse, a friend of Rachel's who had always seemed to me grounded and funny and kind. Another was the doula I'd hired and hadn't ended up needing, a whip-smart, high-energy mother of six who had brought us a lasagna after Fiona was born. And yet another was Sadie. This was not a surprise, but it was still painful to see her jubilation, and then to look over at Fiona's growing stack of children's books in the bookcase next to our bed, where I had shelved the one she'd given her: *In My Heart: A Book of Feelings*, which talked about the range of emotions Fiona would feel and struggle to understand as a child: fear and sadness, hope and joy.

Just as the barista finished grinding the beans, Abby emerged from the kitchen in her apron, carrying a gift bag.

"There you are," she said, thrusting it toward me. "I've been trying to give this to you for weeks."

"I can't believe you got her a gift," I said, moving aside to let the patron behind me order.

"Are you kidding?" she said. "Of course I did. I'm gonna miss you guys." She peeked into the carrier to look at the top of Fiona's head. I dipped forward to give Abby a peek at her face.

"Oh, she's beautiful," she said.

All my life, whenever I left a place, I had told friends and family that I would miss them. And I had meant it, but I'd never let myself feel it. I hadn't ever quite understood what people meant when they said leaving a place was hard, because, even when I was in New York, I'd always had one foot out the door. But I had become rooted here in order to survive, and even though I was ready to leave, even though there was so much I couldn't reconcile about this place and my time here, it hurt more than I had imagined—to say the words and let myself feel them.

"I'm going to miss you too."

—

Fiona was eight weeks old when we left Georgia. Julia and her husband, Anthony, threw us a goodbye party at their home in Phenix City, where we were staying for our last few days before heading to Washington. Anthony and Andrew had gotten close over deployment. Rachel and Dan, Hailey and Jack, and a few other couples were here, spread across their open kitchen and living room. I had taken up a perch on an over-stuffed armchair with Fiona nestled against me. Sadie, the only person I knew for certain from our circle who'd voted for Trump, was not here.

Now that the deployment was over, I no longer saw her. And now that Trump was the president, Hailey was having an increasingly difficult time overlooking her politics.

At my postpartum checkup, I'd asked to get on something for depression and anxiety. Hailey was right: Life was better with Fiona on the outside. I felt more like myself than I had in months. The baby's arrival had not righted my world overnight, though. Instead, her presence had fully revealed to me just how wrong things were. The Zoloft was already helping, and my first order of business when I got to Washington would be finding a therapist.

After the checkup, I'd spent twelve days alone with Fiona while Andrew was away training. They had been grueling, but also sweet and profound, a slow, helpless tumbling into the deepest love filled mostly with days of staring at the fine fur that dusted Fiona's earlobes and the nape of her neck. The sensory experience of tickling her toes, the let-down of my milk, the sun on my face as I walked around the park with her strapped to me, all gave me a quiet feeling of well-being I had never known.

"I cannot get over how beautiful she is," Julia said, sitting on the floor across from me, her legs tucked beneath her. "She doesn't even look like a newborn. She looks like a fully formed little person." Fiona was an alert baby. That's what people on the street said when they met her. So engaged. So much personality already. "A sign of a high IQ," a couple of people told me when I said she wouldn't sleep. "Uh-huh," I'd replied, sure that she was steadily siphoning off any IQ I had to speak of. I couldn't remember basic words. I couldn't finish a front-page news article. I couldn't conduct a halfway decent conversation with Andrew about this disorienting age of politics we'd entered.

But I did have new room in my mind. It was strange, because my daily life was so small, full of the tedious, painstaking routines of waking, pumping, rocking, and agonizing over what to put in the diaper bag for my first visit to the pediatrician, but my vision had broadened since Fiona was born. I thought less about orchestrating everyone's fates and more about who I wanted to be for Fiona, who I wanted to be for myself. I wanted to be a true and unwavering home base, not overbearing, but steady and full of light, the way my own mother had been those mornings in the bathroom doing her hair and makeup. I had always wondered what home felt like, but the truth was, I knew. It was those mornings I'd sat on the closed toilet seat and watched my mother; it was the sweetness of her voice, the nights I read to her in bed until she fell asleep. It was the view from my father's shoulders as he walked into the ocean. When I'd left home, I'd shut out these memories along with the dark ones. With Fiona's arrival, they'd all come flooding back in. Some part of me had always worried that I was deficient, that because emotion hadn't flooded me wildly the moment I first kissed Andrew or held Fiona in my arms, I was incapable of real love. But my love wasn't deficient, it turned out. It was overwhelming. I had been afraid of loving someone because I was afraid of my love's size.

As the afternoon turned to evening, everyone gathered in the living room and Jack got up to give a speech, a Coors in his hand. Andrew sat on the arm of the chair where I'd remained planted. When he wanted to, Jack could really turn on the charm, flashing a boyish smile, engaging with every person in the room. He talked about how invaluable Andrew had become to the team. "An absolute stud," Jack said as he grinned at Andrew, and I thought of how, just after Andrew's first deployment, Tyler had drunkenly declared that Andrew was a stud, or would be, eventually. I remembered how intimidating and enigmatic Jack had seemed to me when I'd first met him, tight-jawed and laconic and reading *The Power Broker*. He and Hailey and their kids had become like family, in the truest sense—they were people, I was pretty sure, we were never going to get rid of.

"Andrew was my first private," Jack said. "But he was so old, the first time Hailey met him, she thought he was the officer I worked for." The room laughed. "Andrew was different, and that's been a good thing for us, an asset. He and Simone have both been a big influence here." He looked at me then. "They've contributed in more ways than I can say to people's lives professionally and personally. They've changed us." I had never heard Jack say anything even close to that sincere. I knew that everyone in this room had changed me. It had not occurred to me that I might have changed them too.

After he finished speaking, the women sprawled out on the floor with the kids, and the guys sat in a huddle on the couch, recounting stories from deployment. I was contentedly on the outside of it all with Fiona in our comfortable little nest, belonging to neither group, my ear on the men's talk. They were like high schoolers grown up, remembering the good old days, except the days they were recounting had ended just four months before.

At one point, Jack spoke in hushes, all the guys leaning in, and I could hear his voice shake as he pretended to make a call over an imaginary radio, *fuck* and *shit* splicing the rehearsed lines. I knew that tremor in Andrew's voice, and Jack was mimicking it perfectly. He was doing an impression of Andrew losing composure during a mission when things had gone south, and hearing it in the warmth of this living room was confusing, almost out-of-body. Andrew must have sensed what I was feeling, because he left the couch, walked over to me, and sat down on the arm of the chair. The space was big enough that it felt, for a moment, like we were alone together, Fiona's sleeping body between us. He smelled of chewing tobacco and Fiona smelled of baby soap, and the scents mingled in a way that was strangely intoxicating.

Andrew and I had been back to see Gary a few more times, with Fiona sleeping in a car seat between us. Talking through our last few years together had felt like labor, like stretching for something just out of reach. I had learned how to talk to the wives. Now, I was relearning how to talk to my husband. Soon, I would have to relearn how to talk to people on a coast I'd left behind so long ago.

"People like us," I'd said during our last session of therapy, and Andrew had agreed, but then he'd stopped and looked at me.

"Who, really, is like us at this point?" he asked.

It was yet one more question I didn't have the answer to.

I looked out at my friends on the cream-colored rug. Julia was leaning into Hailey, her cheeks red with wine. Rachel was getting up from the floor, casting her gaze around the house, searching for something. Jo was giving a tablet to her son, looking fed up. My love for Andrew had consumed me. Or it might have, if it hadn't been for the wives. It wasn't just that they filled in the gaps, though they did. It was also that, in a way, they were the ones with whom I'd practiced marriage these last four years. From them, or maybe with them, I'd learned not what love was but how to do it.

I understood, now, what Rachel meant about doing life together. It wasn't easier. It opened in you a maw of need, made you vulnerable to overwhelming pain and obliterating loss. It was terrifying to love someone as fierce and fragile as Fiona, as Andrew, as the wives, as myself. But it was so much better than the alternative.

AFTER

Tacoma, WA, January 2023

"And in the end, of course, a true war story is never about war. It's about sunlight. It's about the special way that dawn spreads out on a river when you know you must cross the river and march into the mountains and do things you are afraid to do. It's about love and memory."

—Tim O'Brien, *The Things They Carried*

Fiona is six years old and a natural extrovert, effusive and generous-spirited, the kind of kid who knows everyone on the playground within five minutes of arriving. But she has a vast and mysterious inner world that can be hard, if not impossible, to access at times. Bedtime, in the liminal space between day and night, is when she opens up and tells me whatever she's been mulling. It is always a surprise.

"Mom, has Daddy ever been to war?" she asks me tonight. Her brother, William, who arrived twenty-one months after she did, is already asleep in his bed across the room.

"Yes, he has been to war."

"How long ago?" she asks.

Andrew has deployed four times since we arrived in Washington. "Not that long ago," I say. "He got back from the last one right before your fifth birthday." That was sixteen months ago, two weeks before the final boots left Afghanistan.

I can feel her thinking in the darkness. After a long pause she says, "But, like, a real war." There is skepticism in her voice.

"Yes, they were real wars," I say, though I have no idea what that could possibly mean to her. I have never heard her use the word *war* before tonight. We only distinguish Andrew's absences as short, medium, or long. Over the course of them, he has missed Fiona's first, third, and fourth birthdays; Christmases and anniversaries; emergency room visits; the exhaustion and vertigo of four months of COVID isolation with two children under four. He missed the day, even, that I set eyes on this bedroom for the first time.

We'd been living in an apartment for eight months when our realtor took me and eleven-month-old Fiona to see this place, a Craftsman bungalow a short walk to a coffee shop and bookstore. Andrew had left for Syria a few weeks before. The house was empty and dusty, but it felt cozy and lived-in, with brass fixtures, dark wood paneling, and a small upper half-story with a bird's-eye view of the block. When we made our way to the backyard and Fiona stained her face red with the raspberries planted along the fence line, I knew this was it.

"It is heartbreakingly beautiful," Andrew said when I showed it to him over Skype, and I heard the note of sadness in his voice.

Just as we'd planned, we live a half-hour freeway ride away from base. Tacoma is a gritty, midsized city with natural beauty and a blue-collar backbone. On a clear day, Mount Rainier looks close enough to touch, unearthly, like a moon that has fallen down to earth. Since Andrew summited it with his team, our kids refer to it as "Daddy's mountain." We have been here for nearly six years, longer than we were in Georgia, long enough that it feels like home. I recognize that sensation now, can feel it when I walk through our front door and Will lunges at my knees, still the koala of love and need he was as a baby. Home. It feels like nothing I've ever felt before, like landing and taking off at the same time.

Since we've gotten here, I've deliberately built a life outside of Andrew's world. My career has flourished; I've made writer friends; I have dinner parties with neighbors, a tight community at my kids' school, and a brilliant therapist who has helped me learn to navigate the tightrope of worry and loneliness. Andrew's mother moved up here from the Bay Area, becoming a kind of linchpin in our family unit. After a lifetime of looking for trap doors and escape routes, I don't want to be anywhere but here, lying next to my daughter in her twin-sized bed, looking up at the glowing stars we stuck to the ceiling not long after we moved in.

There are still times, though, that I find myself at my window, wishing for a glimpse of Rachel. Dan got out a year after we left, finding a job with a DOD contractor in North Carolina. He and Rachel have three children and just bought an old house they're going to renovate from the ground up. We text each other pictures of our kids, or nostalgic memories late at night when we're both drinking wine, but we haven't seen each other since I left Georgia, and there is little time for phone calls.

Hailey and Jack wound up moving here a year after we did. Andrew has worked side by side with Jack ever since, but I only see Hailey every few months. They live right on the outskirts of base, and she is student teaching and working toward her credential. Life is fuller than ever for both of us, and mostly in ways that are good, but sometimes I miss the simplicity of the Georgia days, wish I could open my front door to see her holding a cup of coffee from Abby's café. She is my only friend here connected to Andrew's unit, and I wonder if I've swung too far in the other direction, reacted against the insularity of my life in Columbus with too much vigor. Because while I have friends down the street who would open their door to me at 10 p.m., they would do so with a question in their eyes. I don't share a silent language with them like I did with the wives.

Jo and Blake also got stationed here, but they lived on base, and stayed for only a short time. She hated the rain nearly as much as the snow she grew up with.

Anthony got out not long after we left and became a firefighter. He and Julia have two children, a boy and a girl.

Sadie has remained in Georgia. Her husband is now a first sergeant. She has three children. We're Facebook friends. I am rarely on there these days and never comment on her posts when I am.

I can't imagine living in Georgia now, though its memory over-whelms me sometimes—on a late August day when the air is unusually humid; when I walk into Andrew's work and that earthy Army smell hits me, and it feels like I'm inhaling it for the first and the hundredth time; a few months ago, when Dan came through the area for work and wound up at our dining table drinking rye with Andrew, each of them made young by the other, like they were two privates again, their lives a secret shared between them.

The two of them talked, mostly, about the end of the war. We are transitioning to a "peacetime" Army now, which tends to mean more training, stricter rules, shorter haircuts. Andrew relishes none of that, but he is ready for a little bit of certainty in his life, to be here for me and the kids after so much time away. I am ready too, though it's hard to trust it. War, it seems, is always there in the offing, in the headlines and covert meetings. It is hard to imagine what certainty even looks like for us.

The night after Andrew returned from Syria, I watched him break into tears for maybe the fifth time in all the years I've known him. I used to worry that the life we chose would make both of us hard. At times, it has. But, ultimately, a decade in, we've both softened, stretched in places where we were once brittle and unyielding. *No plan survives the first shot.* I have come to know this in my bones. Maybe we all have over these last few years. Life is tenuous, plans are made to be broken, all I can count on is this moment with my daughter in the dark of her bedroom.

"Will Daddy go to war again?" Fiona asks just before she falls asleep.

"I don't know," I say. "But he's home now. We all are."

ACKNOWLEDGMENTS

My time in the Army community has shown me that powerful invisible networks create, support, and run so much of what is most meaningful in this world. Writing and publishing a book has shown me the same. First, my eternal gratitude and admiration to Michelle Brower, the end-all be-all of agents. Thank you for replying to my cold pitch in record time; for gently tricking me into becoming a better, more confident writer; for showing me my worth. Working with you has been a dream I didn't even know I was allowed to have. My thanks, too, to the superb teams at both Aevitas and Trellis, as well as Sally Wilcox at A3.

I am indebted to so many people at Scout. My editor, Hannah Braaten, you brilliant, clear-eyed anxious-person-whisperer, where would I be without you? I don't even want to know. From the beginning, you handled this book with a fierce yet tender care, protecting its heart while helping me weed-whack away at its considerable excess. Huge thanks to Jen Bergstrom and Aimee Bell for their enthusiastic support of this book, and all my gratitude to assistant editor Sarah Schlick, who is a star in the making. Thank you to my amazing publicist, Sally Marvin, and the rest of the publicity team, including Mackenzie Hickey, Lucy Nalen, Julia McGarry, and Sydney Morris. And huge thanks goes to an incredible production and design team that didn't bat an eye at my niggling, last-minute changes: Caroline Pallotta, Emily Arzeno, Alysha Bullock, Chloe Gray, Hope Herr-Cardillo, Lisa Wolff, and, last but not least, Lisa Litwack, who wins the award for most patient cover designer ever. Thanks, too, to Wendy Sheanin for her early support of this book.

My heartfelt gratitude to developmental editor Alexandra Shelley. You have an uncanny ability to see a work's essence, and I think that's because you see its author's essence. Thank you for your wisdom, your generosity of spirit, and your willingness to argue with me when I'm quite obviously wrong. You eased the loneliness and overwhelm that comes with writing a book, and I cannot imagine what much of this process would've been like without your voice in my ear.

The road to becoming a published author would be absolutely untenable without the support of true blue friends. Rufi Thorpe, thank you for reading multiple drafts of this book and saving my ass, as usual. Meeting you at age sixteen is one of the great fortunes of my life. In so many ways, for so many reasons, this book wouldn't exist without you. Thank you for believing in me, especially when I did not believe in myself. I think I will always be writing to you, for you, alongside you, for the rest of my life.

Thank you to Mia Sakai for reminding me to let go and let loose and loving me no matter what. You are my sister, forever, and time with you—there's nothing like it. Thank you to Leslie Kendall Dye, for your listening ear, your frank and hilarious conversation, and your profoundly generous spirit. You have picked me up and dusted me off more times than I can count, and I simply could not imagine my life without you in it. Tara Goedjen, thank you for being the most generous, loving writing buddy a girl could ask for. Meeting you was such an incredible stroke of luck. Thank you to the school yard crew, especially to Josh Clearman and Linda Legnosky, who make me laugh on even the roughest days. I feel like I've known both of you forever, and I hope that I do. Thank you to Sarah Menkedick and Amanda Giracca. Our time together taught me so much as a writer, an editor, a human being, a mother. And, finally, thank you to a remarkable group of writers that came into my life at just the right time: Melissa Petro, Erin Khar, Bess Fairfield, Natalka Burian, Landis Wiedner, Tiffanie Drayton, Debbie Weingarten, Jenn Morson, Shannon Luders-Manuel, Ariel Henley, Lauren DePino, and especially Karie Fugett, my cover ride-or-die, who spent a truly obscene amount of time with me on a weird and exhausting journey. I feel proud just to know all of you.

Thank you to Katie Gutierrez and Stephanie Land for reading early bound manuscripts of this book. Thank you, also, to Danya Kukafka, who gave me insightful notes early on in the writing process. There are so many others who lit the path along the way, too many to count, but I'll name a few: Ms. Parisi, Dyan Pike, Maggie Cornwell (there aren't many people who can say the mother of their husband's high school girlfriend is a devoted reader of everything they write!); Alida Branden-burg; Josey Duncan; Kimberly Cole; Andria Williams; Amy Bushatz, Raleigh Duttweiler; Don Wilson; and, last but not least, Dave Blum, who told me years ago that I should write a book about the woman across the street. I thought it was the worst idea I'd ever heard. Dave, just go ahead and say I told you so.

I am deeply grateful to my parents, who did not ask for a writer in the family, but have always supported me. To my mother, you have given me unconditional love and compassion, and the gentle but con-sistent reminder to stay awake to the quiet beauty of the everyday. I would not have become a writer without those gifts. Thank you to my father for story and language and the life of the mind. You encourage me to go after what I want, even when the venture is clearly foolhardy. Thank you to my brother, Felix, for always cheering me on and having my back. My humblest gratitude to all three of you for braving this book being out in the world.

Thank you to my mother-in-law, Leslie, for helping me survive two deployments during a global pandemic, for being there in nearly every emergency, embodying grace and steadiness, for drinks at the Boom Boom Room, and wild misadventures to the beach in record-breaking heat. Your young heart and resilient spirit inspire me every day. I am so lucky to be able to call you family.

I bow in gratitude to the childcare providers who made the writing of this book possible: First and foremost, Clair Schwem, part-time nanny extraordinaire, this book would simply not exist without you. I am in awe of your many talents, your kindness, and your grace. We miss you. Thank you, too, to the wonderful daycare providers at Montessori in Motion, babysitters Catherine Tran, Rose Dougherty, and the drop-off childcare staff at Tacoma's Morgan Family YMCA, who took excellent care of my baby boy for two and three-hour chunks while I snuck away to the lobby to write the proposal that I sold this book on. To my children's extraordinary teacher, Jo Puree, thank you for the level of attention and care you've given my kids.

During the revision process of this book, a lot ended up on the cutting room floor. That's part of the process, but, somewhere in these pages, I must mention two organizations that did not get their due: the International Women's Media Foundation, who did eventually send me to Congo for that reporting trip, and Empowered Youth of Columbus, who hired me to teach poetry in an after-school program during my last year in Georgia. Thanks, also, goes to Georgia Council for the Arts and the Hambidge Center for Creative Arts and Sciences for their support. To all my EYC kids, your hugs and teasing and poetry carried me through an especially difficult time. I was lucky to have you in my life, and the world is lucky to have you in it.

To the community of people I met during my time in Georgia, knowing you all has been one of the greatest honors of my life. Thanks for putting up with me, for expanding my mind and heart and teaching me how to show up. To M and R, you know who you are—you are both my heroines, and always will be.

To my daughter, Fiona. You made me a mother, but you also made me a writer. Your startling presence in my life gave me the guts to write this book. I am in awe of your golden heart, your fine-tuned attention, and the incredible gift for human connection you've had since day one. And, William, my sweet, earnest, wild and curious boy, you are a marvel, a gift from what feels like another realm. I've learned so much from you.

And, finally, Andrew. I could write ten books about you and never be able to encompass all that you are. The time you spent with me on these pages, the difficult and beautiful conversations you had with me late at night at our kitchen table, the blessing you gave me—these were some of the most precious gifts I've ever received. Thank you for being my one true love in an ever-changing world. Everything begins and ends with you.

ABOUT THE AUTHOR

SIMONE GORRINDO'S writing has appeared in the *New York Times*, *New York* magazine, *Longreads*, *Los Angeles Review of Books*, the *Christian Science Monitor*, *The Best Women's Travel Writing*, and other publications. She holds an MS in journalism from Columbia University, and she has received fellowships and grants for her writing and reporting from the International Women's Media Foundation, the Georgia Council for the Arts, and the Hambidge Center for Creative Arts and Sciences. She lives in Tacoma, Washington with her husband and two children. *The Wives* is her first book.